The Definitive Guide to Shooting Muzzle-Loading Pistols

THE DEFINITIVE GUIDE TO SHOOTING

MUZZLE-LOADING PISTOLS

Derek Fuller

The Crowood Press

First published in 2002 by
The Crowood Press Ltd
Ramsbury, Marlborough
Wiltshire SN8 2HR

British Library Cataloguing in Publication Data
A catalogue record for this book is available from the British Library.

ISBN 1 86126 482 8

Acknowledgements
To Len Allen – gentleman – without whose guidance and enthusiasm for muzzle-loading pistols many of us would never have got ourselves involved in this fabulous, friendly, frustrating and essentially dirty sport.

And also to the whole of the muzzle-loading community, from the humble club shooter to the denizens of European and world events, who provided information, guidance, the opportunity to investigate, dissect and photograph their prized possessions, and provided hours of talk on the subject – shooters beat fishermen to the gift of the gab at any time. It is their wisdom that has been crafted into these pages, for which all thanks.

Typeface used: New Baskerville.

Typeset and designed by D & N Publishing
Baydon, Marlborough, Wiltshire.

Printed and bound in Great Britain by Bookcraft, Midsomer Norton.

Contents

Preface

This book started from a set of notes put together for members of the Cheshunt Rifle and Pistol Club, founded in 1900, who were taking up muzzle-loading target shooting for the first time. It grew to cover the whole of the United Kingdom muzzle-loading pistol scene, with a good look at the international target shooting scene as well. The book delves deep into the muzzle-loading pistol in many of its forms. It dissects the common varieties of pistol and revolver, it suggests an approach to the muzzle- loading disciplines, and it gives guidance where it has been thought expedient to do so.

Nowhere in this book will you find anything but a passing reference to stance, grip, breathing, area aiming, sight pictures or any other of the myriad of techniques and demands made by the shooting coach. You will not find, except in certain circumstances, pleas to buy this or to discard that. Muzzle-loading pistol and revolver shooting has too many interrelated aspects to be adamant about such things. It also has too many muzzle-loading shooters who will prove me wrong if I should be so foolish as to try.

Although many of the 'original' pistols and revolvers illustrated here have considerable market or intrinsic value, they are held for the sole purpose of shooting them in club, national or international competition. In no way are they considered as museum or collector's pieces by their owners.

So here I hope is some guidance and information, with a certain degree of enthusiasm – if only I could, or would:

- practise a little more
- look at the sights
- concentrate
- keep my feet still
- not forget the pricker
- bring the right balls
- and the right powder
- get to the firing point on time
- be thirty years younger,

but most of all:

- practise what I preach.

Having had no Faith or Footsteps to guide me but my own long Experience, I might, with less Vanity and more Propriety than most Writers, take to myself the Title of an Author, were it not the utmost of my Ambitions only to oblige and inform my Fellow Shooters, and to communicate freely and honestly what knowledge I have treasured up in this hitherto unexplained and difficult Mystery.

Extract from the apologia to *Pteryplegia: or the Art of Shooting* by A.B. Markland (St Joseph's College, Oxford, 1727).

List of Plates

List of Figures

CHAPTER 6

APPENDIX I

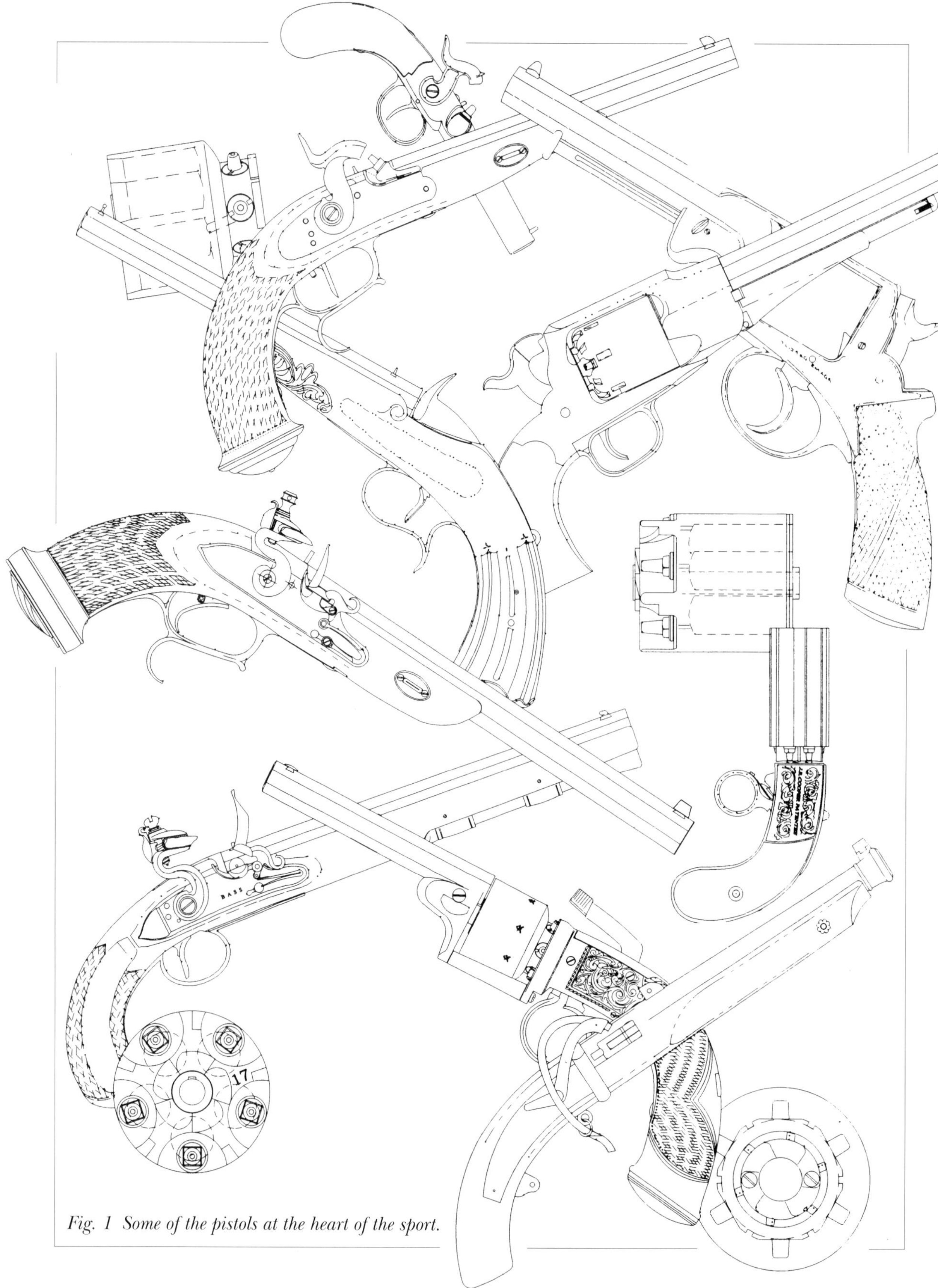

Fig. 1 Some of the pistols at the heart of the sport.

1 The Field of Fire

VARIETY

The thing about this muzzle-loading business is its variety, based mainly on the flintlock and percussion single-shot duelling or target pistols, and percussion revolvers. But you can shoot matchlocks and wheel locks if you have the yen, and mix them up with all the variants of pistol development from the fifteenth to the mid-nineteenth century, when, by and large, the metallic cartridge started to come into its own. You can have fun all day firing combinations of muzzle-loading pistols and revolvers, in a variety of calibres and with a multitude of loads. You go home at the end of the day with the satisfaction of getting it right for a few consecutive shots – ignoring the fact that an hour of gun cleaning awaits you before you can get into the bath and get the smell of black powder out of your hair. You treat your pistols like you treat your horses, you look after them before you look after yourself.

If it is competition you are after there are disciplines for muzzle-loading pistol shooters from 10 to 200yd and from 10 to 50m. There are competitions for revolvers supporting their precision capabilities and their original utilization as weapons of defence. There are competitions tuned specifically for virtually every type of percussion and flintlock pistol that has been developed over the latter half of the last millennium. If the constraints of competition are not for you, an evening of shooting the odd pocket pistol in the local club invites exploration. In the long, dark evenings you can study the history of your favourite gunmakers, delve into the reference books and at the weekend attend an arms fair or auction (keeping your hands deep in your pockets, unless they are deep in their own right). You can gather in, repair and return to the shooting community pistols and revolvers that have long since lost their will to pollute the air with what Shakespeare called 'those noxious fumes'. Or you could immerse yourself in the patents relating to firearms – it used to be said that there have been more patents issued relating to firearms than in any other field of endeavour. In this way you can see, feel and finally dream about the best of the gunmaker's art. The opportunities are endless.

For those of us interested in actually shooting muzzle-loaders, pistols and revolvers are divided into two classes: originals and repros. Originals are as stated – pistols and revolvers made at the time of their original conception, design and manufacture. Most originals used in muzzle-loading shooting were made before 1860, although later examples of design and manufacture might well be accepted by the scrutineers. Copies of such originals – made generally since the early 1950s and conforming to sets of rules that ensure their compliance with the spirit of the originals – were introduced to satisfy the interests of shooters and to increase the participants in the sport. Commercial expediency must also have played its part. Such copies are universally know as 'repros'.

Like any sport, muzzle-loading shooting has its own terminology, which I have tried to apply with consistency throughout the book. Modern pistols and revolvers are often classified by their calibres – the nominal diameter of the bore – and these are quoted in inches. On the other hand, it is common to quote the calibre of original firearms, particularly pistols, as the equivalent 'bore' sizes as they were in the days of their manufacture. Bore size to calibre conversions – in inches and millimetres – are given in Appendix III. In many cases both pistol and revolver calibre sizes are abbreviated, as they are by the shooters themselves, so that a pistol of .44in calibre becomes known as a '44', and one of .36in as a '36' and so on. Strictly speaking, pistols, even when designed to accommodate superimposed loads, have only one breech or chamber and must be reloaded after each shot. Revolvers have five or more chambers, each of which may be fired before reloading is necessary. However, the word 'pistol' has also been used as a catch-all term here to reduce the amount of repetition where both pistols and revolvers are implied.

So let us start to examine those shooting disciplines that form the core of the muzzle-loading pistol shooting calendar. We shall leave behind the collectors who hoard their boxed pairs of Mantons in their hidden vaults, their glistening barrels and ornate decoration fit only to be handled with cotton gloves. No, we visit the realms of the ordinary shooter, who beavers away for half a year to work up a competitive score with his percussion duelling-cum-target pistol, and takes the remainder of the year persuading his wife that it was really an investment not to be missed.

WHO'S WHO IN THE MUZZLE-LOADING PISTOL GAME

Target shooting with long-arms was firmly established by the year 1500, but it was not until the mid 1800s that really organized target shooting with pistols started to take hold. Today there are almost certainly local clubs to support your start in these dark arts, and, as you become proficient, there are organizations at national and international level that can take you all the way to the top. History unfolds, talk abounds all the way, travel awaits and friendships develop in a way so different from many other branches of the shooting sports. Perhaps the peak of the muzzle-loading competition circuit for precision shooting is the biennial world championship run under the auspices of the MLAIC (the Muzzle-loaders Associations' International Committee). The MLAIC is supported in Britain by the Muzzle Loaders' Association of Great Britain. Shooters generally refer to 'the MLA' when no differentiation between the GB and international organizations is necessary.

The current MLAIC pistol disciplines[1] start with both original and repro single-shot percussion pistols, which are named after the famous Regensburg family of gunmakers Kuchenreuter.[2] They also cover single-shot flintlocks, again in original and repro formats, which take their name from the nearly three centuries of Italian gunsmiths Cominazzo. Finally, they cover revolvers. Competitions for original muzzle-loading revolvers are named after Sam Colt, the first to make percussion revolvers in true production quantities. Finally, for repro revolvers we have Mariette, who obtained some Belgian patents on revolver/pepperbox mechanisms in 1837, among his many other achievements.

It is the MLAGB which is the governing body for all MLAIC disciplines in the United Kingdom. They also extend their interest into other, non-MLAIC, muzzle-loading competitions, many of which are detailed later in this chapter. The NRA (National Rifle Association; the British, not the American one) would claim to represent some of the action-packed, muzzle-loading competitions, like the Cavalry Officers' Match and the Bow Street Runners courses of fire (developed to replace the well-established

1. Both the MLAIC and the MLAGB also cover many non-pistol disciplines, including rifles, shotguns and muskets, using matchlock, percussion, flintlock and other systems.

2. Johann Andreas and his successors Johann Jacob, Johann Christoph, another Johann Andreas and Joseph Reims.

competitions for the confiscated breech loaders in the United Kingdom), with still other associations claiming precedence in their specialist disciplines.

The MLAIC acts in a similar way to the UIT[3] which only covers a specific set of rifle and pistol matches shot throughout the world. In a similar way, there are many muzzle-loading disciplines that fall outside the scope of the MLAIC. However, most competitions may be shot equally well with both pistols and revolvers which comply with MLAIC regulations, and so for the majority of pistols and revolvers it is as well to comply with their rules as not.

COURSES OF FIRE – FROM CLUB TO WORLD CHAMPIONSHIP

There are many aspects of muzzle-loading pistol shooting which by their very nature are competitive, and so we start by examining the many shooting disciplines and competitions that are available. This will introduce the reader to the types of pistols and revolvers that might well be used in these competitions, and we shall look at these types of pistol in detail as the book proceeds. A list of some of the major open and closed meetings where these disciplines may be shot, mainly in the United Kingdom, is given in Appendix II.

The MLA 'Deliberate Fire' Competitions

Although many muzzle-loading disciplines have an element of deliberate fire within the complete course of fire, it is the MLA that has the clearest and in many ways the simplest rules. Whether you are firing a percussion single-shot pistol or a percussion revolver, or are endeavouring to persuade your flintlock to perform as never before, the rules for shooting are effectively embedded in tablets of stone. Whether you are shooting Kuchenreuter or Cominazzo in original or repro classes, or revolver in either Mariette or Colt, the course of fire is always the same. Thirteen shots – with only the best ten to count – on the UIT 25/50m target in 30 minutes at 25m. The centre of the shot hole must be at least halfway over the line to count up, which takes care of the variety of calibres that will be shot by different competitors in the same competition. No practice on the day of the competition. No flashing of pans or 'snapping off' the odd percussion cap before the order to 'fire'. If the pistol fails you have to fix it yourself. No coaching, no assistance, no special clothing, no orthoptics (whatever they are). How you might approach these disciplines is addressed in the next three chapters.

As in any competitive sport, it is as well to be completely familiar with the rules, and the rules for both the MLAIC and the MLAGB are clearly published and are available on request from the MLAGB for a small fee. The British rules are issued free to new members.

Out at 50yd, and Beyond

While many competitions are limited by the ranges on which they are shot to 25yd or 25m, there are a good number shot at 50yd and a limited number out to 200yd. Those at 50yd are often shot on the PS13 50yd HBSA (Historic Breechloading Small Arms Association) Classic target. This has a smaller aiming point than the PL7 UIT target, and sports irregularly sized rings – starting from a 4in bull, counting 7, to the 24in outer ring, counting 2 (Fig. 2). Most of

3. UIT (Union International de Tir) – or the International Shooting Union in English – has recently become the ISSF (the International Shooting Sports Federation). UIT is used throughout the book as it is a more familiar acronym to UK shooters.

these are ten-shot competitions, but the Phoenix meetings normally run these as three series of five shots, each in 10 minutes, all to count, which gives the competitor more shooting for his money. Again, with practice opportunities limited to perhaps five shots on the day of the shoot, knowing where your pistol shoots at this range is essential before competition day.

Some of these longer-range competitions have no restriction on the pistol used, making the preferred contender the single-shot percussion muzzle-loader. There are only two questions to answer at this range: firstly, will the ball have enough energy to hold a group at the required distance (with the corollary on whether the 44 will prevail over the 36, and will the shooter need to increase the load?) and, secondly, where will the aiming point be?

This second point is important, as most shooters will prefer to leave their normally non-adjustable sights set for 25m and aim high or low to compensate for the added distance. Guidance can be given only from my own experience of shooting my 36 free pistol and my repro 44 over this distance. For my existing 25m barrel/load/patch combination on the 44, the aiming point is just over the bottom of the 50yd HBSA target, where the combination will happily hold the bull with an 18-grain charge of reasonably fast black powder such as Swiss No.2 ('Swiss' powders are dealt with later).

The common assumption that the ball must be dropping at this distance does not seem to be proved in practice for this pistol/load combination. What happens in your own pistol is, of course, a matter of trial on the range, which is really essential if you expect to come within touch of the leaders. My 36 free pistol, on the other hand, certainly does start to drop at 50yd if I use my 25m load of 12 grains, as Fig. 2 indicates. I also suspect that it does not hold the group as well with this load. I have tried up to 18 grains in the 36 in an attempt to hold the black, which has been quite successful. The best results came from slotting the 44 barrel into my free pistol stock in place of the 36 (*see* Chapter 6), which was rewarding to shoot despite the disadvantage of not having the click-adjustable Patridge sights.

It is interesting to note that the ten-shot holes in the two targets shown in Fig. 2 are in identical positions, but the differences in scoring rings has the shooter dropping 30 points from 100 on the UIT target, but

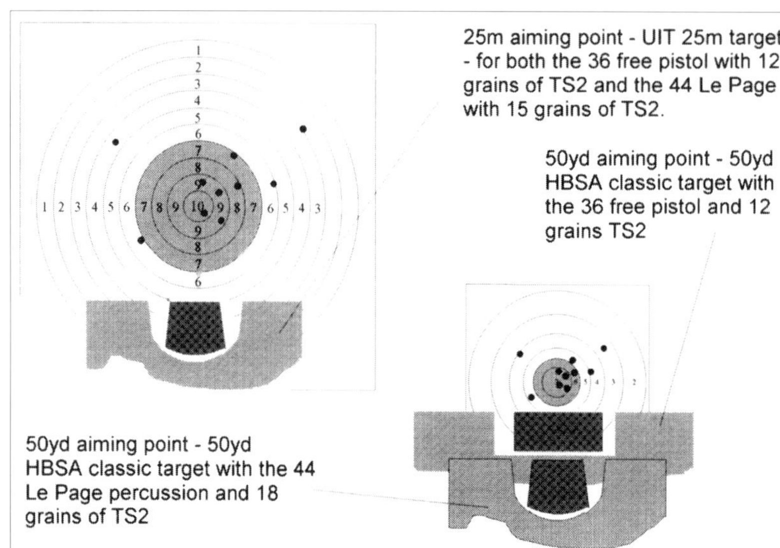

Fig. 2 Shooting on the UIT 25/50m and HBSA Classic 50yd targets.

only 15 from the maximum of 70 on the Classic target.

And for those who wish to shoot at even longer ranges, it is possible to shoot muzzle-loading revolver at 100 and 200yd at the Phoenix and other Bisley meetings. At the Phoenix meeting, the 100yd shoot is at the Wessex target (not illustrated), an oblong black patch on a white target about the size of a piece of A1 paper. You are allowed two sighters, then two series of five shots in 30 seconds. At 200 it is two sighters followed by ten shots to count in 25 minutes. I have never shot at this distance, but am told that the procedure is to increase your normal load of 15 or 18 grains up to 30, and then to aim at the top of the target. The rules don't allow you to stand up and shoot; you have either to shoot in the prone position with the butt resting on a sandbag, or from a 'flying machine', where you can lie back in comfort. A colleague who entered the 100yd shoot in error was welcomed in the true style of the shooting fraternity, was fitted into a borrowed flying machine – and came third! Such is the benefit of a UIT shooting background. Look at the sights, not the target, and squeeze.

You can, of course, shoot cartridge pistols all the way up to 1,000yd at Bisley. Those who do may well be a member of that select band who go in for long-range pistol shooting under ILRPSA (International Long Range Pistol Shooting Association) rules, using breech loaders with esoteric loads in specialist pistols and telescopic sights and lying in their 'flying machines'.

Duelling

The duelling pistol was the forerunner of the single-shot target pistol, be it flintlock or percussion, one seamlessly merging with the other as duelling became more and more unacceptable. Reflecting life, today's duelling discipline is dictated by the rules of the day, with the greatest variable on the range being the targets on which the practice takes place. This reflects the fact that duelling has never become a 'serious' or league competition, and is included in many open shoots as light relief from the traditional MLA deliberate ten/thirteen shots. Neither does it form any part of a two-stage shoot, such as the old UIT Centre Fire course, with its stages for deliberate and rapid fire – the politically correct name for duelling as it was originally known.

In my opinion, by far the most sporting target for duelling was the old, sand-coloured, cardboard target used by the classic advancing target discipline, as it had both shape and lack of any aiming point. The scoring rings were invisible to the shooter, being pressed into the target rather than being printed on it. Shown here, they have fallen by the wayside due to loss of the 'classic and veteran' breech-loading disciplines, together with poor availability and the difficulties of shipping them about the country. This target was

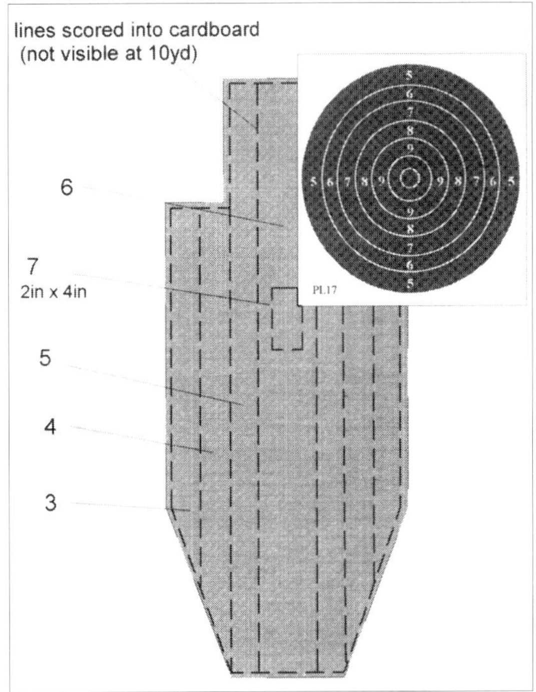

Fig. 3 The UIT PL17 rapid fire and the historic advancing man targets.

based on the original NRA 1913 'Granet' duelling target, itself with links to the even earlier German 'Reichsrevolver' target.

At some recent meetings, duelling has been offered on the round, black UIT Rapid Fire target, the PL17, which seems to be chosen through a mixture of political correctness and availability, rather than applicability to the muzzle-loading duelling discipline. In other cases, duelling will take place on the 1500 Association targets, which have the advantage of their continued availability in their revised form through their current use for gallery rifle. In the recent past I have also shot duelling at Bisley on the old PAA's Combat target, originally used for PP1.[4] For the 1999 Imperial meeting this was continued, but with the more politically correct NRA DP2 target, which is almost the same without the recognizable humanoid features.

The time allowed for each shot is another variable to be taken into consideration. When it was man against man it was not acceptable to take deliberate aim and release the trigger, as we would do in the UIT rapid-fire events. It was *de rigueur* to bring the pistol on aim and to release the shot as if 'snap shooting'.[5] In some meetings the practice of facing the targets for 4 seconds allows plenty of time for an aimed shot, provided always that your shooting technique holds up on the day. In other meetings it has been reduced to 3 seconds – similar in timing to the 'bobber' – which is probably more in the spirit of the discipline. Exponents of the old UIT rapid fire disciplines should excel at duelling, with their training on the positioning of the pistol at the correct angle on the bench, the wrist hardly changing its angle as the pistol is raised rapidly at first and then slowing as it reaches the area aiming point below the bull to release the trigger[6] with half a second or so to spare.

When duelling is included in the shooting programme there will often be two separate contests going on at the same time: the first for rifled percussion and the other for smoothbore flint. The normal sequence of shots is ten, all to count. These competitions are generally shot in quite a relaxed atmosphere, with plenty of time between shots for loading and preparation. However, with no allowance for misfires for either discipline, the winner of the flintlock event may well be the one who has his loading technique so sewn up that he gets all his ten

Fig. 4 The old and the new 1500 target.

4. The very common match for centre fire pistols, now taken up by the muzzle-loading community and the gallery rifle exponents in various forms.

5. Under the pressures of a real duel, the demand for 'snap' shooting caused many shots to go high. It was countered by the seconds urging their man to shoot at the hip so that the expected high shot would have a better chance of hitting the body. Some pistols were even made with barrels bent or ground on the outside to depress the bore line such that the pistol would shoot low. Such originals, even if you could find one, are not allowed in MLA-type competitions.

6. 'Sweetly man, sweetly, you're not yanking at a b.... cannon' was bellowed into my ear more than once during UIT coaching sessions.

shots off, beating his opponents who shoot more accurately but have a misfire or two.

This timing sequence of 3 seconds facing following 7 seconds away is also proposed in a new competition to be held by the MLAGB, following the donation of a trophy by Jim Hallam, a vicepresident of the HBSA among his other appointments in the shooting world. While the form and the venue of the competition are to be finalized, it is proposed that the competition should allow for all forms of single-shot pistol. Here the rifled percussion pistol will be allowed ten shots, its smoothbore counterpart eleven, with twelve shots for the rifled flint pistol and a full thirteen for a smoothbore flint. This format should attract a large entry, as well as raising spectator awareness.

WHAT ABOUT THOSE REVOLVERS?

Are they limited to deliberate target shooting? By no means. With the demise of breech-loading centre fire pistols in the United Kingdom, those who have not been weaned on to centre fire carbines (sorry, gallery rifles) or .22in 'sport rifles', and still hanker for the excitement of turning targets, have a wonderful selection of action shoots to get involved in. PP1 has turned into the equivalent Bow Street Runners course of fire, and Service Pistol into the Cavalry Officers' Match. These shoots require considerable practice, made the more difficult by being shot with single-action revolvers. And you always need some wind to blow the smoke away; the last three shots can be rather hit and miss on a still evening, or, for those of us with the opportunity to shoot muzzle-loading indoors, when someone forgets to switch the fans on.

Many action-based revolver competitions are run under the auspices of the NRA, and reflect their origins in the armed services. Few of their competitions demand the absolute precision required to win the MLA deliberate competitions, concentrating instead on the timing and accuracy consistent with their original role. Some of the competitions also give credit to the potential accuracy of the revolvers used by splitting them into the three classes of 'free', 'target' and 'standard'. This is to give the 'ordinary shooter' a clear chance against the 'super repros' of Hege, Feinwerkbau and others, with their bored-through cylinders and precision lockwork. The definitions of these classes are given under the NRA Revolver Championship later in the chapter.

The rules also support the concept of keeping costs within bounds, since none of these competitions requires the use of more than one cylinder. Although a second cylinder – or presumably more if desired – could be obtained, the shooter so equipped will have to wait for the majority without one, so little if any benefit could be gained.

There is another definition relating to revolvers which is quite pertinent, and this relates to the way the lock mechanism is cocked and released by the trigger. I have tried to keep to the definitions listed below:

- a *single-action* lock is one in which the hammer is drawn back by the thumb until it engages the lock, which is then released by pressure on the trigger; this is also known as 'thumb cocking'. The Remington New Army revolver is typical of this class;
- a *self-cocking action* lock is one in which the hammer is forced back by a long, continuous pull on the trigger, which releases the hammer at some point during its backward travel; it is also known as 'trigger cocking'. The early Adams, like the author's 120 bore, five-shot revolver, is an example of this class. American usage sometimes refers to this as 'double action';
- a *double-action* lock is one which may be used both as a thumb-cocking or a trigger-cocking lock; the Beaumont Adams fits in here; and finally
- a *hesitating action* is one in which the lock is initially cocked by pulling the trigger,

> and is then released by a second pressure being applied to the trigger. Adams made pistols of this type to his patent No.2712, dated 22 November 1853.

So here is a résumé of some of the more adventurous revolver competitions for the revolvers described above. Many have been derived from the original centre fire courses, although some were traditionally shot with muzzle-loading revolvers in any case. The definitive rules for each discipline are normally printed in the meeting programme notes. Note that they may vary slightly from meeting to meeting, especially with respect to the targets used, sighting series and loading disciplines. There is no distinction made between originals and repros in these competitions, unless this is specifically detailed. 'Standard revolvers' are synonymous with the general run of muzzle-loading revolvers and meet the concept of those revolvers shot in MLA[7] competitions. The rest fall into the 'target revolver' category and include the Ruger Old Army (*see* Chapter 3) and repros with Patridge and 'click' adjustable target sights. However, some competitions have further classes to encourage the shooting of different types of originals, with different classes for standard, open-framed and trigger-cocking revolvers within the same competition.

Many competitions will allow re-entry with a second revolver, provided that range space is available, and almost all are inwards gauging with all shots to count, rather than the 50 per cent over the line and the best ten from thirteen of the MLA shoots. Many muzzle-loading revolver competitions are based on five- rather than six-shot series to encourage the use of English revolvers.

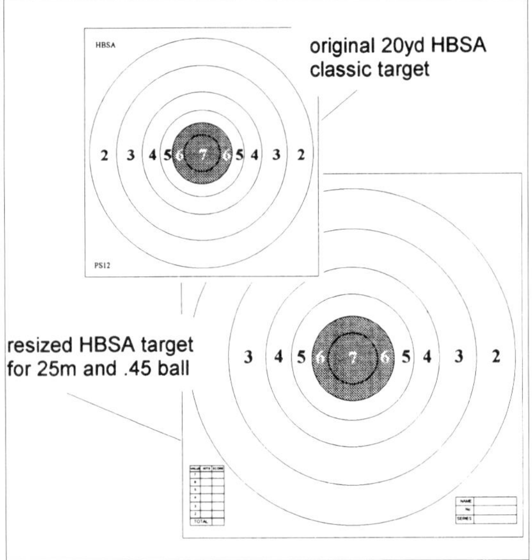

Fig. 5 HBSA 20yd and 25m Classic targets compared.

25m Deliberate and Timed Fire

This series has been a part of the popular muzzle-loading meetings for many years, and is normally shot in three stages. Originally each stage was shot on the HBSA 20yd Classic target, a scaled-down version of the 50yd HBSA target previously mentioned. More recently, the shoot has moved out to 25m using the new HBSA Classic target, which is the original sized down to 25m. The revolver may be supported by one hand only, but both hands may be used for cocking the single-action revolvers.

As shot at the Phoenix meeting in 2001 the first phase was ten shots deliberate, shot in two five-shot series of 3 minutes each, starting with the revolver loaded. Absolutely no problem there, just normal deliberate shooting. The second phase was a single series of five shots in 30 seconds. This timing allows adequate time to cock the revolver, either on aim or by bringing it to the chest to cock with the free hand before presenting

7. The MLA do not recognize these classes in any of their competitions, where classification is either 'original' and 'repro' according to clearly defined rules. Hence the 'specials' and 'target' repros described here have no place in MLAIC-based competition. The so-called 'super repros' are accepted as just another repro.

the pistol to the target again. Practice on the home range works wonders.

At other meetings you may well find three series, the first in 3 minutes, the second in 30 seconds and the final series in 10 seconds. This shorter timing is more difficult, since there is no way in which you can bring the revolver down off aim between shots. Cocking with the thumb is one technique, cocking with the free hand, held high in anticipation, is another. The trouble with this two-handed approach is that it is almost impossible to do unless you are standing square on to the target, which is not the most recommended of shooting stances. The unwary will find that their normal shot group has moved off-centre. The only advice that can be given is to practise. And, with no allowance for misfires, crimp the caps a little so that they stay on the nipples, advice that applies to all the timed fire revolver disciplines.

25yd/m Deliberate and Timed Fire – Ambidextrous

This NRA competition is shot on the DP1 target centre (the programme claims) at the Imperial meeting and the 25m HBSA Classic target when it was shot at the Phoenix (it was dropped by the 2001 meeting). However, experience shows that lack of target availability may present the shooter on the range with the PL7 UIT 25m target. It is normally a twenty-shot event, all to count, with two series of five – unsupported – with the left hand, followed by a further two series of five – again unsupported – in the right. The timing varies from meeting to meeting, but each series is often of 5 minutes duration, starting with a loaded revolver. With revolvers of normally unalterable elevation, it is more than desirable to sort out the aiming point against the anticipated 'blacks' in advance.[8]

At the NRA Trafalgar Meeting this competition becomes much more demanding, and reflects the Army Rifle Association's competition of four 20-seconds series of five shots, starting in the right hand, then the left, right again, then left.

Surprisingly, normally right-handed shooters often achieve better scores with their left hand than their right. Could it be that, faced with an unpractised discipline, they really concentrate on the sights? A lesson for us all.

The 'America' Match – both Slow and Timed Fire

This match has fairly recently been added to the UK competition programme, and is based on the well-established series of the pistol courses of the NRAA. This match pushes the first stage out to 50m, which is not often shot by the muzzle-loading revolver fraternity, since the availability of ranges at this distance is limited. This is a thirty-shot match, shot in three stages, the first at 50m, the others at 25m, all stages being shot on the PL17 UIT rapid-fire target. The course of fire is:

Stage 1. Following an optional sighting series of five shots in five minutes, starting with the revolver loaded and capped, there are two series of five shots, each in 5 minutes. Normal slow-fire technique is applicable here.

Stage 2. No sighters as the shooter moves down to 25m. This stage comprises two series of five shots in 30 seconds.

Stage 3. This stage is again at 25m, with two series of five shots in 20 seconds.

In this sort of discipline, practice makes perfect. All the practice in the world is negated on match days when you fail to draw the hammer right back (to allow the cylinder stop to drop in the notch in the cylinder)

8. Unless, that is, you set up your revolver for point of aim and shoot into the centre of the black. With this approach, you certainly have a better sight picture for the Advancing Target, Bow Street Runner and the Cavalry Officers' Match, and even on the competitions using the all-black PL 17, the UIT rapid fire target.

or forget to squeeze the percussion caps to stop them falling off during the speed shoots. Remember, there is no malfunction allowance in these competitions.

Advancing Target (Previously Known as Advancing Man)

Advancing Target always was shot with single-action muzzle-loaders, but it may be difficult to set this up in the average club. The only place where I have seen this practised is on the Gallery range at Bisley, where the necessary track and carriages are in place. It can also be shot on ranges with 'wind in' targets, but these are not common in the United Kingdom. In this competition, the target is drawn towards the shooter from a distance of 25yd (or 25m, depending on the meeting) 'at a walking pace'. This pace is generally dictated by the willingness of the winder and the heat of the afternoon (the pace tends to become slower as the day wears on). Starting with the target in the facing position, the shooter is given the command to fire. On reaching 10yd, the target is edged by a device on the side of the carriageway on which the target runs. The shooter has about 10 seconds in which to release his five shots: it is up to him whether he starts firing at long distance or waits until the target is nearer.

In this competition the shooter normally gets three series of this sequence. It is often shot in two classes: single action and trigger cocking. With the visually broken image on the target, which seems to change in appearance as the target approaches, the shooter has the problem of where to aim on the target, as well as the problem of cocking the revolver and releasing the shot. There is normally a 5-minute free-form practice session with the target facing at 25yd before the action starts.

This discipline used to be shot with anything from Webley Fosberys to pocket autos, and provided an outing for many pistols for which specific competitions were not available. Their classic replacement is a trigger-cocking pistol such as the Tranter (Plate 27), the trigger-cocking Bentley (Plate 26), or the double-action Beaumont Adams (Plate 28). These pistols allow the shooter to retain his correct shooting position without having to turn the body to bring the free hand into play to cock the revolver. This may appear an unfair advantage when in competition with a single-action Remington. However, most meetings split this discipline into separate classes to obviate any potential advantage. However, the 2001 Phoenix ran this as three series of six shots, which excluded the use of English revolvers. It is hoped to correct this in the future.

The Bobber

The Bobber has always been as applicable to muzzle-loaders as to centre-fire revolvers. It has been shot since the 1890s, when the target faced the shooter and hinged forward as if falling on its face between shots. The timing was quite short in those days, with 3-second exposures and a 3-second gap. The timing is now similar to that in the old UIT duelling sequence and is shot as two series of five shots on turning targets, with 3-second exposures and 7 seconds edged. This was traditionally shot on the old UIT duelling target (looking like the centre of the 1500 Association target without the head), but the 1999 Imperial meeting changed that to the restyled PPI target, the NRA DP2.

The Bow Street Runner

This is the revised version of the three-stage, thirty-shot PP1 match for muzzle-loading revolvers. It gives muzzle-loaders the opportunity to shoot on the restyled PP1 target, designated the DP2 by the NRA. With this new target it is just as difficult to find a consistent aiming point as it was with the original.

In the centre-fire PP1 match there was a requirement for fairly rapid reloading

(Right) *Fig. 6 The NRA DP1 (the restyled service pistol target).*

(Far right) *Fig. 7 NRA DP2 (the restyled police pistol target).*

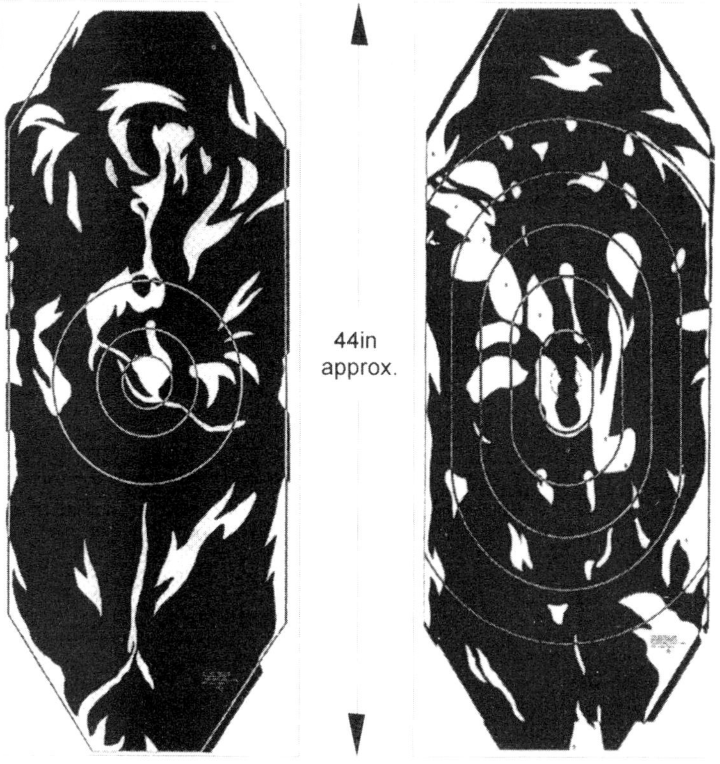

during the 2 minutes allowed for the first-stage shoot at 25m. This has naturally been extended for the muzzle-loading discipline on the principles of both safety and practicality. All stages may be shot single- or double-handed, and start with the revolver loaded.

Practice 1. For this practice the shooter has twelve shots in as many minutes, including a reload, at a distance of 25m. Since even a leisurely reload should not take more than 6 minutes at the outside, this timing is quite generous.

Practice 2. In Practice 2 things start to get faster. The shooter has two separate series of six single shots on turning targets, with each exposure taking 2 seconds. Basic two-handed techniques are used, cocking between shots with the left hand (keeping the trigger finger on the side of the trigger guard) while the revolver is held at the 45-degrees ready position between shots. Only 15m for this practice.

Practice 3. This final practice is shot at 10m. The shooting sequence is three 4-second exposures, two shots per exposure. Here you really need some new techniques and a good deal of practice to get it right. There is not time to take the revolver down between shots, and so it is either a choice of thumb cocking with the right hand or reaching over and using the left thumb. Much depends on how you handle the recoil from the first shot. Once you have a technique worked out which suits you, practise it time after time, since this is the stage where matches are won or lost.

The Cavalry Officers' Match

This is, not surprisingly, the revised version of Service Pistol for muzzle-loading revolvers. The original Service Pistol target for the centre-fire course has recently been updated to lose its humanoid features to become the NRA DP1 target. However, this makes no difference to the aiming point in the centre of the target, which is as elusive as ever.

This match comprises four separate practices of six shots from 25 down to 10m. As with the Bow Street Runner's course of fire, we start each practice with a loaded and capped revolver, with shooting double-handed throughout being a favoured method. A major difference between this and the Bow Street Runner's course is that certain practices are shot on adjacent targets, which halves the number of shooters on the line at any one time. The ready position is also different, with the revolver held at the waist with the barrel parallel to the ground, reflecting the traditional pistol training for service personnel. The course of fire is as follows:

Practice 1. Six shots in 30 seconds at 25m, all on the left-hand target. There might just be enough time to bring the revolver down into the ready position between shots, or at least after the first three, for a brief respite.

Practice 2. Down to 20m and 20 seconds for this shoot. Three shots on each of your two targets. Turn the whole body for the second target or there will be a group to one side or the other.

Practice 3. Back to a single target, this time at 15m. Three exposures each of 4 seconds, with two shots per exposure. Your single-action cocking technique has to be smooth and reliable, with no time to reposition the revolver in the right hand if you lose your grip.

Practice 4. Down to 10m for this stage. Here you have three shots at each of the two targets in a total of 15 seconds – so close that you may feel that you can poke the shots into the bull, but the scores may show otherwise.

The Surrenden[9]

This well-established course of fire is a great test for the muzzle-loading revolver shooter, combining the needs of speed and accuracy. Originally shot on the HBSA Classic target at 20yd (but subject to change now from meeting to meeting) you have three five-shot series against the clock. A marker behind the shooter records the time from the command 'fire' until the shooter releases his last shot. The time in seconds is deleted from the target score. Shoot too slowly and you may record a negative score.

The NRA Open Championship for Percussion Revolvers

This major revolver meeting was originally held by the NRA about the beginning of August, but has now been incorporated into the Imperial Meeting. It is a combination of existing disciplines, although some are shot on targets chosen for this particular match. The competitor shoots all the stages; they cannot be entered separately. The competitor may enter with almost any type of percussion revolver, with some limitation on how it may be cocked and presented to the target. The types of revolver will fall into one of the following classes:

- *'Free Revolver'*: described as virtually any safe revolver, with a two-handed grip allowed throughout. Into this class go the Feinwerkbau and the Hege revolvers from the expensive end of the market, together with revolvers such as the Ruger with its click-adjustable sights and modern lockwork.
- *'Target Revolver'*: as described above for 'free' revolver, but held in one hand at the moment of discharge.
- *'Standard Revolver'*: described as being of nineteenth-century design and manufacturing standards. This would include

9. Surrenden was the 'house' occupied by Walter Winnans for many years. Winnans was the doyen of early twentieth-century pistol shooters, who is now immortalized by having the Gallery ranges at Bisley renamed after him.

all the original revolvers shot in the MLA Colt competitions, plus most of those shot in its repro equivalent, the Mariette.[10] There is a sub-group for 'English Revolvers', which gives an opportunity for the trigger-cocking revolvers to make their mark. What these notionally gain in rapid fire is lost in their reduced accuracy. The revolver must be held in one hand only at the point of release of the shot.

All the stages of the competition are based on five-shot series rather than six to enable the 'English Revolvers' to compete. The stages are as follows:

Stage 1. The 'Bullseye' stage: this starts with two series of slow fire on the NRA 25m Classic target, each series to be shot in 3 minutes with scoring after ten shots. This is followed by a single series of timed fire in 1 minute, and the stage is completed with a single series of 'rapid fire' in 30 seconds.

Stage 2. The 'Ambidextrous' stage: the target changes to the NRA DP1 (the new 'Service Pistol' target) where the shooter has two series of timed fire in 20 seconds with the right hand, followed by a further two series with the left. This is a true right hand–left hand competition, as the free hand cannot be used to assist in cocking the revolver.

Stage 3. The 'Bobber and Surrenden' stage: another target change here, this time to the NRA DP2 target. The strong hand may be used at the moment of discharge and the free hand can assist in cocking the revolver. The timing has reverted to the original timing of 3 seconds facing and 3 seconds away, and the revolver must be at 45 degrees or touching the bench between shots. The competition is concluded with the Surrenden series. Apart from the target used, the Surrenden part of the match – two series of five shots against the clock – is as previously described.

This competition requires a truly competitive approach and favours the shooter who practises and has his revolver and loading tuned to a fine art, with no allowances for misfires or malfunctions at any stage.

The Historic Revolver Competition

This discipline has been introduced by the MLAGB as a postal league competition. It is shot on a new MLAGB Racetrack target (the 11BP) which is based on the dimensions of the old 1500 target. Alternate rings are shaded and the target finally sports a round 'X' ring. The course of fire is loosely based on the old PP1 discipline, changed to suit the requirements of single-action, muzzle-loading revolvers. The sequence of shots is:

Practice 1. After an initial 4 minutes for loading, a timing repeated at each reloading stage, the competitor has six shots in 1 minute at 25m. Following a reload, a second series of six is fired under the same conditions.

Practice 2. Down to 15m for this stage, there are two further series of six shots, with single shots at each 2-second appearance of the target, with a 5-second period with the target edged.

Practice 3. Down to 10m for this shoot, for a final series of six shots, with two to be fired at each of three 4-second appearance of the target.

Recent scores have climbed ever closer to the maximum 300 mark, which is excellent shooting for a single-action, muzzle-loading revolver. This competition is obviously attracting some of the top black powder

10. Note that there is no restriction on the use of the Hege and the Feinwerkbau revolvers in MLA Mariette competitions.

shooters. Entries are accepted through the MLAGB from both individuals and teams and are open to both members and non-members of the MLAGB. Shall we see the 'Racetrack' target used for other competitions in the future?

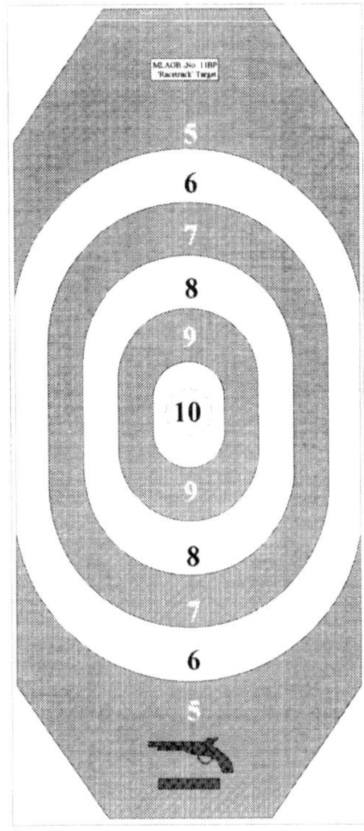

Fig. 8 The MLAGB racetrack target.

SHOOTING THOSE POCKET PISTOLS AND REVOLVERS

There are even competitions for nineteenth-century style pocket pistols and revolvers. For pocket revolvers[11] there are classes for 'any pattern', including repros, single-action revolvers (thumb cocked like the 1848 and 1862 Colts, 80 and 120 bore Tranters, for instance), and finally for the trigger-cocking revolvers, such as the smaller Tranters and Adams. Even the tiny North American Arms 'mini-revolver' in .22 calibre muzzle-loading revolver is eligible.

The series for these revolvers is not easy, even when shot on the HBSA 20yd target at 10yd. Small revolvers are by no means easy to hold on target, being very light and generally with the most rudimentary of sights. The series of five shots in each of 120, 60 and 20 seconds is testing.

The series devised for the Imperial for pocket pistols (Plate 29) is based on duelling at 10yd on the DP2 target centre with 2-second exposures. To achieve some degree of fairness between the many variants of pocket pistols, a handicapping system has been devised. This gives more or fewer shots from the nominal thirteen allowed, depending upon whether the pistol has rifling, sights, a side hammer, is percussion or flintlock, and so on. It is intended as a catch-all to enable the interest in these small pistols to flourish.

The handicapping rules are as follows. It starts with a smoothbore flint pistol without sights, which is allowed thirteen shots. The number of shots allowed is then reduced by one for each of the following: rifled barrel, sights, percussion ignition and side hammer. Some examples follow:

Smoothbore boxlock flint without sights	13
Smoothbore sidehammer flint (–1) with sights (–1)	11
Rifled barrel (–1) percussion (–1) with sidehammer (–1) and sights (–1)	9

Chapter 6 describes some of the peculiarities of these small pistols and revolvers.

11. Pocket revolvers are generally classified as a revolver in which the height plus the length does not exceed 15in. Pocket pistols are defined in a somewhat more arbitrary manner, being required to be 'reasonably able to be fitted into an overcoat pocket'. If in doubt about the eligibility of your piece, bring your own overcoat.

THE *SCHUTZENFEST*

Many meetings throughout the world give themselves the general or specific title of *Schützenfest*, but the intention here is to highlight the original targets used for these shoots. The original targets were hand-painted on wood, with pictures of soldiers in uniform (presumably a depiction of the enemy of the day), cherubs holding vases or maidens disporting themselves in unlikely poses. Some of these were beautifully painted, the common factor being some form of target buried unseen off-centre.[12]

The competition, still competed for in the same way, was traditionally a single shot per competitor at the target. The shot holes were marked by named pegs passing through the holes, the nearest to the centre of the set target being the winner. The names of the competitors would be painted on to the wooden frame, with numbers against them to identify the shot holes.

Persuading the artistic to paint pictures on wooden boards for your local shoot will not be easy, especially since these will last in their pristine glory for only as long as it takes to fire the first shot. The cost of the turned wooden frame would be enough to put off many clubs. However, round backgrounds are not essential and many a competition is held on more prosaic hardboard squares with the paintings replaced by poster-sized copies of old soap or other beauty advertisements, with the target rings drawn on afterwards. This technique was often used with early lithographs in the nineteenth century, where they were glued on to a backing board. Not aesthetically appealing, but they keep the spirit of the competition going, which is the prime purpose of the competition.

THE OPEN AND THE CLOSED SHOOTS

The final question is when and where you are going to shoot these muzzle-loading pistol disciplines. Luckily, within the United Kingdom there is an increasing number of shoots attracting the muzzle-loading pistol aficionados. Most of these are open shoots, with restrictions applying only to the MLAGB National Pistol Championships, normally held at Bisley towards the end of June, and the MLAGB team trials for the European and the world team, which are held in September and March at the Association's national range at Wedgnock, near Warwick.

Not all the meetings have a wide choice of shooting disciplines. Appendix II indicates the typical competition schedule at the current national and international meetings. These will vary from time to time, with shoots for open frame revolvers, pocket pistols and cavalry flintlocks (with minimum loads and trigger pressures) being added to test demand.

Remember that many of these meetings have competitions not just for pistols and revolvers but long-arms as well, including anything from matchlocks to chassepots and the 'brown bess' to rook rifles, with some matches being shot out to 1,000yd. It is wonderful to watch these matches being shot, even if you do not take part yourself.

The following chapters look at the pistols and revolvers that can be used in these competitions. We start with the typical single-shot pistol, and follow this with the revolver and then the flintlock. There follows a chapter on the recovery of original and repro pistols, and then some of the more esoteric pistols and revolvers that you might find on the muzzle-loading circuit.

'EVERY DAY'S A BONUS. EVERY DAY YOU MIGHT GO SHOOTING.' (COLIN JACKSON).

---

12. There is a book on these, for any interested parties, called originally *Historische ZielSchieben* by Anne Braun and released in English following the translation by Max Stanton as *'Historic Targets'* way back in 1981. There is a marvellous collection of such targets in the range in Pforzheim, Germany, some of which go well back into the last century.

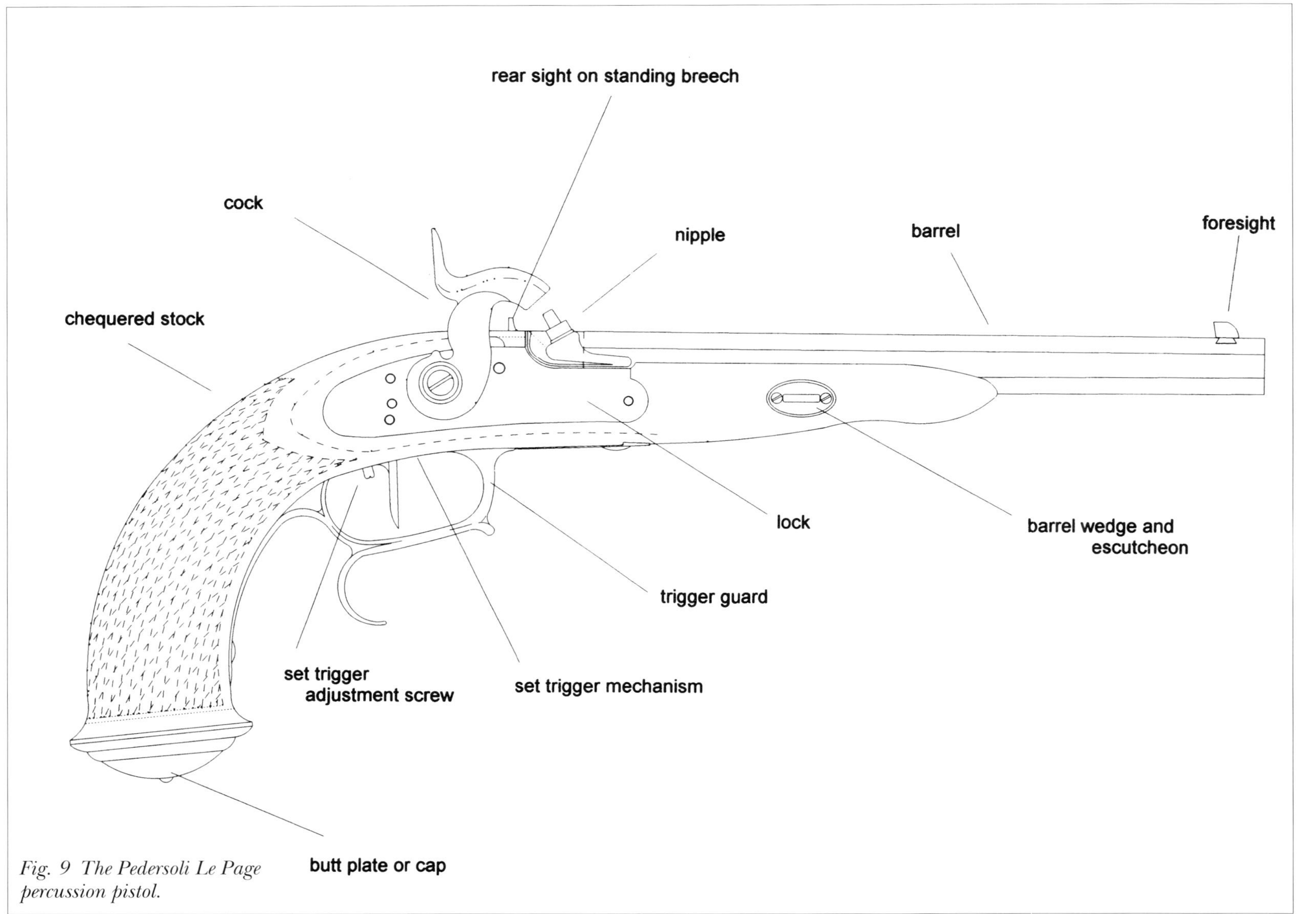

Fig. 9 The Pedersoli Le Page percussion pistol.

2 The Classic Single-Shot Percussion Pistol

STARTING OFF

In the last chapter we examined a number of competitions and courses of fire for a range of pistols available to the muzzle-loading shooter. Now we start looking at these in detail, how they are made and how to get the best out of them.

If you are dipping your toe into the muzzle-loading pistol waters for the first time there are many pools that you might try, but probably the most rewarding is one containing the single-shot percussion duelling or target pistol. If you are already experienced you will know that they are reliable, very accurate, safe and satisfying, and the repros are comparatively cheap even if the originals are not. The number of people who have got into the sport through the muzzle-loading single-shot repro route must be legion.

When starting off, you will find many manufacturers making a variety of repros of original single-shot pistols, but they all follow the same principles of loading and shooting. One of the best known competitive repro is the Hege Siber (Plate 2), based on a Swiss original and, along with other Hege products, comes at the top end of finish and accuracy, and is priced accordingly. There are also the under-hammers, a well-known supplier in the United Kingdom being Greathead Restorations (Plate 24), with others from both Italy and Germany, which provide a fascinating alternative to the normal duelling pistol format. Notwithstanding the many possibilities here, by far the most common reproduction on the single-shot percussion scene is the Pedersoli Le Page (Plate 4), a pistol that gives full value for its modest price in the hands of the pro and the tyro alike. It is this pistol on which this chapter is based, but the comments apply generally to others, whether repros or originals.

THE PISTOL ITSELF

Both the percussion and the flintlock Le Page will shoot straight out of the box if they are the finished versions. However, you may well have picked up a second-hand pistol, or may have started, as I did myself, from an unfinished kit of parts. Whatever the source, there are likely to be things wrong with it or which can be improved, or which just need to be learned, and it is therefore better to check it and do anything necessary before you start shooting with it.

THE LOCK

To remove the lock (Plate 9) from the percussion Le Page you first need to put it at half cock. This is to raise the free end of the mainspring – which connects to the link – as this is lower than the aperture in the stock when the lock is in the fired position. Then loosen the single lock retaining screw, traditionally know as a 'pin' or even further back in time as a 'side nail', a couple of turns. Tapping the head of this screw with the heel of the screwdriver will 'unstick' the lock from the woodwork. Finish undoing the screw and lift out the lock. This technique of removing the lock should be used on all single- shot pistols, be they percussion or flintlock, original or repro. You have to be careful with some originals because many of them, including the author's Nock flintlock, have a hook at the front of the lock-plate (Plate 20) requiring the lock to be slid backwards and outwards to release it. Some of the older originals may have a second screw at the front of the lock, either right through the stock as the main screw or as a short wood screw in place of the hook.

THE WOODWORK

You will find that the pistol gets dirty and oily very quickly, especially when you start cleaning it on the firing point. Cleaning fluids and oil mix with the inevitable residues from firing the pistol, which can easily be absorbed into the stock.

To protect the pistol against this problem strip everything off the woodwork. Note that screws on muzzle-loading pistols often have wider than standard heads for the thread size and narrower than standard screwdriver slots for the heads. So, before you go too far, ensure that the tips of the screwdrivers[1] you are using fit both fully into and right across the slots. Failure to do so will certainly result in chewed-up screw heads or, even worse, stocks with slots cut into them by slipping screwdrivers. With many originals costing £1,500 and upwards at the end of the last millennium, you can well do without this happening. Once the pistol has been taken apart, clean up the inside surfaces of the stock, particularly those around the inside of the lock, with fine glasspaper. Then coat every visible and not-so-visible area of the inside surface of the woodwork with a layer of thinned polyurethane varnish. Let it dry for 24 hours. Rub down and repeat until a seamless and waterproof skin of varnish covers these internal surfaces. Do not forget the area under the barrel. All this will take a week or more if you are to do it properly.

THE SIGHTS

While you are letting the varnish dry, have a look at the fit of the rear sight in its slot in the standing breech. The design of the percussion Le Page allows for vertical adjustment on the rear sight, whereas the one on their flintlock allows for no adjustment at all. While these rear sights may reflect nineteenth-century design, the detailed manufacture of some samples is not up to the level of nineteenth-century workmanship. The fit of the blade of the rear sight in the author's percussion kit was loose, and it was necessary to fill the gaps with a piece of brass shim, held in place with Araldite.

A 36 percussion[2] and a 44 rifled flint (.360in and .440in bore, respectively), purchased some twelve years later, were unfortunately little better. The method of retaining the blade of the rear sight in the flintlock by passing a square lug through a round hole compounds the loose fit of the blade in the standing breech. Even with normal handling pressures on the rear sight, the corners of the lug are soon rounded and the sight starts to flop about. The rear sight on the author's original Kirner is also devoid of adjustment, but the blade in the standing breech is retained by a tight fitting wedge and there is no rear sight wobble at all.

So, if you have this problem on any of your single-shot pistols, percussion or flint, the possible answer lies in inserting a 2.5mm locking screw through the front face of the standing breech to bear on the blade

1. I am not in favour of turnscrews, those beautifully made screwdrivers with flat ebony heads and polished blade, unless for show as part of a boxed pair of pistols. They are too short for normal work: the shorter the shank on the screwdriver the greater the wobble at the screw head. A properly ground full-length screwdriver is a much better proposition.

2. The minimum bore for a rifled percussion pistol under MLAGB rules is .30in, but there is no minimum for pistols being shot under MLAIC rules.

of the rear sight. A slot in the screw please, since one fitted with a socket head for use with an Allen key would hardly be in the spirit of the original. Pack with grease to stop it from being corroded in.

The rear sight as supplied probably has a very small V notch in the top, which is pretty useless for serious target work. Open it up to get a wider V or a U picture. It is not acceptable to make it look like a Patridge rear sight with its square notch, as used in UIT shooting, since it would not be 'in the spirit of the original' (*see* Fig. 11). At the same time, check the top of the foresight. This can be flat. Some pistols as delivered need some work with a file on them.

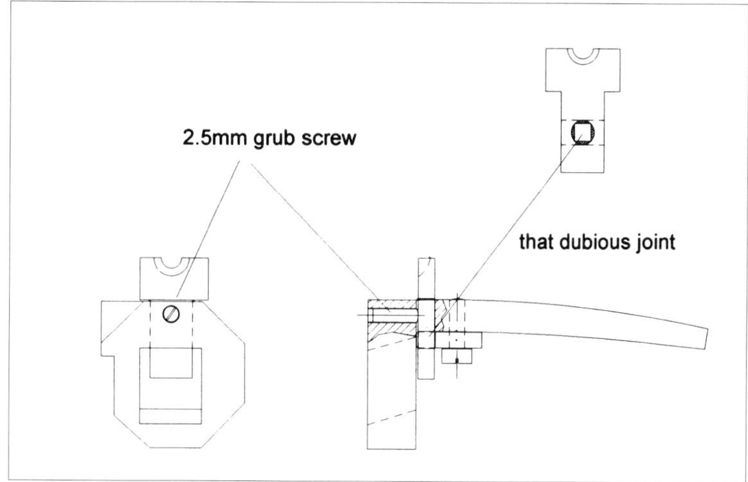

Fig. 10 Possible modifications to the flintlock rear sight.

(Below) *Fig. 11 Front and rear sight combinations for single-shot pistols.*

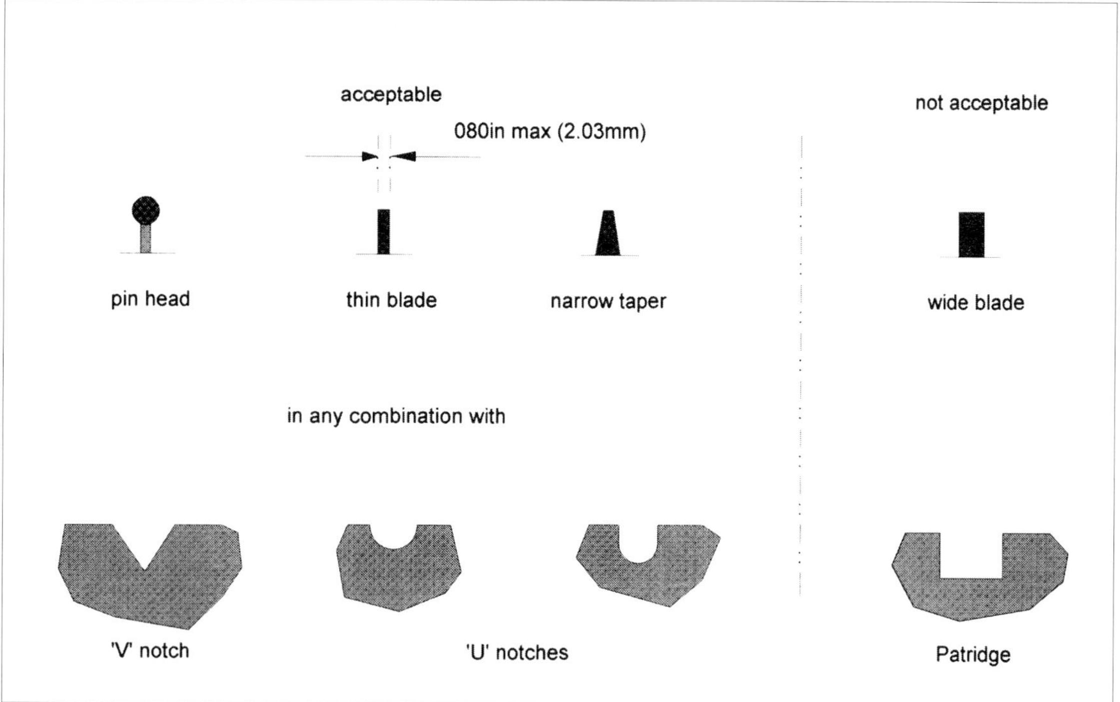

Note that the profile of the sights on single-shots as viewed from the rear normally needs to conform to one of those shown in Fig. 11 to be within the spirit of the original. Scrutineers would expect a repro to conform closely to these profiles. The 'pin-head' shape is sometimes referred to as a 'barleycorn' or 'Paine' foresight.[3] However, you may well pick up an original which does not match any of the above. For instance, the original sights on the author's Nock flintlock, shown in Fig. 12, certainly don't conform to the regulations, but you can't get more original than a Nock.

Windage on both the percussion and the flintlock Le Page is changed by tapping over the foresight in its dovetailed slot, as shown in Fig. 13. The wings on the foresight do not have to be removed for competition rules compliance, unlike service pattern revolvers. This applies to any single-shot pistol with the foresight fitted into a tenon on the barrel.

THE TRIGGER

Both original and repro single-shot muzzle-loading pistols have quite strong mainsprings. With heavy mainsprings it is almost impossible to get a low trigger pressure which will last for more than a dozen shots combined with a 'safe' lock, that is, one that will 'hold' during normal handling. To get around this problem a 'set trigger' is fitted. The set trigger provides a light and crisp trigger release, leaving the safety aspects to be handled by the main lock. Both the Le Page percussion and the flintlock are fitted with such set triggers, as are many good quality originals. On the Le Page, the trigger is 'set' by pushing the trigger forward until it clicks. The trigger pressure is controlled by the little screw behind the trigger: the farther it goes in, the lighter the trigger pressure and the sweeter the release. However, it takes only a turn to go from not holding at all, through something sweet to something quite the opposite. This screw has both a slot in the top for a screwdriver and a hole through it to take a thin rod for adjustment. This hole is inevitably in the wrong place, and screwdriver access to the screw slot in the head is at an angle. The answer to this is to find a small screwdriver and to drill a hole in the bottom of the trigger guard to suit its shank. This enables the screwdriver to go

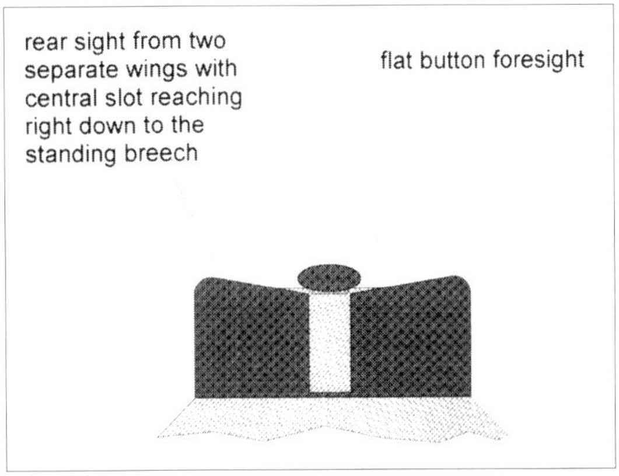

Fig. 12 The Nock foresight.

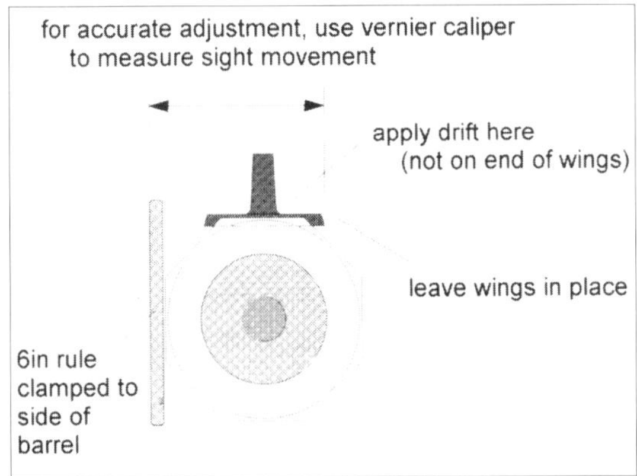

Fig. 13 Drifting over the Le Page foresight.

3. Named after a certain Chevalier Ira A. Paine, a professional marksman prominent in the 1880s. The square form 'Patridge' sight was first described in a letter to *Shooting and Fishing* by E.E. Patridge dated 13 January 1898.

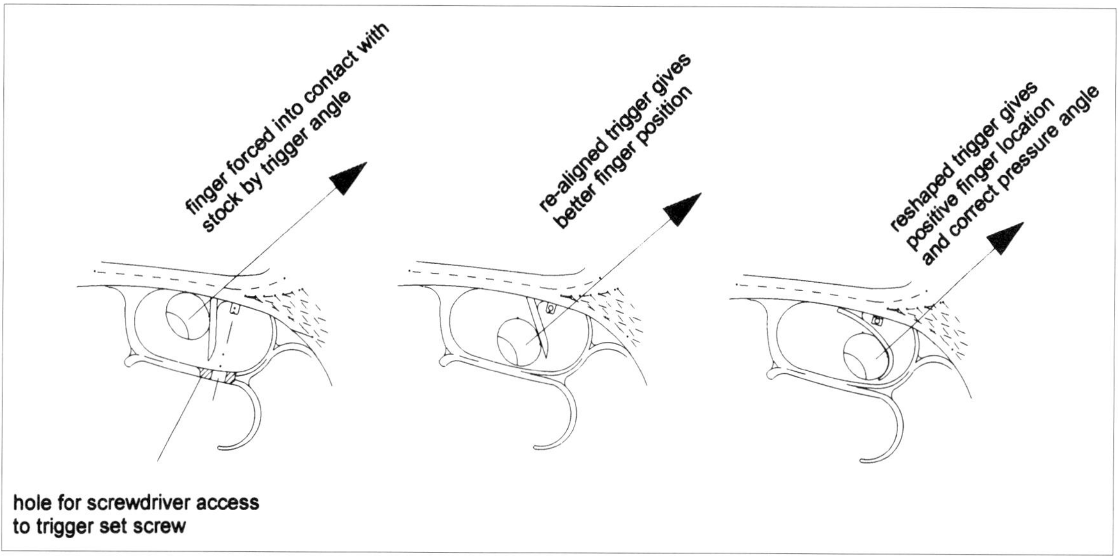

Fig. 14 Possible Le Page trigger variations.

straight on to the top of the screw and results in much easier adjustment.[4]

On the Le Page the angle of the trigger in relation to the stock seems to assume that you are going to hold the pistol well down the butt. If you are like me and prefer to get the sight line as low over the wrist as possible, the trigger angle is some 15 to 20 degrees too close to the vertical, which forces the trigger finger upwards against the stock. It helps if it is changed to one with a less acute angle. Trying to bend the existing trigger backwards is a dangerous procedure, since it is cast steel and will break without warning. It also interferes with the set screw, which needs to be shortened. If you make it really hot it will bend, but then promptly covers up the already shortened set screw. Hence if you do attempt to bend it back you will need to put up with the hole in the set screw or to file flats on it to match a small, open-ended spanner. Perhaps the ultimate answer is to replace the trigger with a curved one, such as is fitted to the author's 'free' pistol, shown in Fig. 14.

BEDDING DOWN

When putting the pistol back together, the barrel wedge should be reasonably tight. The wedge, which holds the barrel down against the stock, will bed down and loosen in time. This will result in a change in shot pattern. When this time comes, do not pack the woodwork[5] but take out the barrel wedge and put a slight curve in it by tapping the *top* in the middle with a hammer.

4. *See* Appendix I for a description of the Le Page set trigger operation. Note that some repros, as well as many originals, have the set screw to the front of the trigger, and, in consequence, may differ in which way the screw should be turned to lighten the release pressure. Set triggers are not a recent innovation. They were first used on long-arms in the mid sixteenth century.

5. If you do have to rebed the barrel of your original pistol, you should note that modern glass fibre/resin or similar products are not allowed under MLA rules. You are limited to contemporary materials, which means animal glues and sawdust, as used in the nineteenth century.

You need only a fraction of an inch to get it tight again.

CHECKING THE COCK

On replacing the cock, check that it lines up squarely over the middle of the nipple. The one I had supplied with the kit was off to one side to such an extent that the cap would ignite before the cock was properly covering the cap. It took some reworking to get it to line up properly, but was well worth the effort. If you try bending it in a vice be aware of its brittle nature, as this, like the trigger, is cast steel.

THE GRIP

Few people who shoot the Le Page seriously – and many people shoot them in internationals – use the spur on the trigger guard, as they prefer to get a good hand position reference by getting the middle finger nestled behind the trigger guard and against the woodwork. This position will, unless you have a large hand, leave a lot of butt under the heel of your hand. However, the flare on the butt of the Le Page may be used as a rudimentary palm shelf, and those with a steady hand can cut a section out of the butt and bring the flare on it right up to the hand for this purpose. This gives a much better chance of getting a reproducible grip between shots, especially when the hand is wrapped around the butt in the approved UIT training method – as it should be – every shot.

The technique, shown in Fig. 15, is to cut across the butt on the bottom line of the chequering and then to make sure that the mating surface of the cut-off end is absolutely flat by lapping it with a piece of glass paper stuck to a flat wooden surface. Then, with the pistol on aim, have a colleague mark the butt at the heel of the shooter's hand. Cut this off as shown in Fig. 15 and flatten the mating surface of the butt as before. Try the fit by sticking the butt cap to the shortened stock with a dab of super-glue. Depending on the size of the shooter's hand, it may be necessary to shorten the back strap on the trigger guard. Once you have cut off the correct amount make a good job of the joint between the two parts. Use the smoke from a candle to blacken one surface of the

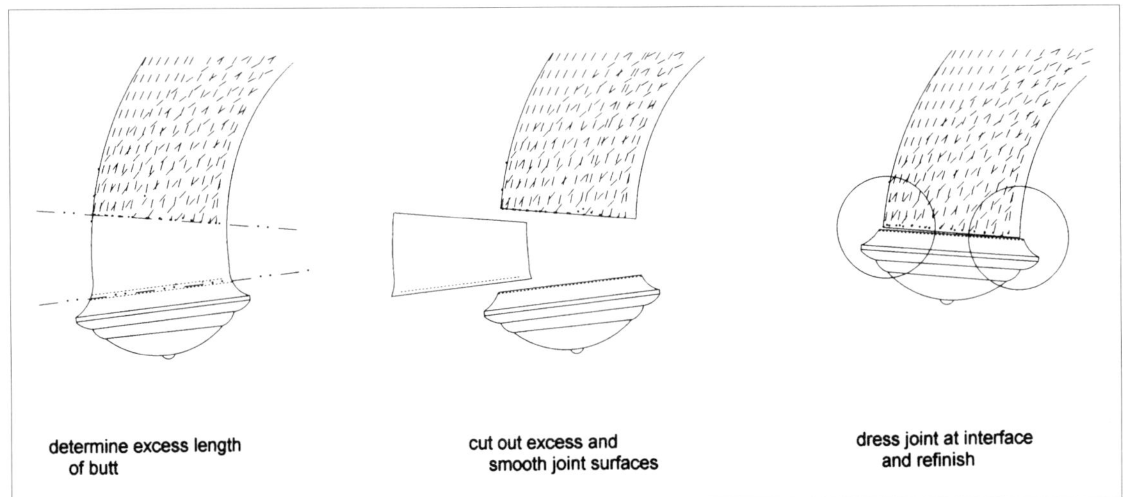

Fig. 15 Shortening the butt on the Le Page.

wood and then rub both parts together to see where it should be filed down to get a more perfect fit.

Finally join the two parts permanently by using white PVA glue, and then replace the screw which normally holds the metal butt plate in position with a longer one. When the glue has dried, say after 24 hours, blend the contours with a round file, keeping the file away from the chequering as much as possible. Cut a thin line around the joint with a needle file so that it forms a gutter to terminate the chequering and extend any lines on the chequering to meet this gutter. A final wipe with a little varnish over the bare wood and the job is complete. This type of modification, even if you were so tempted, should not be carried out on an original pistol. The 'original' concept is that the pistol (or revolver) should be shot in the form in which it was originally made.

CLEANING

Cleaning after shooting will often take place in two stages. The first is on the range, with a quick clean of the exposed surfaces with a damp cloth and the inside of the barrel with a wet patch, followed by a generous squirt of WD-40.[6] This should be followed by a more rigorous clean at home.

Now black powder residues are not corrosive in themselves; however, they are highly hygroscopic, extracting moisture from the air or from the dampness left by a wet patch. This moisture combines with any remaining residues to form corrosive acids that will quickly take the shine from polished steel, and ultimately dig deep and irrecoverable pits. WD-40 prevents the moisture from getting at the salts to produce acids and is an effective short- to medium-term protective. It is also designed as a lubricant. Mechanisms such as locks may be lubricated with a minimal spray and will remain in good condition until the WD-40 residue is washed off or otherwise removed. There are also a number of products marketed to clean back-powder guns, and some are very effective. However, when none are available and all else fails the most readily obtainable and cheapest alternative is warm water with a small amount of Fairy Liquid or some similar washing-up liquid in it.

The Le Page lock is not completely encased in the stock (unlike, for example, the Hege Siber or the author's original Kirner) and so corrosive gases and residues get blown into the lock, as well as the underside of the barrel. For this reason it is particularly important to take both the lock and the barrel out of the stock for cleaning after the end of shooting. This will also enable you to clean the internal parts of the woodwork thoroughly – which you have already sealed with polyurethane varnish. Forget the oft-repeated advice in shooting magazines where the writer says there is no need to strip pistols for cleaning. You will end up with a corroded pistol. I would agree that there is no need to take the lock to pieces, although I sometimes remove the cock to clean behind it. Put the complete lock into warm, soapy water and scrub with a toothbrush or a washing-up brush. Finish off by pouring boiling water over it and then shake or blow the remaining drops from inside the mechanism. Some people put the lock in the oven for a few minutes to dry it completely. Apply a little WD-40; most of this will evaporate from the surface of the hot lock, leaving the essential protective and lubricating film. Before putting the lock back into the woodwork, check that the screws holding the bridle (the bridge over the lock parts) are still tight, since they have the tendency to work loose with time.

---

6. The WD-40 (WD = Water Displacement) provides both rust protection and lubrication. It is not effective in removing black powder residues – you need plain water for that. Other water-displacement sprays are probably as effective.

The set trigger assembly drops out of the bottom of the woodwork once the trigger guard and the long screw holding down the standing breech are removed.[7] I do not take it out every time I shoot, but tend to give it a squirt of WD-40 before the lock is replaced. When you do drop it out, clean it in the same way as the main lock. Before putting it back, check that neither of the two very small transverse screws in this lock has started to loosen: they are only held in by a couple of threads. You will not be able to set the trigger properly if they are loose.

The barrel should be placed, with its nipple still in place, in soapy water or some other black-powder cleaner and the bore scrubbed with a phosphor bronze brush. After the mid 1790s it became common to add a small chamber connecting the touch hole to the barrel. This concept, patented by Henry Nock, was intended to improve the speed and efficiency of the powder's burning. It was almost universally adopted in duelling and 'target' pistols. This design is a standard feature of nearly all repro pistols (*see* Fig. 17). This small chamber may become partly clogged in time. Use a smaller brush (a .32 brush is ideal for the Le page, especially if you get a new one and solder the central wires before cutting them off in line with the first row of bristles) to get to the bottom of the 'patent' breech. Alternatively, use the brass scraper if one has been provided. When the expelled water is quite clear, remove the nipple and brush around the nipple hole. Dry out the bore with a tight fitting patch; this will be quite clean the second time around. Brush the threads on the nipple itself and put it aside for final assembly. Finally, pour a pint of boiling water through the barrel and let it drain out of the touchhole. You will be surprised how much more fouling this releases. Warning: this produces a very hot barrel. Hold with a thick rag or oven cloth, and

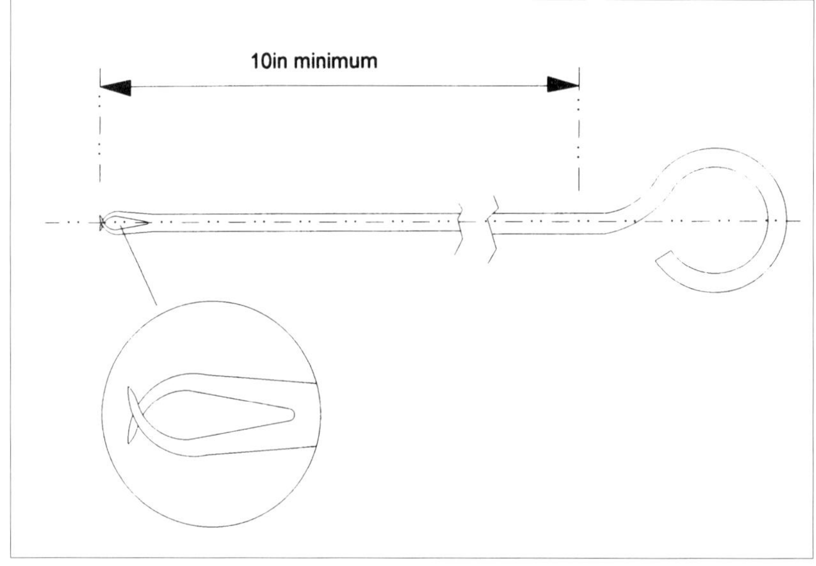

Fig 16. Patch puller.

7. There seems a great reluctance by many top pistol shooters to even consider removing the set trigger from the stock, let alone taking it to pieces. This seems to be based on the theory that the set trigger mechanism must be as delicate as a Swiss watch. This is just not so, as the modern set trigger is quite a simple assembly of lost-wax steel parts and as such is just as susceptible to corrosion and wear as the main lock. The only 'precision' part of it is the reasonable finish at the scear/bent interface.

use more 4-by-2[8] until the patch is quite clean. Finally, protect the bore with a lightly oiled patch or a nylon brush.

When cleaning a barrel I have found that it is better to use a piece of 4-by-2 wrapped over an old .38 phosphor bronze brush, as this seems to force the patch to the bottom of the rifling and the patches never fall off. Use a piece of 4-by-2 over a .32 brush for the '36'. Trying to use 4-by-2 over the traditional diamond-cut jag in a barrel with a closed breech invariably results in the patch falling off inside the barrel. This is when you need a patch puller or 'worm', a length of rod with a pair of fingers or a coarse screw thread at the far end to grip the miscreant patch. It is well worth making or buying one from the black-powder accessory suppliers.

All but the early versions of the percussion Le Page have the barrel plated 'London Bright'. This does protect the external finish of the barrel, but the rule is that the sooner it is cleaned the better. Originally, the barrel on the standard Le Page percussion was supplied as polished steel (it has always been browned on the de luxe models and the flintlock), and here the effects of corrosion may be particularly noticeable. Even if you clean the barrel thoroughly but do not clean the woodwork properly you will soon find a line of corrosion down each side of the barrel. So if you pick up a second-hand pistol, check whether it is plated or not. If not, have the barrel blued (*not* blacked – it does not look right), or blue it yourself using the cold blue sold in gun shops, or even use the technique outlined in Appendix V. Now, unless you are meticulous with your cleaning and bluing techniques it may not last too long, but it will finally settle down to a thin covering that does protect the barrel's surface to some extent. It also gives the pistol a rather antique look.

THE FINAL CHECK

A major advantage of stripping the gun every time is that you can check the parts that the eye does not always see.[9] One of the things to watch on the Le Page is that the knurled lock nut under the standing breech holding the rear-sight blade in position is not loose. Also check that the top surface of the trigger, which is mounted in the set trigger assembly and pops up under spring pressure to clip the scear bar as the set trigger is released, is not becoming burred. If it does, you will have trouble in getting the set trigger to 'set' properly. The top surface of the trigger is soft enough to remove any burr with a needle file.

POWDER SELECTION

Use good quality black powder. The use of commercially made powder (and no alternative[10]) is required in all MLA-controlled competitions, as well as those for original pistols shot under NRA rules. In the United Kingdom a common black powder is Nobel's TS2. There are some cheaper powders available, some even labelled 'TS2 type', which might be acceptable if you are not too particular, but for competition use I recommend that you use the original, which has been very consistent in the past. Since you will be using only 15 to 18 grains in the Le Page 44 percussion and a mere 12 grains in the 36, the cost of the powder – all 15,400 grains of it per kilogram – should not be a factor.

8. The ubiquitous 4in × 2in flannelette patch used for cleaning the British service rifle and obtainable in rolls from many shooting outlets.

9. This examination is particularly relevant to muzzle-loading revolvers; *see* Chapter 3.

10. You need a special licence to make even small quantities of black powder (gun-powder) in the UK.

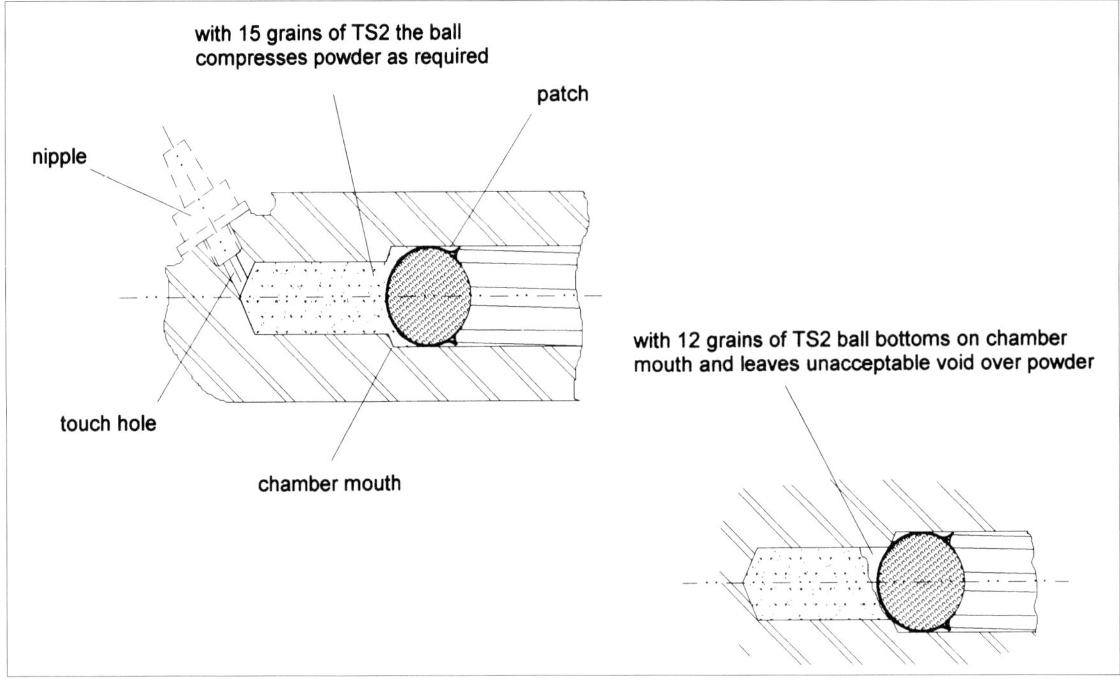

Fig. 17 The Le Page 44 percussion chamber.

We now have available in the United Kingdom 'Swiss' powders,[11] which are of excellent quality and are being used more and more widely, even if they are a little more expensive. They have the reputation of being some of the best on the market and they 'burn clean', that is, without excessive fouling. This is of particular interest to revolver shooters, whose pistols tend to get rather clogged with fouling. Swiss No.2 is perhaps a little faster than TS2, with No.3 being a little slower. Swiss No.1 is faster still, and as a result is the de rigueur powder for many British flintlock shooters. However, many British shooters still prefer the somewhat slower powders for their percussion pistols and revolvers. This is not to say that there are not other manufacturers whose powders are just as reliable, but it is not appropriate to propound the virtues of one against another, as some powders seem to work well in some pistols, and badly in others.

Because of the fairly voluminous chamber on the Le Page (particularly when compared with some originals), you cannot go much below 15 grains on the 44. If you do, you risk bottoming the ball on the lips of the chamber (*see* Fig. 17) rather than allowing it to compress the charge slightly, a cardinal sin if ever there were one. The minimum on the 36 is about 11 grains. However, some pistols may shoot with accuracy with as little as half these loads as described in Chapter 6.

In some non-MLAGB open meetings Pyrodex is allowed for small calibre arms. We all tried Pyrodex,[12] believed by many to be a

11. Entreprise Suisse de Munition, Poudrerie fédérale, CH-1170, Aubonne, Switzerland. Imported into Britain by Edgar Bros. and available from their authorized distributors, including the MLAGB.

12. Made by the Hodgson Powder Co. of Kansas and also imported by Edgar Bros.

'black powder' that was safer to handle when it first appeared in the United Kingdom. However, its failings on the competitive muzzle-loading pistol range did not make up for its main attraction, which was that you did not need a black-powder licence[13] to purchase it in the UK. One of its reported disadvantages is that it will explode on impact (although not very easily, I may add), which black powder will not do. Its biggest drawback is that it has a steep volume/pressure curve, which makes it dangerous if a firearm is overloaded in error, for example, by double loading. It is certainly more difficult to ignite, and you may get a small but disturbing lag between the cap going off and the main charge igniting. This was probably the prime reason for the wider groups that seemed to be experienced at the time of its introduction. The ignition difficulties and the delay make it quite unusable in flintlocks, which are slow enough anyway, unless you use a black powder 'starter' under the Pyrodex (known as duplex loading). Finally, it comes out second best as regards corrosion since the residue is corrosive, wet or dry, and will even pit 'stainless steel' pistols unless action to clean them is taken immediately after shooting. All in all, it has little to recommend it in competitive target shooting.

DISPENSING THE POWDER

Powder is dispensed by the uninitiated from a powder flask. This is unacceptable under MLAIC match conditions for safety reasons, where it is mandatory to load from pre-filled phials. This procedure is not mandatory under MLAGB rules, but it is generally encouraged, even at club level. The smallest of the glass sample tubes provided by pharmaceutical supply houses or friendly nurses come with a neat nylon top. They last for ages. Plastic tubes were originally rejected on the grounds that the black powder would stick to the sides, but current supplies to the muzzle-loading fraternity do not have this problem. They are certainly less vulnerable to breakage than glass.

Fill the required number of phials from the flask. When dispensing the powder from the flask into the phials it is essential to check that all the powder has left the spout and dropped into the phial. Some powders, Swiss No.1 being a prime culprit, do not flow easily in a narrow spout and will sometimes 'ball' at the end closest to the flask. This results in incomplete charges being transferred to the phial. Trying to trace the cause of the resultant wild shots is difficult since all the evidence has already been blown out of the barrel. To obviate this problem, or if you are just fussy about your charges, fill the phials at home where you can drop a slightly smaller charge from the flask into the scale pan and bring it up to weight with a powder trickler. I calculate that I throw a charge from a flask to about ± 0.5 grain. With the 18 grains often used in the Le Page percussion you will not see any difference in this group. With pistols with smaller bores and loads (such as the .33 Siber, which will happily group with only 8 grains of powder) this variation may have more effect.

Now there are flasks and there are flasks. The common flask, used by most people, has a single shutter between the bottom of the spout and the powder canister itself, and it has to be said that some of these flasks, available from normally reputable distributors, leave a great deal to be desired. The problem is that the shutter inside the flask is so poorly fitted that the powder

13. Available free on request from the constabulary to any shooter with a muzzle-loading firearm on his firearms certificate. However, this gives you the authority only to purchase and store. The EU demand that you have a document allowing its 'transport' from the point of purchase to the point of storage, and from there to the range and back. This document, called a Recipient Competent Authority Transfer Document, is issued automatically on receipt of a copy of the black powder licence by the Health and Safety Executive; this is also free.

trickles back into the flask as it is turned upright. This results in light loads being delivered from the spout, which is of no help to anyone. When it comes to shooting muzzle loaders, check, check, and check again. There are so many more things which can go wrong that are in the hands of the shooter compared with, for example, small-bore rifle shooting. The answer in this case is to use an original flask with a 'patent top', that is, one which has two shutters and has been fitted with a much greater degree of precision. The double shutter also improves safety overall in the highly unlikely event of a blow-back from the pistol when loading it direct from the flask.

Under MLA rules for precision courses of fire you will be shooting fourteen shots per detail, a 'fouling shot' into the bank and thirteen scoring shots into the card, and so a block holding fourteen phials is good practice.[14] However, you need to have at least one spare to hand, since you may realise that you have not loaded correctly. Here it is acceptable to empty the barrel (or the chamber on a revolver) or blow the misloaded shot into the sand without losing the shot. In MLAIC or other controlled shoots, penalties are incurred for extra shots. In these competitions each and every shot is logged by a 'verification officer' or marker, and any discharge of this type must be agreed with the range or verification officer first.

The powder is not simply poured into the muzzle but goes into the chamber through a drop tube. This is intended to improve accuracy by avoiding the problem of the powder hanging up on the fouling in the barrel left by the previous shot. The drop tube is just a long aluminium or brass funnel. Aluminium is the favourite since brass quickly tends to be discoloured by black powder. Get the tube to settle into the patent breech before pouring in the powder. Once poured, lift the drop tube a little and tap to ensure that all the powder has been deposited into the breech end of the barrel. Withdraw slowly to avoid pulling some of the powder back up the barrel. Keep both the inside and the outside of the drop tube clean and dry. I use a piece of string attached to a length of piano wire to clean the inside.

THE PATCH

Having settled the powder into the breech of the pistol, place a pregreased patch centrally over the muzzle. Patch! What patch?

It is normal practice in any single-shot muzzle-loading pistol to use a cotton/linen patch – typically tight weave calico – to fill the space between the ball and the bottom of the rifling.[15] Do not be tempted to use nylon or any other plastic-based fabric since they will melt and foul the bore. Most people cut their own patches from large sheets of calico cut from the roll in the local market. However, you can also buy them from your local gunsmith or from those who publish their wares in the black-powder journals. Calico is available in different thicknesses, and you need to get the thickness right for ease of loading as well as accuracy. I happen to use a 13 thou patch with a .44in ball for my 44 Le Page percussion. A good patch diameter for a 44 is 1in. For my 36 I use a 10 thou patch of ¾in in diameter. If you use a patch which is too small you may have the occasional problem of the ball bedding off-centre on the patch as you force it into the rifling, and then you will not know if it has

14. You will need larger blocks for a number of the revolver shoots; thirty-five are required for the America Match, including the allowed five sighters at 50m, for example.

15. The use of patches of various sorts in rifled barrels had begun by 1600 and possibly earlier. Their use applies equally well to pistols with smooth-bore barrels. Exceptions may be found in very small calibre pistols such as the 4mm Zimmer-Pistolen (*see* Chapter 6).

made a good seal or not. If it does not seal down one side the shot is guaranteed to go off line.

The easiest way to cut patches is through sixteen layers of material at the same time by using a patch cutter, a hollow steel punch hit firmly with a 2lb hammer when supported on a firm but yielding base. Plywood is unsuitable for this base because it delaminates at the first blow, and lead sheet needs to be reworked between sessions. Try fibreboard covered with three or four copies of *The Times* (for a superior patch) supported directly on a concrete floor – this operation is definitely not for the dining room table. The layers of paper help to stop the punch from cutting right through the board and chipping the cutting edge on the concrete below. Keep the cutting edges of the punch really sharp otherwise you will find that the patches refuse to be parted from the sheet material.

The best technique is to cut the cloth so that each layer lies flat, rather than folding the sheet over and over again. Pin the edges to the cutting board with carpet tacks through the paper backing sheets. If you do not do this, the layers of cloth slide over each other and you lose workable material as you get to the end of the stack. Depending upon on the material used, patches cut in this way come out of the patch cutter in little stacks. Leave them like this since they are much easier to handle in the next stage of patch production, which is lubrication.

Patches need not be round. Square ones will work just as well. They may be a little more difficult to control as regards size, but this is a satisfactory way to make a few patches for a pistol with a new calibre before you go looking for another punch. It is not really practicable to cut patches at the muzzle as is often done by the long arms exponents – you need a third hand to hold the pistol.

Some people lubricate the patch on the firing point. The traditional method for the odd shot or two used to be to wet it in the mouth. Some people use soapy water or black-powder solvent, or even buy modern substances such as Spit Patch, one of a number of commercial patch lubricants. In my opinion it is more convenient to do it back at home, using something like Spry, Trex or some other vegetable fat, which works just as well. Put a lump of the proposed lubricant into a glass bowl and put this into the microwave to melt. This is a much cleaner operation than melting the fat in a frying pan. As soon as the fat has melted, take it out of the microwave, immerse the stacks of patches in the fat, and then make piles of sixteen or so fat-laden patches. Making sure that they are not too hot, gently squeeze the pile to expel the excess fat, and return the excess to the bowl. Squeeze most of the lubricant out of the patches – you only need a very small amount. Too much lube, especially on a hot day, will get into the powder as the ball is seated, and cause misfires. This especially applies when you are lubricating the patches on the firing point and have less control over the amount of lube applied.

Leave the patches in their piles, and stack the piles in an open plastic-topped box (like the old Remington .22 boxes). Peel them off one at a time as required on the firing point. If you have the right amount of lube on the patches, they almost 'dry' and are quite easy to handle.

Check the state of the shot patches at the end of the detail: they will be 3 or 4m down range. They should still be in reasonable condition. If there is any indication of a hole burned in the centre of a patch or cuts at the edge of the rifling marks, the problem is almost certainly that you are using the wrong sort of material, although a patch which is too thin can have the same effect. The periphery of the patch is bound to be frayed to some extent. If the fraying extends to the rifling marks (or the ring left on the patch as it was forced down the barrel by the ball on a smoothbore flintlock) the patch is too soft and another source must be found.

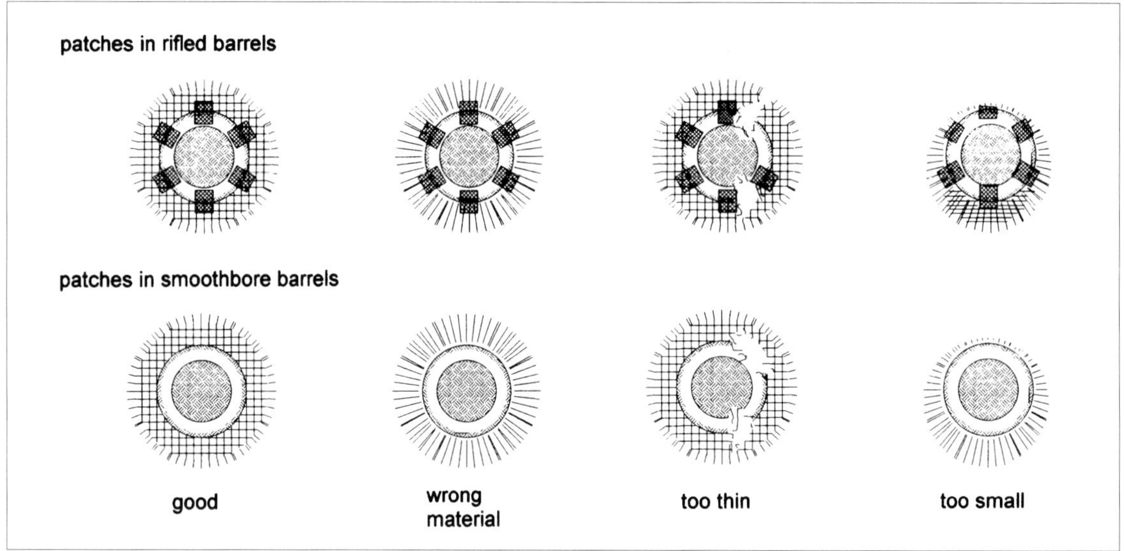

Fig. 18 Good and bad patches.

LOADING THE BALL

Place the patch, making sure you do not have two patches stuck together, centrally over the muzzle, and press the ball – of which more later – into the centre of the patch until it is retained firmly in the mouth of the barrel. Tap the ball firmly with a soft-faced hammer so that the ball, with the patch now wrapped tightly round the back half, is positioned just below the muzzle. An 8oz. leather- or rubber-faced hammer is ideal, or you can use a soft lead-faced version if you care to make one.

Then using a starter, which is in effect a 2 or 3in-long ramrod, push the ball down the barrel as far as it will go. Starters are sometimes made as part of the hammer, and sometimes as part of a full-length ramrod, which reduces the number of items spread about the shooting bench. You will have to see what arrives with the pistol and then decide on the hammer/starter/ramrod combination that you intend to use. To get enough leverage you tend to do this against your chest, and the front of your shooting jacket will become very dirty by the end of the day in consequence. Some people wear a butcher's apron or an equivalent garment to absorb the dirt.

As an alternative to the use of a traditional starter, some inventive shooters use a home-made guide with an integral rammer (*see* Fig. 19). It has the advantage that the patch is held in position at the muzzle, and that the rammer can be given a smart tap with a hard-faced hammer to get the ball started in the barrel. Profile the rammer to fit the ball. The top circlip should make contact with the brass body before the bottom circlip can hit the muzzle. At a recent continental meeting some sophisticated moulded versions of the above were on display; it will be interesting to see whether they become available in the United Kingdom.

Whatever type of starter you use, complete the job with a full-length ramrod, pushing the ball down the barrel and on to the powder. The ball needs to be firmly seated, but not so hard as to crush the powder grains. If you do crush them, each firing will create a different pressure and the group will suffer. When a patched ball is forced down a barrel, such a good seal can be made that it acts as a pump. In some pistols, particularly those with a larger than average hole in the nipple, this can force the main charge powder out of the nipple, reducing the charge. Lower the cock onto the nipple to stop this happening. If the nipple fills with powder, use a nipple pricker to push the powder back into the breech, or you may experience slower ignition times.

The Pedersoli ramrod supplied with the 44 has a useful nylon guide to stop the ramrod from wearing the barrel's muzzle. This was missing (or is not normally supplied) on the 36 I recently acquired, and I thought it worthwhile to make one out of brass as an alternative. You may also find suitable alternatives from the black-powder accessory manufacturers. These ramrod guides pick up the patch lubrication, and this in turn picks up grit and hard fouling. Check and clean them regularly.

As shooting proceeds it is possible to get a hard ring of burned powder about an inch or so up the barrel from the breech.[16] After a long series of shots it is quite easy to drive the patch and ball down only as far as this ring and then you will be left with an air gap over the powder. This results in uncontrolled burning of the powder, which seriously affects accuracy. It may even cause a shock wave to be generated, which can 'ring bulge' the barrel. Check this every time, either by marking the ramrod level with the top of the barrel or get used to judging that it is fully home by placing the fingers between the end of the barrel and the top of the ramrod and noting the distance.

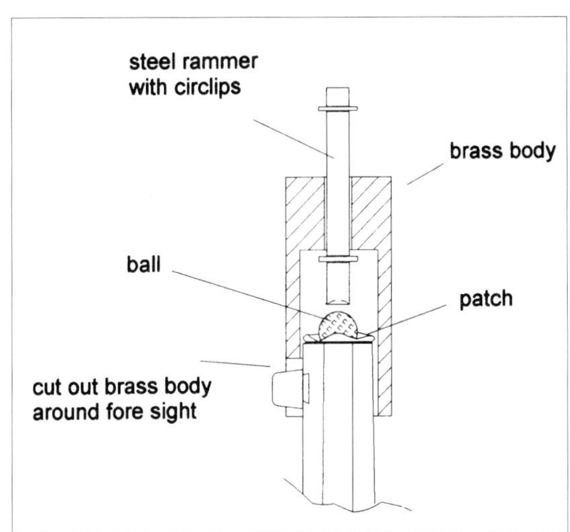

Fig. 19 Ball loading device.

THE BALL[17]

Soft lead is essential. Use lead from old, small-diameter water pipes or really old lead flashing from domestic premises. You can also buy cast ingots of pure lead from the MLAGB at Wedgnock or Bisley. It is difficult to get balls made from even half hard lead to cut into the rifling. Some sources of lead, such as church roofs, may be surprisingly hard, so it is advisable to test the lead first. Old centre fire heads picked up from the indoor range are just as hard and unsuitable.

A pistol described by a supplier as a '44' may have a true bore varying between .435 and .457in. This is particularly true of revolvers. Even the single-shots differ to some extent, as the majority of these pistols have barrels made in comparatively small batches and the bore diameter may differ as a consequence. The ball and the patch must match the individual barrel. It must be said that the diameter of the bores on the 44 Le Page do not seem to vary significantly. However, while I need a .360in ball for my 'free'

16. Multi- or poly-grooved barrels are prone to this problem. Such rifling seems to be found on originals only since I do not believe that any manufacturer has had such rifled pistols on the market since the nineteenth century.

17. In MLAGB percussion events, balls may be replaced by 'any type [shape of shot] within the spirit of the original'. In MLAIC events, balls must be used in Cominazzo and Kuchenreuter competitions.

36 percussion pistol, a club member with a 36 'Kentucky' from the same manufacturer cannot get a .360in ball down the barrel and is currently using a .350in ball.

So before you buy a mould, borrow balls and patches from your fellow shooters and check out the fit. My Le Page started off with a .437in ball and an 11 thou patch as recommended, but I now use .440in balls with a 13 thou patch. The main reason for this change of ball size is that it did not make any difference to either the ease of loading or the accuracy, and it is possible to buy a two-cavity .440in Lee mould. For some reason Lee only markets a single cavity .437in mould, so the .440in mould halves the time of a casting session. It would be helpful if Lee made all moulds under .500in double-cavity; the small price increase would be far outweighed by the reduction in casting time.

Lee moulds are of aluminium and have a great advantage over steel or brass moulds in that they yield good balls right from the start of casting, with no sprue. I am able to cast something like 250 to 280 44 balls in the first hour using a double-cavity Lee mould. I use a propane-heated, stainless steel tea pot and a sauce dipper as an alternative to the more commercial, bottom-fed electric melting pot, which, I am told, takes forever to reach working temperature.

SHOOTING THE BEAST

If you are properly prepared, shooting the Le Page, or any other single-shot percussion for that matter, is just full-bore free pistol. In any normal MLA-controlled shoot, you have thirteen shots, the best ten to count, in 30 minutes. For a percussion single-shot this is more than sufficient time. The flint version may take up more of the allocated 30 minutes, as the ignition system has a greater tendency to misfire (*see* Chapter 4).

Before anything else, and ensuring that the range is clear, try the set trigger when on aim. The 'set' can change with time, and it is not unknown for the trigger set screw to work loose, increasing the trigger pressure and increasing creep. Once you have the trigger pressure somewhere near the way you like it, it is a good idea to put a spot of Screwloc or something similar on the setting screw. It does not lock it solid, and permits further adjustment without the problem of the screw working loose.

Shooting with a set trigger needs some practice, but, once mastered, is a dream. Muzzle-loading pistol set triggers do not work by firing a separate lever or 'fly' to hit the scear, but by flicking the trigger upwards under heavy spring pressure as the set is released. In common with most makes of pistol, the Le Page does this with quite a snap. Do not expect to release the shot with the precision of a .22 free pistol or one of the carbon dioxide or air pistols used for precision target shooting. You could not use a trigger stop even if it were allowed, because the trigger has to travel most of the way back before its top hits the scear bar.

Having put a piece of 4-by-2 through the barrel to get out the remains of the WD-40 or other barrel protective (you may need a somewhat more rigorous cleaning technique for the flint version), 'cap off'. With the barrel pointing down range, put a cap on the nipple and squeeze off the trigger to blow any residues or oil out of the nipple and the patent breech. Failure to do this may well result in the first shot failing to 'go off' and you will be faced with the problem of what to do about it (*see* Chapter 4 on flintlocks). Warning: in some matches you may be informed that you have a 2-minute preparation period, but the old rule allowing capping off during this period has been recinded. This means that you may only cap off once the 30-minute detail has started. There are, however, no MLA rules that require that this preparation period be announced. In most NRA matches, the permission to cap off will be given before the start of the series, but capping off is treated as 'firing' and may only be carried out with the permission of the range officer.

When shooting under MLA rules you have the option of a 'fouling shot' into the bank. Always take it, as it is the nearest thing that you will get to a practice shot. Some people claim that, without a fouling shot, their first shot always goes low. In serious matches you declare your intention to fire your 'fouling shot'[18] to the marker before shooting commences. Put it into the sand over or under your target. In the United Kingdom we do not favour the continental practice of putting it into the ground between the firing line and the targets: the ball could strike a stone and go anywhere.

Once the ball is down on the powder, take the grip in the approved UIT fashion, pull the cock into its full cock position, slip a cap over the nipple and push down firmly to ensure that it is fully seated. If it is not, you will get an unmistakable click/bang as the cock pushes the cap all the way down on to the nipple before it sets it off. Many people in the United Kingdom use RWS No. 11 red caps (No.1075) on their Le Page.

At this moment I like to line myself up to take the shot, with the barrel of the pistol on the bench pointed down range. With the trigger finger on the trigger guard beside the trigger, 'set' the trigger by pushing the trigger forward with the thumb of the non-shooting hand until it clicks. Getting into the upright position and with the head still, bring the pistol up on aim, feeling for the set trigger. Despite the light let off, I prefer the traditional method of steadily increasing pressure to set off the lock. Trying to 'touch it off' as soon as the sight picture looks right may work for some, but for me this technique tends to give three good shots followed by one in the white. If your trigger release technique is really good, the trigger finger is left in mid-air as the set is released and the trigger jumps backward under spring pressure. This is a good check on your technique when you are doing dry firing practice. If you have not mis-loaded – and you will soon recognize by the recoil if you have – a shot that goes into the white is the result of pointing the pistol in that direction as it went off.

In domestic circles all thirteen shots go on to one diagram, but in internationals or their trials you are presented with a wide card with two diagrams side by side. Here you shoot six shots on one diagram and seven on the other. If you have your phial holder arranged in two rows of seven, it is easy to put one in the bank and then put six shots on one diagram and change over to the other as you come back down the row of phials on the other side. (You use a slightly different technique for revolvers.) Leaving yourself seven shots on the second diagram is a measure of insurance in case you put a seventh shot on the first diagram in error during your final seven-shot string.

Treat every shot as if it were the first. Trying to keep your feet in the same place for seven or more shots on the trot is not practicable. As soon as you start to wobble, come down off aim. You have plenty of time. Do not think, 'Well, I only have to count the best ten shots.' The last five shots have a nasty habit of going nowhere near the group set up at the beginning of the card as the eyes get tired and the arm weak. A similar effect occurs when the shooter on the next firing point finishes early and you are aware of his packing up while you still have six shots to go.

It is essential to get the sights right well before the competition starts since no practising is allowed on match days. Besides, to try to change your sights during a match is almost impracticable on non-click adjustable, muzzle-loading pistol sights. Once the windage is set, scribe a reference line across the flat of the foresight and the

18. *Flambage* (singeing) in French and *Öl Schüss* (oiling shot) in German.

top of the barrel. Check this as soon as you get to the firing point. It is not unknown for the foresight, with its overhanging wings, to be dislodged during cleaning, storing and transporting, and nothing is so galling as to put the first three shots into a 1in group in the white at 9 o'clock before you check the foresight. Once you are quite sure of the group you can reduce the width of the wings, which resolves this problem to a large extent.

SIGHT ADJUSTMENT

To achieve vertical group repositioning on the percussion Le Page you need to reset the rear sight. To do this you have to take the pistol to pieces to release the knurled lock nut under the standing breech, change the elevation, retighten the lock nut and then put it back together again. To get accurate vertical sight adjustment you will have to use a vernier calliper to measure the space between the top of the rear sight and the top of the standing breech. Having done this, add or subtract 10 thou for every ring on a PL7[19] target that you need to move the group.

Changing the group laterally can only be done only by tapping the foresight across in its mounting (*see* Fig. 13). Using the same measurement technique, you will need to clamp a plate – a 6in metal rule is as good as anything – to one side of the barrel to get a reference for lateral sight adjustment. Remember that the foresight is moved in the opposite direction to the required change in the centre of the group on the target. For lateral sight adjustment, foresight clamps, similar to those used on the old Lee Enfield rifle, would be useful, but I have never seen one in use on the muzzle-loading pistol range.

If this seems complicated, have a thought for those shooters who have originals with a rear sight without any adjustment whatsoever, like the author's Kirner.[20] When this was first tried on the range it dropped shots into the three ring at 6 o'clock, virtually 'point of aim', but far too far down to 'aim off'. As the foresight had a beautifully proportioned pinhead shape, it could not be filed down to raise the group. This meant having to raise the rear sight, which was luckily no more than a plate dropped through the standing breech and retained with a small pin. The only way to tackle this was to make a completely new rear sight, mounted in the same way as the original, but some 70 thou higher, so that it could be finally filed down to size.

HOW DO THEY SHOOT?

The Le Page has the reputation of having a superb barrel and will group consistently better than you will ever hold it. Credible scores in repro percussion are no less than 93. British team trial qualification scores are steadily rising above this level, with the Kuchenreuter repro team for the 2000 World Championships all shooting 96 or above. So you will have to be shooting in the high 90s if you expect to be pushing for the first three in internationals. The Le Page, properly handled, as well as many other comparable repros, such as the Mang and the Siber, will put you into this class.

In competitions run strictly to MLAIC rules, which for British shooters extends to

19. The PL7 is the standard UIT 25 and 50m target, used for all MLA-based 25m deliberate pistol competitions. Shooting deliberate at 50yd or 50m (outwith MLAIC competitions) is often done on the 50yd HBSA Classic target, the PS 13. With only ten shots, all to count, the maximum score is 70. Such competitions are often won with a 65 or so, which indicates the superb accuracy of these pistols over this distance. Scoring is usually by the outside of the ball, not the centre, in these ten-shot matches.

20. This pistol, quite by chance, takes the identical ball, patch and load as the author's repro Le Page. It is marked on the barrel 'JOZSEF KIRNER – BUDAPESTEN', and is No.1 of a pair.

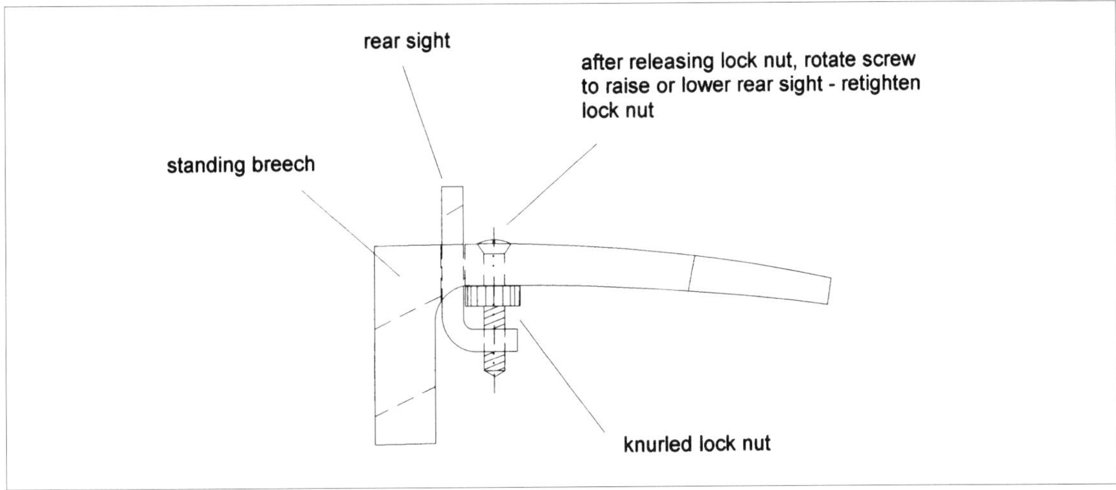

Fig. 20 Rear sight adjustment on the Le Page percussion.

the European and the world championship, as well as some European countries' national open championships, you cannot shoot both repro and original percussion pistols in the Kuchenreuter[21] competition. This restriction also applies to the Cominazzo (flintlock) competitions. However, MLAIC rules have always allowed individual entries in the repro and original revolver competitions – the Mariette and the Colt.

Any original percussion in good condition with a set trigger and reasonable rifling will cost the purchaser over £1,500 as the new century starts – provided that he can find one. The sights may be rather different and there will be variations in the form of the grip compared with the shooter's repro, but they all need to be treated with the same care and attention if you are to get the best out of them. When you do, your scores should be no less than with your repro.

From then on it is a question of constant practice. The world record for an original percussion was set at 100 by Welsch of Germany, and his compatriot Balk took the repro record with a 99, both in 1987. Remember that the centre of the ball must be on or inside the line to count up, unlike UIT rules where the periphery of the shot has only to touch the line to count up. A 'possible' in muzzle-loading is therefore much more difficult to achieve than in other branches of the sport. Germany was very successful in the world championships in that year, the only occasion on which MLAIC world records can be set.

THERE WAS BY NO MEANS GENERAL APPROVAL OF THE INVENTION OF THE PERCUSSION CAP. TO QUOTE A CONTRIBUTOR TO THE *GENTLEMAN'S MAGAZINE* IN 1817: 'IF, HOWEVER, THIS NEW SYSTEM WERE APPLIED TO THE MILITARY, WAR WOULD SHORTLY BECOME SO FRIGHTFUL AS TO EXCEED ALL BOUNDS OF IMAGINATION ... IT IS HOPED THAT MEN OF CONSCIENCE WILL MILITATE MOST VEHEMENTLY FOR THE SUPPRESSION OF THIS NEW INVENTION.' THERE WAS LITTLE HOPE OF THAT, THE SAME WAS SAID OF THE CROSSBOW.

---

21. I recently saw two pairs of very similar originals side by side, one engraved 'IoH Andre Kuchenreuter' and the other 'IoH Andre Kuchenreiter'. They could be by the same man, since spelling was more erratic in the eighteenth century. For IoH read Johan, and for Andre read Andreas. But which one?

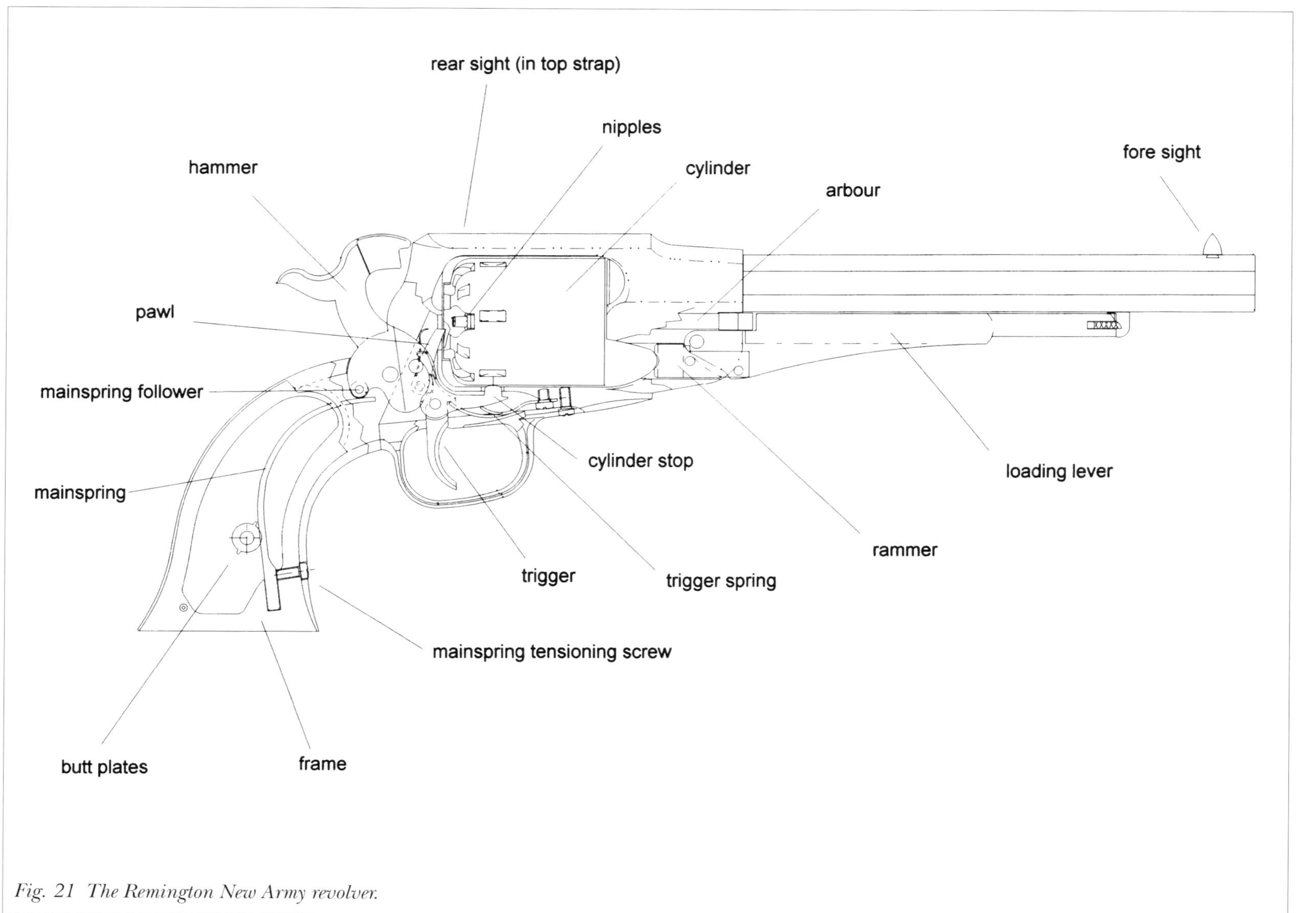

Fig. 21 The Remington New Army revolver.

3 Those Muzzle-Loading Revolvers

INTRODUCTION

Revolving chamber or magazine arms have been in use since the seventeenth century, and limited numbers of revolvers were still being made to Collier's patent (flintlock revolvers that is) until the early 1820s. However, revolver shooting really came into its own in the 1830s when Sam Colt started making his now legendary open-framed percussion revolvers. Colt was the first revolver manufacturer to use state-of-the-art production methods (backed up by an equal amount of hand fitting) on any scale, allowing his products to spread through the world and stay ahead of the rest for twenty years or more.

A hundred and fifty or more years later by far the largest number of revolvers seen on the muzzle-loading range are not of Colt origin or pattern but variations on the Remington 1858 New Army (Plate 10) or the equivalent Rogers and Spencer (Plate 23). This is not to say that the English did not make some excellent percussion revolvers in the 1850s. For instance, there is the much sought after double trigger'd Tranter[1] which should be a natural choice for revolver timed shots. And then the massive Kerr[2] (that great beast of a 'double action' revolver with its hammer on the outside of the frame – like a single shot), with many thousands being exported to the colonies and being adopted by some European countries (such as Portugal) as their official side arm. And then there were the later versions of the Adams, which eventually found favour over the Colt after some four years of acrimonious rivalry. The Adams's ultimate acceptance by the British government[3] was one of the reasons that Colt stopped manufacture in London and subsequently supplied the European market by exporting from his newly expanded facilities in Hartford, Connecticut. However, the availability of sufficient numbers of affordable English originals and the complete lack of repros – mainly due to the pressures of the American market – makes the appearance of English muzzle-loading revolvers in deliberate competitions very rare. It is good to see that in some 'Schützenfests' a separate competition for English muzzle-loading revolvers has been introduced. This includes shoots such as the Imperial and the Trafalgar, in addition to the well-established MLAGB shoots. It must also be said that the typical English revolvers of the 1850s were mainly intended to be loaded with 'paper cartridges' or loose powder with wadded balls (*see* Fig. 68), and the tapering of the mouths of the chambers to aid their loading did not enhance their accuracy, although they were more than accurate enough for their original defensive purpose.

1. Patented in 1853, five years before Beal's patent which was utilized in the design of the Remington New Army.

2. Kerr went into partnership with Adams after Adams split up with Deane in 1856, and their company, the London Armoury Company, made both Adams and Kerr revolvers, the latter to a patent dated 1858.

3. Adopted as the double action Beaumont-Adams. It also found favour with both the Dutch and the Russian governments. Beaumont's patent was dated 1855, complimenting Adams's original patent of 1851.

There are any number of muzzle-loading revolvers about, of which the Ruger Old Army (Plate 11) is one of the most common. The Ruger is made quite unashamedly as a modern muzzle-loading revolver rather than as a 'copy' of a nineteenth-century original, and meets the demands of its own market. Such pistols tend to have modern designs of locks, use coil rather than leaf springs and are often fitted with click adjustable sights of Patridge form. Not being made 'in the spirit of the original' they are not allowed in the Mariette. However, such revolvers are allowed in many of the open competitions held, for example, at Bisley, such as the Trafalgar and the Phoenix meetings, in which the shooter may use almost any safe percussion revolver in the 'free revolver' competitions. In the Ruger we have one of those revolvers which are often bought by British shooters starting off in the discipline of muzzle-loading, only to find out too late that this particular revolver does not qualify for the MLA precision shoots.[4]

This chapter covers both originals and repros, since they are (or should be) virtually identical. Details are based on an original 44 Remington New Army (made about 1862 for the private market) and the well-known repro made by Pietta, of which there must be thousands in the United Kingdom alone (Plate 10). Pietta are by no means the only producers of such repros, with suppliers such as the Pedersoli (which has a feel quite close to the original), Euroarms, Uberti and many others. Manufacturers also include the Feinwerkbau and the Hege Remingtons, advertised as being exact copies of the original but made by the most modern manufacturing techniques. These pistols fall into the category of 'free revolver' as far as the NRA is concerned, but are accepted in the Mariette by the MLA.

At the end of the last century you could pick up a shootable original 44 Remington from £500 upwards. The general key to the asking price is the finish, with some examples with a good covering of original blueing commanding prices in the region of £1,200 or more. If you want one for putting away and expecting it to appreciate that is one thing. However, you really do not need to pay that sort of money for a perfectly acceptable and shootable original revolver, especially if you are prepared to do a little work on it to bring it up to a competitive standard.

As the new century starts, you can buy a new repro from £250 upwards, depending on the source and the bargaining power of the purchaser. There are also a number of repros on the second-hand market, and it is quite possible to pick one up for well under £100. However, much of the second-hand stock on the gun shop shelves needs to be looked at in detail, which we shall go into later, a major problem being that some have been woefully mishandled by their previous owners.

Remington also made a 36, mainly for the US Navy (Plate 12), which has a driftable foresight for windage adjustment. There are a limited number of repros in this calibre: the Pietta New Army is one (also Plate 12) and originals are pretty scarce. The frame is virtually the same as the 44, with the Navy barrel being some ½in shorter than the army model. The original has tapered mouths to the chambers like the Rogers, and takes a .370 ball, while the Pietta takes a .375 ball (reflecting the sharp edge of the chambers), despite their designations as a 36. (A .360in

4. In addition, the Ruger shooter will occasionally meet some problems which detract from the pleasure of shooting. One is that, without using a plastic or silicon rubber cap guard, the remains of fired caps often used successfully on other revolvers in Europe all too frequently find their way into the mechanism, and can only be removed by stripping the complete gun. This problem is also reported by open frame Colt shooters. The Ruger also has a fundamental weakness in the arbor, which is easily bent. This may occur if the shooter tries to load balls of too large a calibre or when the rammer is allowed to get out of line with the chamber as the loading lever is depressed.

ball will just roll out of the chambers on both of these examples). These variants are the same weight, give or take a little, as the 44, which should make them ideal for target shooting with their reduced loads and recoil. However, they are rarely seen on the international circuit, so perhaps they are more difficult to get to group properly.

A high percentage of muzzle-loading revolvers on the second-hand shelves are repros of various models of the Colt, easily recognizable as having no top strap over the cylinder (Plate 22). Colts are not normally renowned as being serious contenders in the target stakes. The lack of the top strap permits the barrel to wobble from side to side with respect to the frame as the barrel key loses its initially tight fit and the arbor starts to wear where it mates with the recess in the barrel lug. Also, it takes only a little wear on the hammer-bearing pin for the rear sight, cut into the nose of the hammer, to take on a different lateral position between each shot. This is not helped by the rear sight only remaining visible when the revolver lock is in the full cock position. This causes the rear sight to vanish as the shot is released. None of these 'defects' are aids to good shooting. However, the occasional pistol that has been reworked and tightened up shows that really respectable groups are possible. I think that these Colt repros end up on the shelf when the unsuspecting shooter finds that they are not competitive and trade them in for a Remington or a Rogers and Spencer (*see* Fig. 35). However, separate classes for open frame revolvers, such as the Colt M1851 and the M1860, have been offered at the Imperial meeting for some years, and this is bound to happen at other meetings as time goes by.

If you do want to shoot a Colt original, be prepared to pay premium prices for one in good condition. Colt revolvers are extremely collectable in the USA, with the prices obtainable there drawing them away from the United Kingdom and the rest of Europe.

Repros are invariably claimed to be accurate repros of the originals, but I have never found one of the cheaper repros that has that genuine feel of an original. There is always something about the weight or the size or both which is never quite right. Of the many manufacturers; some are inevitably much better than others. Some are definitely made on the cheap, and one I encountered was about 90 per cent of full size, making it difficult for me to get my not so large middle finger between the butt and the trigger guard.

WHEN IS AN ORIGINAL NOT AN ORIGINAL?

The MLA definition of an 'original'[5] precludes 'any alteration to an original firearm which would spoil its historical value', and goes on to require the pistol to have the original and unsleeved barrel.[6] Repairs are allowed, where they must 'assimilate the original construction of a style contemporary with the period of manufacture'. Although this apparently allows for considerable leeway, a scrutineer also has leeway in saying whether a repair is within the spirit of the rules or not. It is as well, when planning anything other than minor repairs or replacements to pistols and revolvers destined for use in MLA competitions, to discuss the proposed changes with one of the MLAGB's

5. See the Constitution, Rules and Regulations of the MLAIC.

6. On the establishment of the MLAIC, classes for original and repro revolvers were included. At that time the only single-shot pistols recognized were those of original manufacture. However, this was changed (under commercial pressure) in 1981, which dramatically increased participation in the Kuchenreuter and Cominazzo competitions. However, pistols or revolvers with sleeved barrels are not eligible in either MLAGB or MLAIC competitions, other than MLAGB competitions allowing the use of 'free pistols'. In internationals a beta or ultrasonic tester is used to test for sleeved barrels, which can result in instant disqualification.

experts on the subject. The secretary will put you in touch. Nevertheless, many things may be replaced without compliance problems, including the hammer, the mainspring and other parts of the lock work. Almost all Remington 'originals' have something which has had to be replaced, perhaps the most common being the little bifurcated trigger return spring, which is exposed when you take off the trigger guard. In almost all cases the foresight will have been replaced – or at least reworked – to get the pistol to shoot into the middle of the target without 'holding off'. Such changes are allowed under MLA rules. Any modern replacement parts must conform closely to the original.

Another definition of an original is set out in the recent British Firearms (Amendment) Act and is for a muzzle-loading firearm produced before 1939. However, original revolver shooters are unlikely to be interested in designs conceived after the mid 1860s, when cartridge revolvers started to make themselves available. It should be noted, however, that solid-frame percussion revolvers continued to be made up to the early years of the twentieth century.

TO BUY OR NOT TO BUY, THAT IS THE QUESTION

If you are contemplating buying an original – or even a second-hand repro of any of the Remington-type pistols, including the Rogers and Spencer – there are two places to examine carefully before you decide to purchase. The first is the inside of the barrel, which should be reasonably clean with the rifling being clearly visible. A few minor pits down the barrel, provided that they are not close to the muzzle, will probably not detract from the accuracy of the revolver to any real degree. If you cannot see the bottom of any of the pits, start looking elsewhere.

Now, you can't see what is going on in the barrel without dropping the cylinder out. If the vendor is not happy about your doing this, look elsewhere. The cylinder is removed with the hammer at half cock by unclipping the loading lever and sliding the arbor out as far as it will go and then rolling the cylinder clockwise as the cylinder is pushed from the frame to the left-hand side. If you do not roll the cylinder it will catch on the pawl (also known as the hand), damaging both the pawl and the back of the cylinder.[7]

Having got the cylinder out, look at the ratchet or 'star' at the back of the cylinder. The ratchet on all revolvers is vulnerable to wear from a chipped or misshapen pawl. You cannot expect the edges of the ratchet, shown in Fig. 22, to be absolutely sharp, but if they are worn away and rounded, or there are deep scratches between the edges of each indent, give it a miss. It is possible to upset the back of the cylinder with a small cold chisel and push metal towards the bearing edge on each segment of the ratchet and dress to shape, but results in very mangled looking cylinder. So, unless you already own the pistol and decide that you want to rework it in this way, again it would be better to look elsewhere.

The reason for this scoring on the ratchet is that the top edge of the pawl either becomes chipped or is worn away, or someone decides to repair it and does more harm than good. These problems can produce a sharp edge on the pawl, which will quickly chew up the cylinder. This is one of the reasons why I recommend that the revolver be stripped after every shoot so that the tip of the pawl can be properly examined and dressed to remove burrs if necessary. Almost anything else is replaceable,

7. Exceptions to this may be found on small pocket revolvers, such as the author's 120 bore Adams, where the ratchet extends out to the periphery, and the 1863 .315in five-shot Remington, where the ratchet is cut into a projection on the back of the cylinder. On withdrawing the arbor, these cylinders will simply drop out of the right-hand side of the frame.

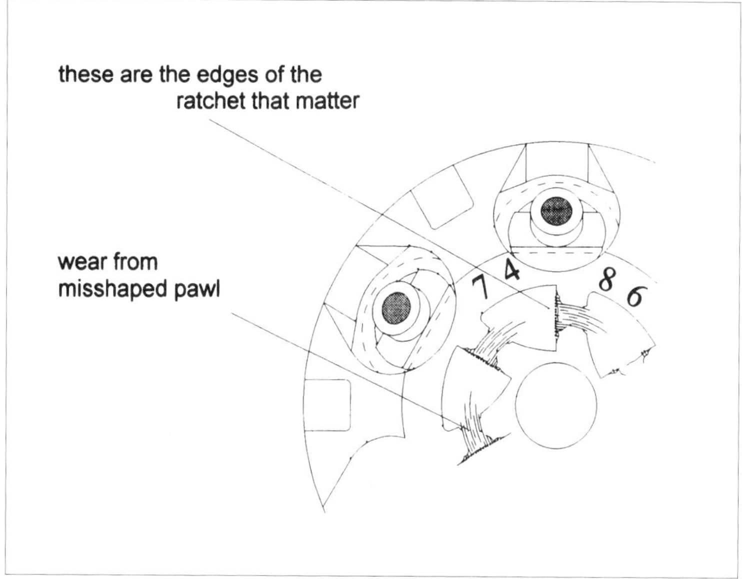

Fig. 22 Typical wear on Remington cylinders.

from weak springs and worn cylinder stops to missing front sights and cracked butt plates, all at a quite reasonable cost.

Many 'English' revolvers have the ratchet made as a separate piece and fitted to the rear of the cylinder with two screws (*see* Fig. 55). Both the author's 120 bore Adams and his unnamed 'transitional' pistol were made in this way. In theory, this should enable a replacement to be fitted, but it is not an easy thing to make without the proper machine tools.

Do not be caught out by thinking that stainless steel repros are not vulnerable to problems. Much of the stainless steel used in repro revolver manufacture is softer than normal steels, especially at the cheaper end of the market, and problems associated with wear can quickly make themselves apparent.

TAKING IT TO PIECES

When taking the Remington to pieces for cleaning or general maintenance you have the same problem as with other pistols regarding the tips of the screwdrivers used. It really is important to get these right, both with regard to the width of the blade and its thickness to ensure maximum purchase and minimum slip in the screw slot. The same applies to the nipple key: you have to get the right size. For instance, the nipple key for the Le Page is far too big for the Remington. Before you start to disassemble you will need to find a couple of glass dishes to put the parts in. This enables you to see what is in them and they are easy to clean after the revolver has been reassembled. The sequence of disassembly is as follows:

1. Drop the cylinder out of the frame as previously described. Wipe off as much of the oily black fouling as possible and then unscrew the nipples with the nipple key, putting the nipples and any associated washers into a dish for cleaning. A nipple key for this task is essential. A pair of pliers, even if modified to fit around the nipple, will inevitably slip and round off the edges, making the removal of the nipple more and more difficult as time goes on.
2. Remove the wooden butt plates by unscrewing the single screw in the middle of the butt. Put the plates to one side for cleaning with a dry rag since they will

be dirty both inside and out. Don't wash them. They will quickly distort.

3. Release the tension on the mainspring by unscrewing the mainspring tensioning screw, almost at the base of the butt, until it is clear of the mainspring. Tap the mainspring out of its slot in the frame. It will slide out from under the little wheel on the hammer and can be wiped and put in one of the dishes. On the author's original the mainspring is a tight fit and I normally have to tap it out using a brass drift with the butt resting on a sand-bag.
4. Next, unscrew the screw forward of the cylinder which retains the loading lever and slide out the loading lever, followed by the arbor. Note that the flat on the arbor is on the underside. Gas cutting is not limited to centre-fire revolvers so check for excessive gas cutting on the arbor at the point opposite the end of the cylinder.[8] The arbor and its mating hole in the cylinder quickly fill with fouling on the range, so get used to giving it a quick wipe between details as well as cleaning it thoroughly at the end of a shooting session.
5. Unscrew the single trigger guard retaining screw, lift the front and slide the projection on the back of the trigger guard out from its slot in the frame. This reveals the bifurcated trigger/cylinder stop return spring. If this is the first time you have dismantled the lockwork, note how this spring locates on the flats on the trigger and the cylinder stop since it will help you when you come to put it back again. With the hammer fully forward, release the screw retaining the bifurcated flat spring and lift it out. You can now unscrew and remove the trigger pivot screw, which permits both the trigger and the cylinder stop to be withdrawn through the bottom of the frame.
6. Nearly there! Unscrew the one remaining screw in the side of the frame, this one going through the hammer. To get the hammer out, you need to drop the bottom of the hammer out of the base of the frame and unscrew the little screw that acts as the pivot for the pawl. Once this is out the pawl drops out of the bottom of the frame and the hammer slides out of the top (*see* Fig. 23). On my repro the pawl pivot screw always seems to come loose during firing, but it can't go far since it is stopped by the inside surfaces of the frame.

CLEANING

Once you start shooting, every piece of the revolver becomes progressively covered with black oily fouling, together with your hands (and the front of your shooting jacket too, if you are not careful). Wipe off as much as you can with a dry cloth on the firing point as soon as you have finished your detail. Once you have finished the shooting session, give the complete pistol a brush out, wipe off any residues with a damp cloth and finally give it a generous spray with WD-40.

As soon as you have time give the gun a thorough clean. My favourite technique is to drop each part into hot water mixed with a small amount of washing-up liquid, but you can use any of the professional black-powder cleaners for this purpose. If you are really the sort of person who can't take things to pieces and put them back together, at least take out the cylinder and remove the wooden grips and trigger guard. Brush

8. Gas cutting is caused by a high-speed stream of hot gases which erodes the steel, cutting a quite distinctive slot in the arbor opposite the gap between the cylinder and the barrel cone. Long arms users, with their increased loads and pressures, also report gas cutting of the nipple hole, their threads and seatings. They counter this by wrapping the nipple threads in PTFE tape and fit thin copper or stainless steel washers under the nipples. This is not normally reported as a problem on revolvers, with their much lower loads and pressures. However, many an English revolver, such as the Tranter, will sport copper washers under the nipples, and thin ones will certainly do no harm if fitted.

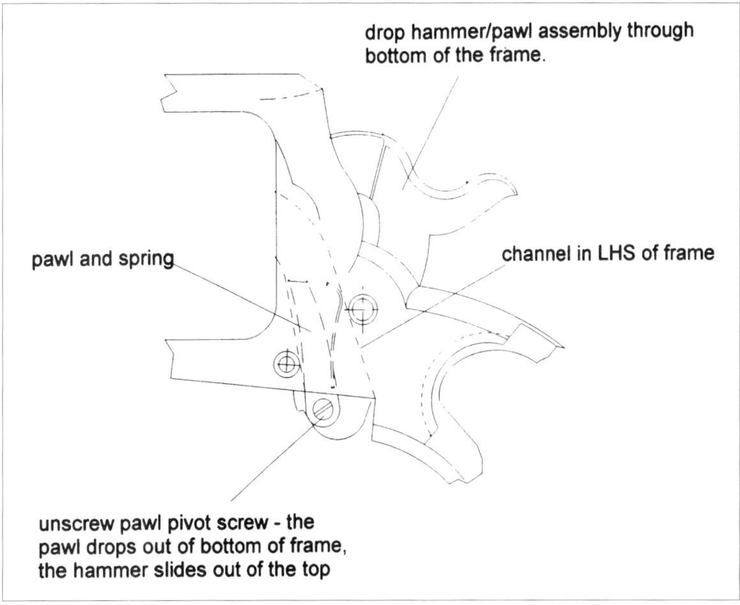

Fig. 23 Remington hammer and pawl removal.

everything except the grips in soapy water, getting right into the recesses of the frame, flush with boiling water, apply a dry cloth and finish drying in the oven before applying WD-40 in and out.

Watch out: it is very easy to lose a screw. From long experience, I put the plug in the sink, put the smaller parts in a glass bowl and the bowl in the washing up bowl, and do not empty either the bowl or the sink until the pistol is completely reassembled, oiled and returned to its safe. You only have to remove the trap under the sink to look for the little pawl pivot screw once, praying that it has not got into the drainage system, to see what I mean.

Brush the frame inside and out with a toothbrush. The frame has many odd corners where fouling accumulates. You can use a phosphor bronze brush in the barrel and even the individual chambers of the cylinder if you can get one that gets to the bottom. Use a cut-down cleaning rod with a wire brush on the end. Degrease and solder the central twisted wires and then cut them off as close to the bristles as possible. Only then will the brush get to the base of the chambers. Dry parts as you clean them and put them to one side. A chamber cleaner (*see* Fig. 24), made from a piece of slotted dowel, is also useful.

I favour finishing off the cylinder and the barrel by pouring boiling water over and through them before drying them off, since this releases the last vestiges of black powder residues. Note that they rust quickly after this treatment since all traces of oil will have disappeared. Oil each piece as you finish drying it. Put the parts back into the frame in reverse order, examining parts for burrs or high spots as you go, and taking any action to remove them as necessary. I suggest that you judge for yourself any claims that it is not necessary to take the pistol apart for cleaning before adopting the practice as standard. As a trial, just drop out the cylinder, clean the revolver with your favourite cleanser and put it back together. Then start again. Strip it completely, wiping each part on a clean rag. See how much fouling has remained and make your decision accordingly.

The only problem you may encounter during reassembly is with the mainspring.

On my repro it is easily reassembled by hand, but with the original external leverage is required to get the much stronger mainspring back into its slot in the frame. You can make a little tool for this yourself, either from a couple of screws or by silver soldering two 3/16in studs into a 1/2in × 1/8in steel bar to act as the lever (*see* Fig. 25). A large pair of pliers also works, but these will chew up the spring in time.

As you reassemble the cylinder, check that the tops of the nipples are not starting to be peened over. You may get advance warning of this problem on the range when you find that spent caps on one particular nipple become more and more difficult to remove. Nipples should be through hardened and tempered and will not generally deform in use. However, you may get one that missed the hardening process or was tempered improperly, and the end slowly distorts as shown in Fig. 26. Replace completely or file back to the original contour. Be careful not to take too much off or the caps will shake off as other chambers are fired.

All the nipples on the revolver should have touchholes of similar size – about 40 thou (about 1mm) is typical. Note that the hole in the repro Pietta Remington, as well as in most other repros, is tapered outwards from the cap towards the cylinder. The original Remington and some original English revolvers may not follow this pattern. The Tranter is one, which is tapered the other way round. Reverse tapered nipples can be bought for the repro Remingtons, but do not seem to offer any advantages.

Finally, when you are putting pistols or revolvers back into a safe, do not wrap them in cloth unless you are sure that the cloth is absolutely dry. It is much better to let the air circulate around them, otherwise you will end with a rusty pistol despite all your good cleaning techniques.

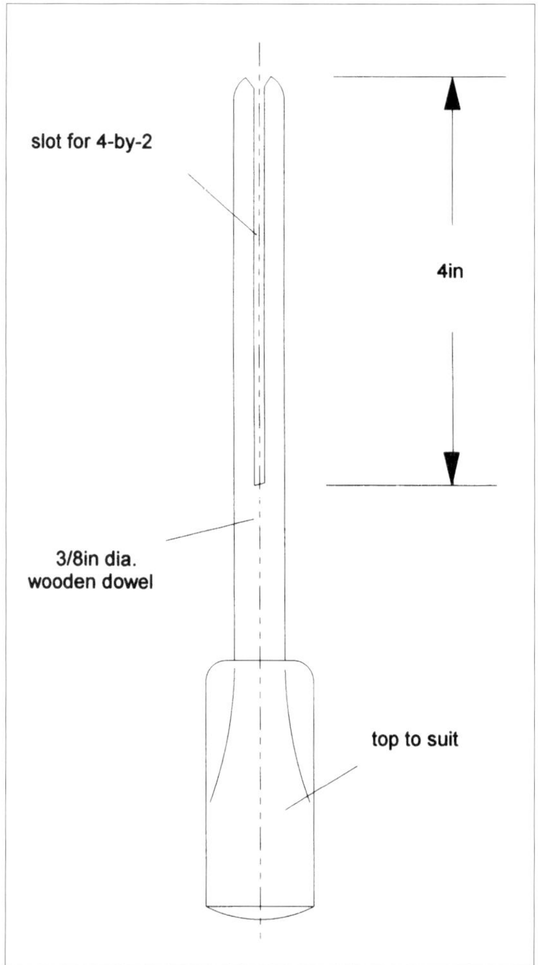

Fig. 24 Cylinder cleaning dowel.

Initial Inspection of New or Second-hand Revolvers

Unfortunately, we cannot rely on the perfect manufacture of repro revolvers, especially those from the cheaper end of the market. They are made down to a price, and final inspection seems to consist of 'if the hammer goes down and the cylinder goes round, that's good enough'.[9] This suggests that the first thing to do when you get your

9. For a classic example of this type of problem, see the rework found necessary on a virtually new .315in Remington Model 1863 in Chapter 5.

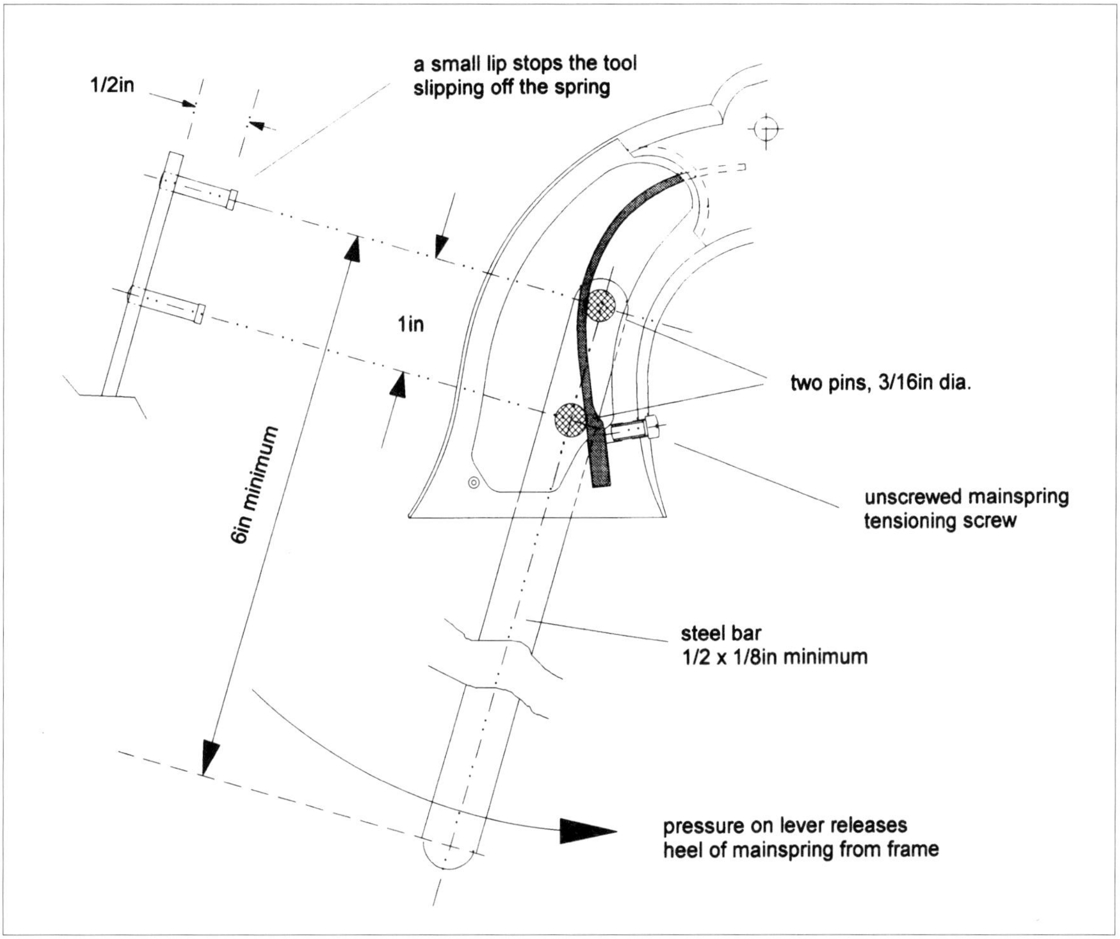

1/2in
a small lip stops the tool slipping off the spring
1in
6in minimum
two pins, 3/16in dia.
unscrewed mainspring tensioning screw
steel bar 1/2 x 1/8in minimum
pressure on lever releases heel of mainspring from frame

(Above) *Fig. 25 Revolver mainspring compressor.*

prized possession home, be it new or second-hand, is to take it to pieces. In any event, it is a good thing to get used to its maintenance before you have a problem and are faced with having to take it apart on the range. Secondly, it does allow you to carry out some post-delivery checks, which may improve the initial functioning of the revolver and ensure its long life. Remember that, during any competition run under MLAIC rules, you and you alone may service the pistol if it goes wrong during the detail. This means that familiarity with the internal workings of all your pistols and revolvers is of prime importance.

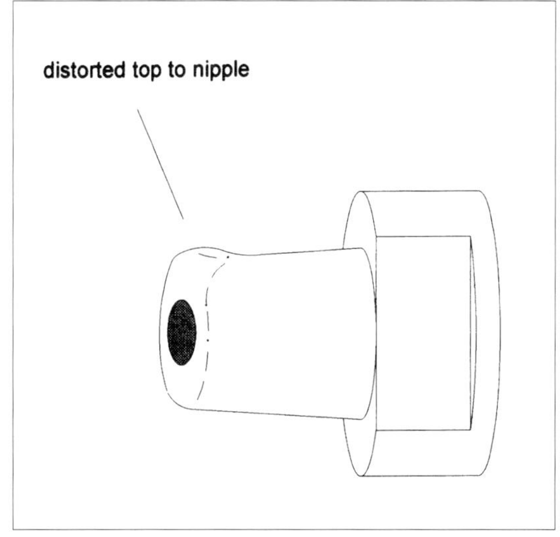

Fig 26. Distorted nipples.

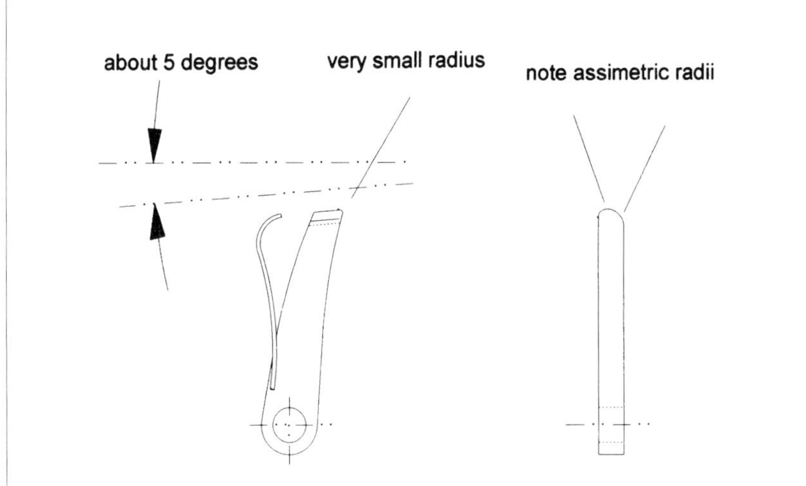

Fig. 27 Remington pawl.

Typical things to watch out for are:

1. Burrs on just about everything inside the frame. Favourites are the edges of the trigger/cylinder stop return spring and the edges of the hammer. Making sure that there are no burrs inside the frame is also important.
2. Check that the mainspring follower (the little wheel on the hammer) actually goes round. A favoured production process from the cheaper end of the market is to blue the hammer and its follower *after* assembly, resulting in the follower being stuck solid.
3. Check that the arbor is straight. On one pistol I had it looked as if the arbor had been both chewed up during manufacture and was visibly bent. Also check that the end of the arbor where it fits into the frame is bevelled – it ensures easier assembly. Finally, if it is a second-hand revolver, check for gas cutting opposite the end of the cylinder, as previously described.
4. Make sure that the tip of the pawl is not burred. The shape of the tip of the pawl should be properly profiled and polished, as shown in Fig. 27. This allows the pawl to roll along the surface of the ratchet to push the cylinder round.
5. Following reassembly, check the lock timing by ensuring that the cylinder is pushed round until the cylinder stop pops up into the indent in the cylinder just before the hammer is stopped by the frame. If it doesn't, it indicates that the pawl is not pushing the cylinder all the way round. This may result from either a worn ratchet on the cylinder, a worn pawl pivot screw or a pawl that is worn and is consequently too short. The latter problem can be rectified by taking out the pawl and tapping smartly with a hammer to stretch it slightly until the length is right. Another option is to replace the pawl; but you may be faced with the opposite problem of the pawl being a little too long, in which case it will have to be shortened to length and repolished.
6. When the hammer is released and is not stopped by the nipple it can go all the way forward until it is stopped by the step on the frame. On some revolvers that have seen hard useage the hammer has upset the edge of this step to form a burr. This slows the hammer down as it falls, resulting in light strikes. Remove any burr from this area of the frame. It

is also a good thing to look at the nose of the hammer. This inevitably gets burred with time. Dress off the burr where necessary.

VARIATIONS – ORIGINALS TO REPROS

One of the most common makes of repros is the Pietta, which was generally considered to be one of the better and more affordable variants of the type on the market when I bought one more than ten years ago.[10] However, the difference in 'feel' between my original Remington and my repro is quite noticeable. Although both are almost the same size and weight, individual parts of the pistols are quite different. For instance, the cylinders are not interchangeable. Neither are the pawls nor the trigger/cylinder stop return springs. Another major difference is the cubic capacity of the chambers, with the original being nearly 15 per cent higher than the repro. I noticed this when I used my usual measure to drop the filler into the chambers of the original Remington for the first time, and it disappeared farther into the chambers than with the Pietta. On checking the dimensions, I found that the original chamber was over 1.4in deep with the Pietta being almost 0.25in less. This led me to check the dimensions of some of the muzzle-loading revolvers that I could find.

The table below confirms that many original English revolvers had cylinders bored somewhat larger than the true bore diameters since they were often designed to receive paper wrapped 'cartridges' which were inserted by hand. They were made without a rammer as a consequence.

REVOLVERS: CHAMBER SIZES AND LOADS			
Revolver manufacturer	*Chamber diameter (in)*	*Chamber volume (in^3)*	*Maximum charge (grains)*
repro Colt Dragoon .44	0.440	0.235	49
54 bore Beaumont Adams	0.451	0.230	47
Remington .44 New Army	0.449	0.226	46
Ruger Old Army .44	0.450	0.215	43
repro Remington .44	0.454	0.198	37
56 bore Tranter	0.434	0.178	34
Remington .36	0.365	0.149	32
repro Remington .36	0.367	0.143	30
120 bore Adams	0.340	0.081	15
70 bore 'transitional' revolver	0.433	0.065	11
repro 1863 Remington .31	0.312	0.057	11

10. Quality changes in all manufacturers over the years, and sometimes even from batch to batch. Ask around for the best of breed at the time you are contemplating the purchase of a new repro. Expect to pay a considerable premium for the really professionally made repros from, for instance, Hege and Feinwerkbau.

Another thing that affects the feel is the grip, with even small changes in profile from the original making quite a difference. The 'feel' of my original Remington is quite different from my repro, and the reason why is easily seen if one set of butt plates is offered up to the frame of the other. This, by the way, is one of the major handling differences between the Remington and the Rogers and Spencer. The Rogers' grip is slightly wider at the heel than the Remington's and this gives a substantially different feel, which is preferred by some shooters. Some repros are significantly smaller than the originals on which they were based, and anyone with large hands may find difficulty in getting their middle finger comfortably between the trigger guard and the frame.

Some less obvious changes between originals and repros are the mainsprings, the trigger return springs and the pawl pivot screws. Here is one of the hidden variances between the original and most repros, since on the original Remington the pawl pivot screw is screwed into the pawl and on the repros it is screwed into the hammer.

As regards accuracy, both repros and original Remingtons have progressive rifling, whereas nearly all modern centre-fire revolvers have rifling with a constant twist. I have never seen a comparison of the merits of the two systems. I suspect that both will hold groups better than the shooter can ever produce, all other things being equal.

COMPLYING WITH THE MLA RULES

One of the key inspection points in official MLA competitions is the shape of the foresight. Foresights on repros must conform to the profiles used on the original pistols on which they are based. There are essentially two versions of the profile on the Remington. One, common to versions for both service

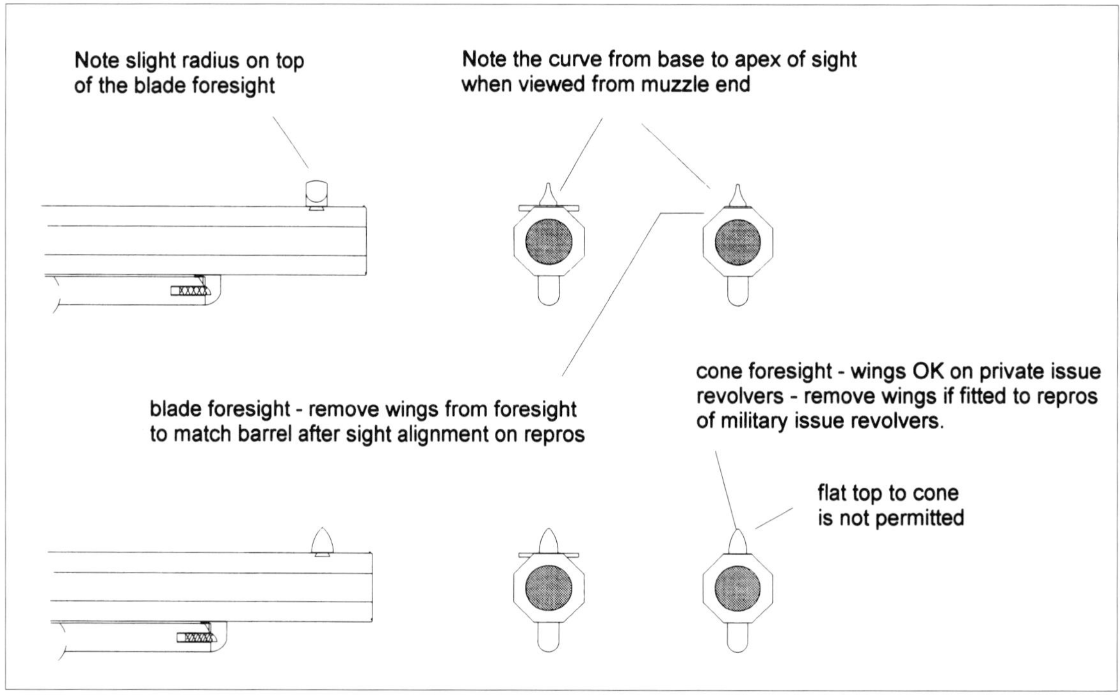

Fig. 28 Remington foresights.

and private use, is the truncated cone, originally made in German silver. The second, found on the versions made for Army service, is a curved blade. The only service foresights adjustable for windage were the original Beal's Remington in 36 calibre made for the US Navy, whereas the truncated cones on most of those for private purchase are mounted on a dovetail and are easily adjusted.

The shape of the foresight matters to the scrutineers, and you must have the right profile for the version you are shooting. It must be said, however, that there were many variations on the originals, so, if you have a revolver with an apparently non-standard sight, do not change it but be prepared to give evidence to the scrutineer.

Most of the Remington repros are provided with an approximation of the 'blade' profile, while the Rogers and Spencer repros are, quite correctly, fitted with a very thin cone. However, most of the blade foresights on repros do not have the 'original' profile when viewed down the barrel, and some scrutineers will reject a revolver on these grounds, even though only the top 20 to 30 thou of the foresight is visible when on aim. These profiles will have to be corrected for competitions run under MLAIC rules. Although the 'original' service pattern foresights were not driftable, many of the repros certainly are. This is acceptable in competition provided that, following the alignment of the sights to suit your shooting grip, load and so on, the wings on the foresight are filed back to the original contour of the barrel.

The only alternative for those with fixed foresights and 'windage' problems is to build up one side of the foresight and to file down the other. This will effectively move the centre of the foresight in relation to the centre line of the barrel. There are many variations used for this, from shims glued or soldered on, the building up one side with filled resin, to the manufacture of offset foresights to replace those originally fitted. Those with round post foresights fitted straight into the top of the barrel, which are standard on the Rogers and Spencer and common on the Remington, have a problem. Here you can't file off one side and retain the required height and correct profile. The only answer here is to make offset posts, but this is not a job to be tackled at home. If you really want to do the job properly, have a gunsmith remove the existing sight and replace it with one mounted on a dovetail, remembering, of course, to remove the wings before competition day. So if you are contemplating buying a second-hand repro for target shooting, the ease of correction of the windage on the foresight should be carefully considered.

The rear sight is formed by a V slot cut into the top strap. On both originals and repros this slot is often extremely small, and, when taking aim, only the tip of the foresight can be seen. Many a slot has been opened up on both originals and repros to get a better view of the foresight. This does not seem to worry the scrutineers, which is surprising since only the tip of the foresight can be seen whatever the foresight profile, whereas the width and the depth of the slot forming the rear sight make a considerable difference to the sight pattern.

LOADING

The original 44 Remington was made to Beal's patent in the late 1850s with the prime intent of 'personal protection'. Here, the cylinder would be loaded with 45 grains of black powder, producing an almighty bang, plenty of recoil and a decidedly uncomfortable effect on the recipient of the ball. Most shooting would have been at really close range, with instinct and self-survival being of much greater prominence than the careful alignment of the sights and a gentle increase of pressure on the trigger. Such full loads are not necessary for good accuracy nor conducive to the nerves of the man shooting beside you.

Whether we are shooting 'precision' in MLA competitions or 'service disciplines' under NRA rules, we only need to shoot with the minimum load to get the required accuracy. This keeps the noise down while the maintainability of the revolver is much enhanced. Most people shooting 44s use about 18 grains of TS2 or Swiss No.2, with some down as far as 15 and some up to 21 grains. On both my repro and original it does not seem to make much difference to the size of the group and not too much to the recoil. What matters more is that, once you have settled on a load, you should keep the variation in load down as much as possible (±½ grain being reasonable) to keep the group in the same place.

However, the original Remington loading lever was designed for fully charged chambers, and the stroke is not long enough to seat the ball on to 18 grains or so of black powder. To fire the pistol with the resultant void between powder and ball would result in uncontrolled powder burning, and is not to be tolerated (*see* Chapter 2 on single-shot percussion pistols). We also know that, for the greatest accuracy, the ball should be set as close to the face of the chamber as possible. The answer is to fill the space between the top of the powder and where the ball should be with an inert filler of some kind (*see* Fig. 29). By far the most common filler in use is ground, dry semolina ('cream o' wheat' in America).

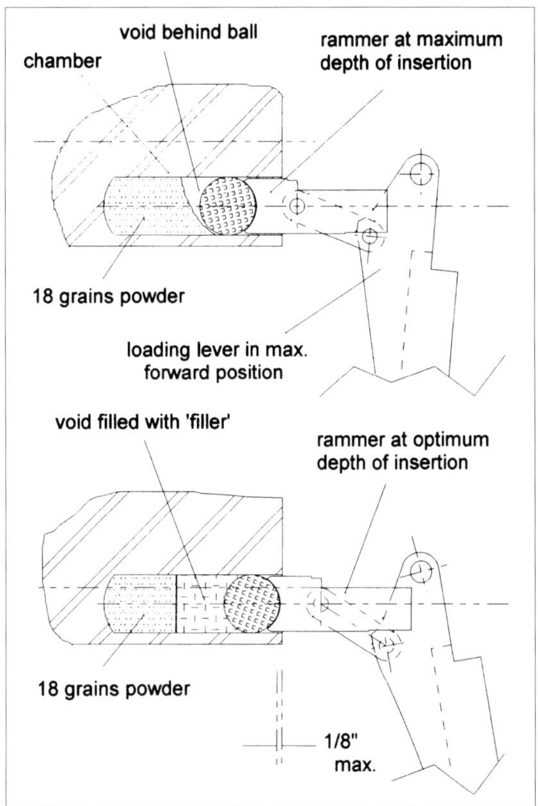

Fig. 29 Use of filler in Remington revolvers with reduced loads.

A less common but increasingly attractive alternative to powdered fillers is the use of foam plugs. Loaded directly on top of the powder with the ball on top, they perform the same function as the filler in keeping the ball close to the end of the chamber. They may also limit the fouling in the barrel in the same way as the patch limits fouling in the single-shot pistol. Obviously they must be of the correct length or the ball will be too far down the chamber for maximum accuracy. The plug follows the ball down the range for 15 to 20yd, but it is not biodegradable like natural powder fillers. They are certainly a cleaner alternative for those who shoot black powder indoors.[11]

Once the black powder has been dispensed from its glass or plastic phials into each chamber[12] the filler is ladled in with a

11. A point should be made about shooting black powder pistols indoors. Photographs showing sparks galore shooting out of the end of pistol barrels are indicative of the almost complete burning of the charge, and not of unburned powder being discharged from the barrel. This is confirmed by examination of the floor sweepings from in front of the firing point. This debris will not ignite if touched by a flame, in complete contrast with the remains of the smokeless powder spread across the floor after a session of shooting gallery rifles. This situation should not be confused with debris found at the firing point itself, where any spilled black powder should be carefully gathered and disposed of.

12. The rules forbidding loading direct from a flask in MLAIC competitions apply to revolvers just as much as they do to single-shot pistols.

scoop, dispensed from a plastic bottle with a wide nozzle or, preferably, from a second set of phials containing a weighed or measured amount of filler. This last method is by far the most reliable. It is all too easy to ladle too much or too little filler into the chamber, and one ball may be ¼in below the mouth of the chamber while, on the adjacent chamber, the ball projects over the lip. For the most accurate loading, the ball should be seated, with reasonable pressure on the loading lever, just below the lip of the chamber. In the uncompressed state, the semolina filler will normally come to about ⅛in below the top of the chamber. However, the amount the semolina compresses varies from brand to brand and this should be borne in mind when changing supplier.

If you do decide to use a scoop, you can make one easily from a .38 S&W case superglued to a small wooden handle and filed to size. Note that, because of differences between the size of the chambers in originals and repros, you will need filler scoops of different sizes. Lee used to make a useful set of scoops for centre-fire reloading, but they were probably all discarded in the United Kingdom when centre-fire revolver target shooting was banned.

If you do overfill a chamber, blow a little filler out before seating the ball. If you do not, the ball will project above the lip of the chamber even after it has been 'rammed' into place. If you try to get away with this, you will find that, when the projecting ball gets round to the barrel as the cylinder is rotated, it will not go any further and the mechanism will jam. The answer is to anticipate the problem before you get this far, slip the cylinder out of the frame and cut the top off the ball flush with the surface of the cylinder with a sharp knife. This knife is one of the key contents in the shooter's 'ready for use' box. If you fail to take this action in time, you either have to trim the ball *in situ* or force back the pawl to remove the cylinder.

The proper size of the ball[13] for a revolver varies from make to make, and, I suspect, from date to date, except that all the original 44 Remingtons I know use a .451 ball. My Pietta Remington repro takes a .457, and a Euroarms version I once owned used a .454 ball. The size of the ball is determined by the size of the chamber rather than the size of the barrel. The ball should be a reasonably tight fit, without having to lean on the loading lever. Some revolvers with sharp edges to the chambers will shave off a thin ring of lead as the rammer is forced home. This is quite acceptable – just remember to flick away the shaving to prevent its getting into the lock mechanism. Again, this is a question of borrowing balls to start with to get the right ball size before you buy a new mould.

Ease of loading can differ between versions of both repros and originals. Some revolvers have, as do most Remington originals, a square end to the chamber. Others, the Rogers is one and I seem to remember that the Euroarms Remington repro another, have a slight taper at the mouth of the chamber. While this taper might reduce the loading pressure, it is important to link the size of the ball with the parallel part of the chamber and not its mouth, otherwise you could be trying to force an oversize ball into the chamber. Many English original revolvers have tapered mouths to the chambers to ease the loading of paper cartridges.

With the ball settled firmly just below the lip of the chamber, the final act before capping is to apply lubricant over each ball as it is sitting in the chamber. In the first half of the nineteenth century, when revolvers were starting to be commercially developed, this lubricant acted not just as a ball lubricant and residue softener, but also as a

13. There is nothing in the MLAIC or MLAGB rules to prevent you using 'picket'-shaped bullets in Colt or Mariette competitions. They rarely are used, however, as it is difficult to align the bullets to the centre line of the chambers when loading, which leads to the odd wild shot on the target.

barrier to stop flashover from the fired chamber to the adjacent one. One has only to watch the flashover between all chambers on the pepperbox pistol in the BBC television series 'The Gun'[14] to show the result. However, in normal target-shooting today, inter-chamber flash-over is completely prevented by the plug of inert filler between the ball and the powder, and ball lubrication and residue softening is all the lubricant is left to do. The task of lubrication should not be underestimated: get the lubrication wrong and the group will be all over the card.

You can buy lubricant for this purpose, but virtually all shooters make up their own. In the wilder parts of the West, they used a mixture of tallow and goose grease, if they used anything at all.[15] The key property is a reasonably high melting point since the flash from each chamber can easily melt and blow away the lubrication in the adjacent chamber. You also need something that does not form a hard deposit in the hot barrel. My current favourite is a vegetable fat such as Trex or Spry mixed with 5 to 10 per cent of beeswax. The beeswax and fat can be blended if they are warmed in a saucepan – lack of water in the beeswax precludes the microwave oven. Too much beeswax and it is difficult to scrape it out of its tin – or some similar open-top container – on the range; too little and the melting point is too low. Lolly sticks are ideal for its application. Fill the gap between the top of the ball and the mouth of the chamber with the lube, wiping off as much as possible anywhere else on the pistol before taking it up for firing.

CAP SELECTION

Cap selection for revolvers is important, both from the point of view of brisance (energy developed over time) and especially of the fit of the cap on the nipples. If the caps are too large in diameter, they will fall off as soon as the first chamber is fired. If they are too small, the falling hammer may not be able to push the cap down on to the top of the nipple to effect first-time ignition. For instance, many European shooters will use the RWS No.11 cap (their number 1075) or its equivalent on their Remington repro revolver, but prefer the somewhat longer No.11 cap from RWS (their number 55) for the Rogers and Spencer. I use the CCI No.10 cap on my original Remington, which still has the somewhat smaller diameter original nipples. But be warned, for there is poor standardization of cap sizes between manufacturers. For instance, the American supplier Remington's No.10 caps are virtually of the same internal diameter as the RWS No.11s, but are significantly shorter. They do not seem to split so easily either and are much less likely to break up and drop fragments into the otherwise vulnerable Ruger Old Army revolver.

Getting caps to fit the original nipples on English revolvers is a problem. They are generally a good deal smaller than anything available today. My answer to this problem has been to make complete new sets of nipples to fit available caps, putting the original nipples carefully aside against the day when the complete revolver is put up for sale. The biggest problem here is to match the original thread form and size. There was little standardization of threads either in London

14. The documentary series on pistols screened by the BBC, not the film of Gregory Peck and the vicissitudes of his full-bore cannon on the way to Avila. The pepperbox as a genre often had nipples protruding at right angles to the barrel array, and was mainly without flash guards between the nipples. This is undoubtedly where the majority of flash-overs occurred, and not chamber mouth to chamber mouth. On a pepperbox, with its lack of frame in front of the 'cylinder', the balls had somewhere to go. On the transitional revolver (*see* Chapter 6) and more advanced full frame revolvers, it was a different matter. I am reliably informed that the 'flash-over incident' in the BBC programme had to be fabricated to show the effect.

15. The reported state of the average cowboy's side arm was described by one historian as 'deplorable – with as much chance of killing the shooter as the intended recipient of the ball.'

or Birmingham – the two main centres of the British firearms industry in the 1850s. It was common practice to cut a tap, make a die from it and use the resultant tap and die as a set until one part broke or was worn out. It is normally easy to tap out the original thread in the cylinder to match a new set of nipples, but to refit the old nipples at some time in the future will then be a problem.

HOW THE SINGLE-ACTION PERCUSSION REVOLVER WORKS

The mechanism of the Remington is simplicity itself. Being single-action – that is, thumb cocking – reduces the number of moving parts to a minimum.

The Cylinder Stop

On drawing back the hammer, the initial action is to drop the cylinder stop from its engagement in the indent in the cylinder wall before the pawl comes into contact with the ratchet on the back of the cylinder. This is caused by the little stud on the hammer pushing on the back side of the inner wing on the cylinder stop, rotating it about its mounting pin in a clockwise direction – from the right-hand side of the revolver, as shown below. Well before the hammer reaches the half cock position, the cylinder stop has dropped down into the frame, enabling the cylinder to be rotated anti-clockwise (from the front) for loading.

As the hammer reaches full cock, this wing slides off the side of the stud and on to its sloping top, which allows the return spring to pop the cylinder stop back out of the frame and into the waiting indent in the cylinder. There it remains as the hammer is released, the bevel on the stud passing under the sprung wing of the cylinder stop until it drops back into its original position.

When cocking the pistol it is essential that the hammer is pulled back as far as it will go. As the hammer is rotated, you can

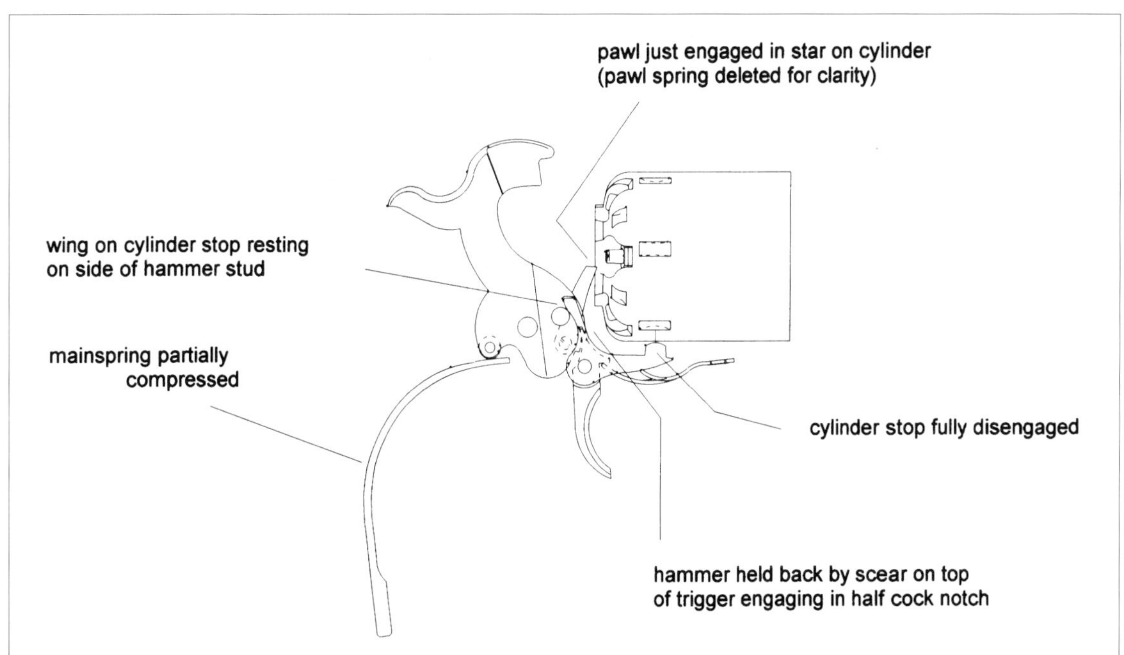

Fig. 30 The Remington lock mechanism – at half cock.

hear the scear on the top of the trigger 'click' as it slips over the half cock notch and then the full cock notch. However, the cylinder has to go round a little further before the cylinder stop drops off the side of the stud on the hammer. If you pull the hammer back only as far as the full cock notch, the cylinder stop will not engage in its indent in the cylinder and the cylinder will actually be 'floating' as the hammer drops, reducing accuracy and endangering safety. The moral of this is 'cock firmly, not gingerly'.

The Pawl

The pawl is mounted on its own pin on the left of the hammer below the main hammer bearing. With the hammer in the forward position, the pawl is hidden in the frame. As the hammer starts to be drawn back, the pivot of the pawl is rotated anti-clockwise. The pawl is pushed against the front face of a slot cut in the left-hand side of the frame by its own small, flat spring bearing against the back wall of this slot. Further hammer rotation causes the pawl to emerge from the frame and locate behind the flat face of the next available segment of the ratchet cut into the rear of the cylinder.

As the rotation of the hammer progresses, the tip of the pawl continues to press against this face, which rolls round the top of the pawl until the cylinder stop drops into place. This rolling action should be quite smooth, and a properly shaped and polished top on the pawl will enable this rotation to be completed time after time without marking the cylinder or damaging the pawl. If the top of the pawl is misshapen, it scratches repeatedly at the flat faces of the ratchet segments, resulting ultimately in an unusable cylinder.

A soon as the hammer starts to drop, the pawl pivot pin rotates clockwise and the pawl is withdrawn first from the face of the ratchet and finally back inside the frame. Note that the pawl does nothing to help to

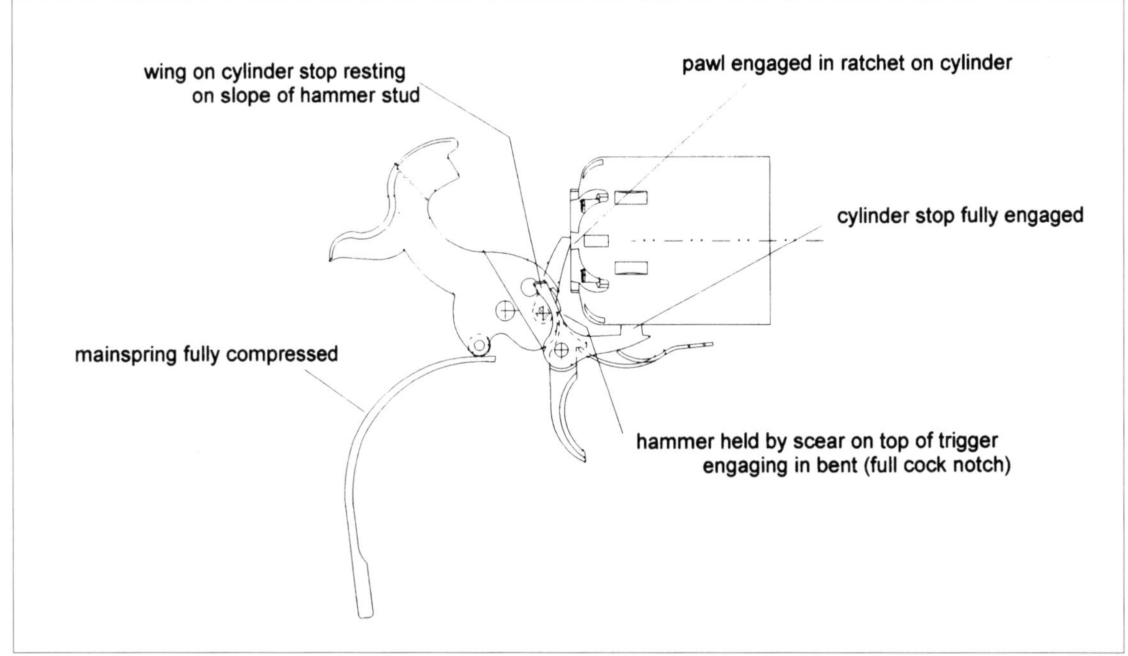

Fig. 31 The Remington lock mechanism – at full cock.

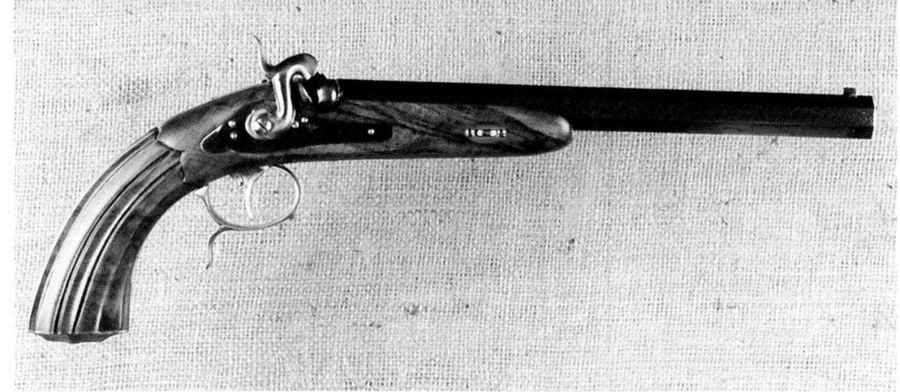

1. Pedersoli's Mang in .38 calibre. Note the similarity in form to the original Kaminecek in Plate 3.

2. The Hege Siber in .33 calibre. Neat, uncluttered lines are coupled with top-of-the-range workmanship and accuracy to match.

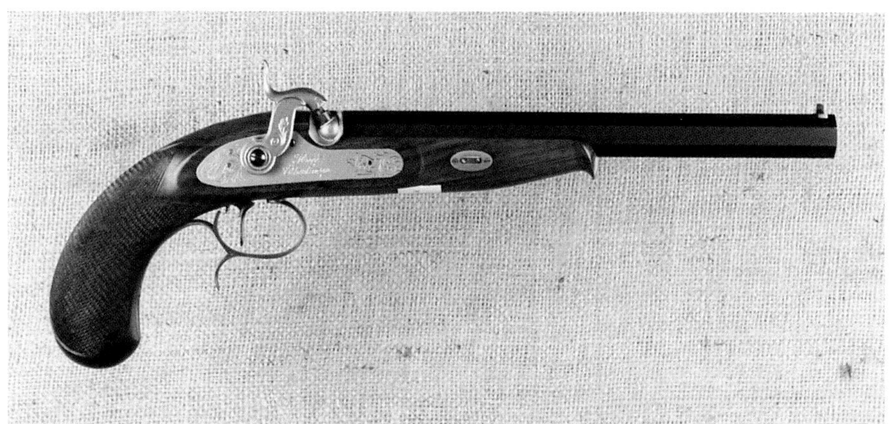

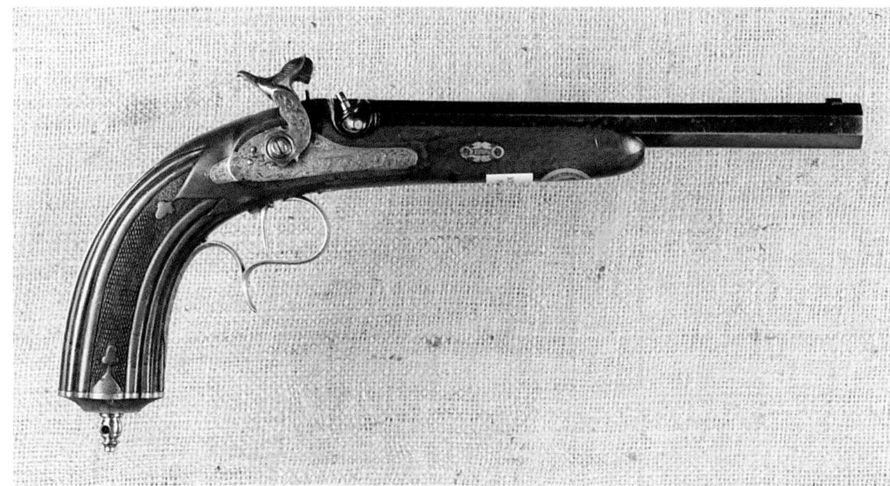

3. The original Kaminecek, again in .38, proudly bearing an international sticker or two.

4. Pedersoli's Le Page percussion, supplied in .33, .38 and .44 calibre. A great workhorse for tyros and those aspiring to greater things; note the reworked butt on the author's .44.

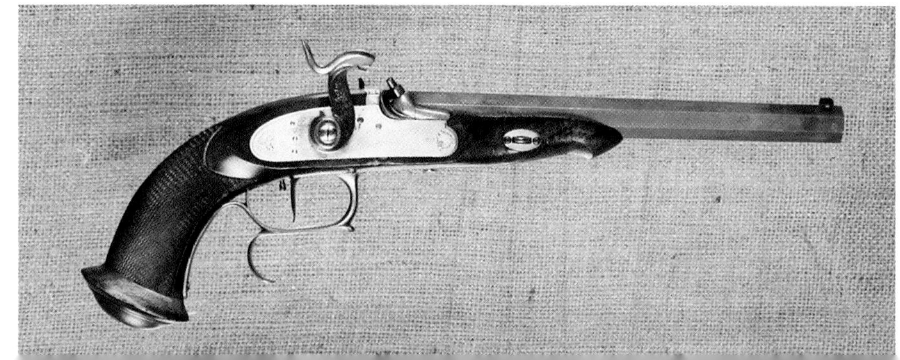

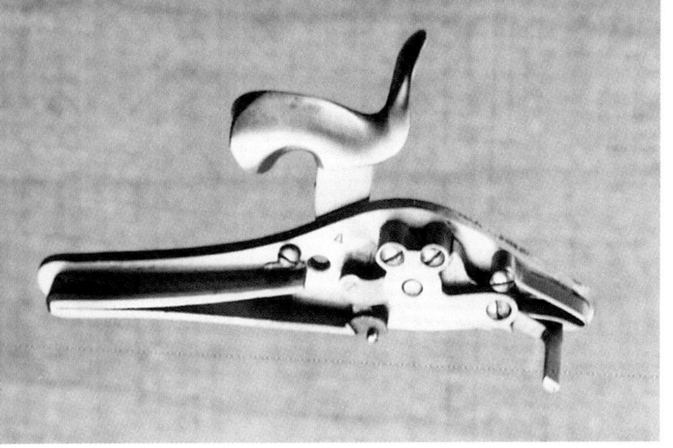

5. A lock's a lock for a' that. The following plates show the remarkable similarity between original and reproduction locks. The Mang lock is shown here.

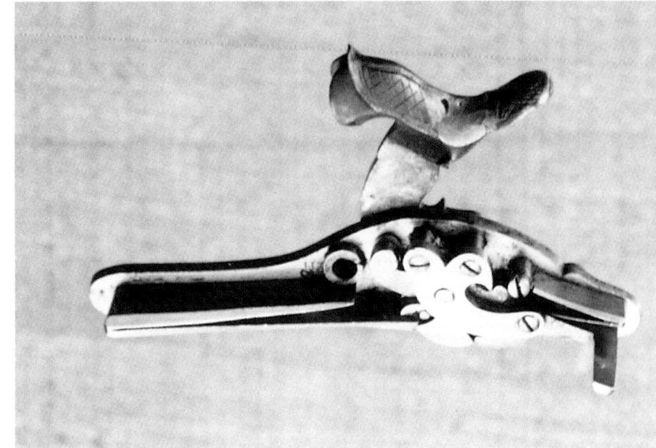

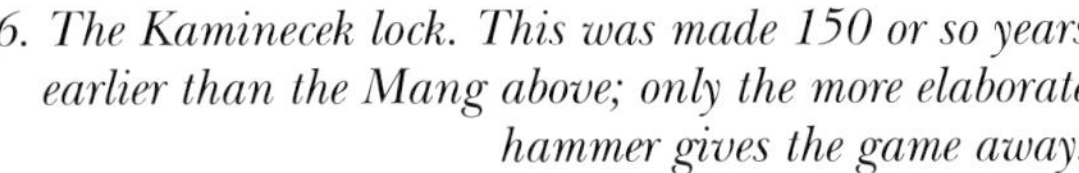

6. The Kaminecek lock. This was made 150 or so years earlier than the Mang above; only the more elaborate hammer gives the game away.

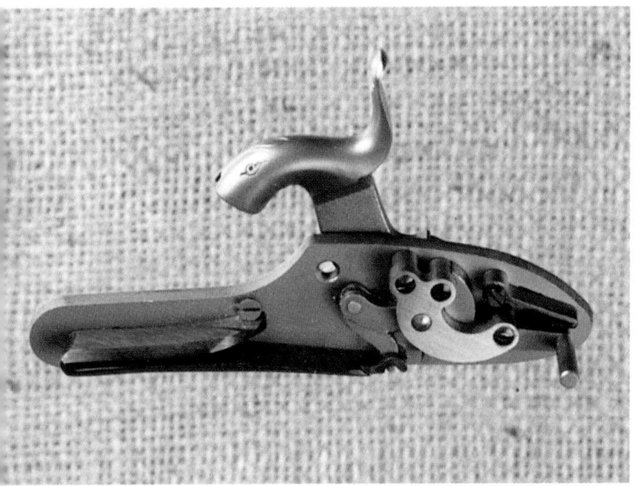

7. The lock from the modern Hege Siber.

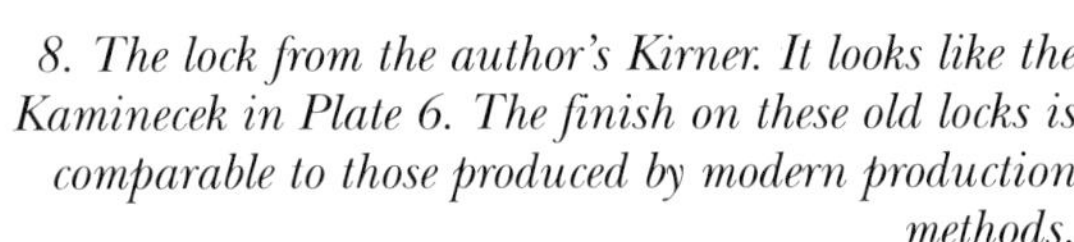

8. The lock from the author's Kirner. It looks like the Kaminecek in Plate 6. The finish on these old locks is comparable to those produced by modern production methods.

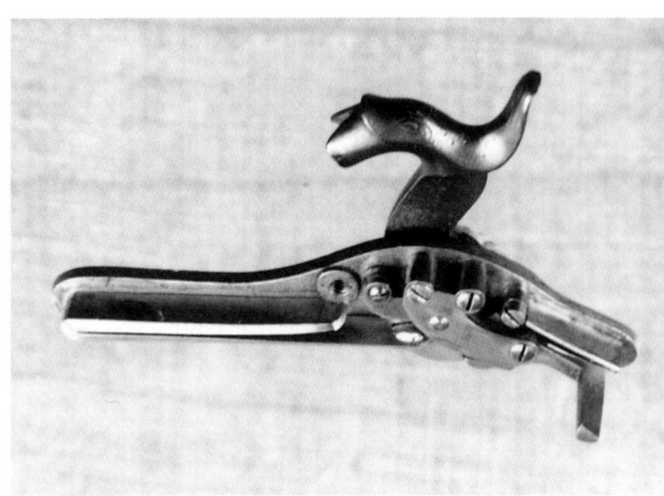

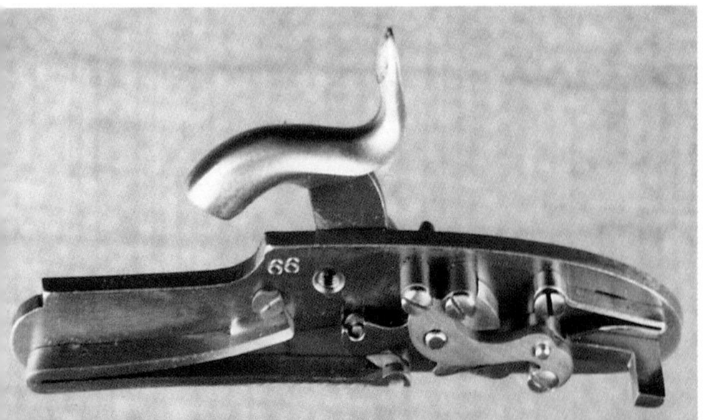

9. The Le Page lock. This is unchanged in principle since the single-shot percussion lock took over from the flintlock during the 1820s. Nearly all percussion locks used the same technology as the flintlocks in the eighteenth century, when the link between the mainspring and tumbler and the detent were added.

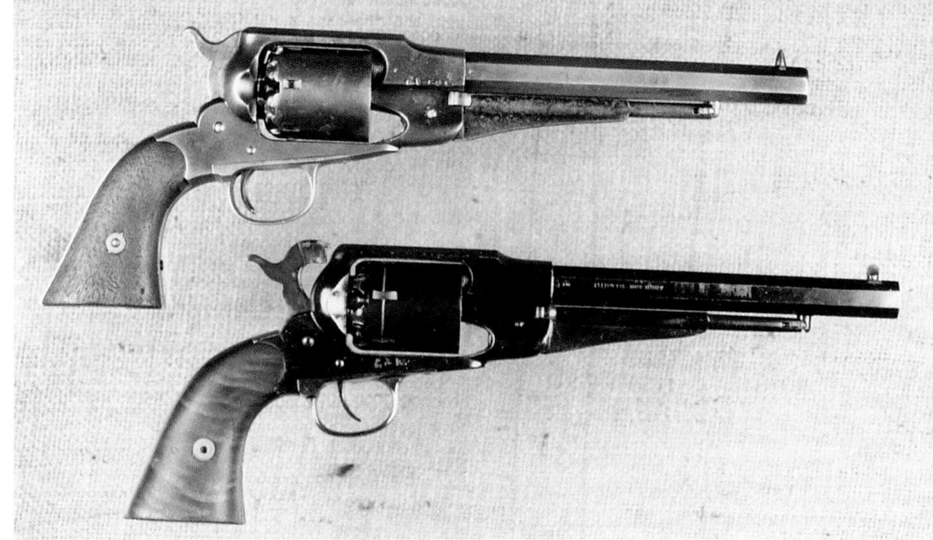

10. Probably the two most common muzzle-loading revolvers seen on the range. At the top, an original Remington New Army model, with its driftable cone foresight; below is the Pietta version, a repro with the traditional blade foresight. They handle in much the same way, but do not expect one set of component parts to fit the other.

11. The Ruger Old Army, a modern response to the mainly American shooters' expectations. Its use in Britain is limited to 'free' revolver shoots as it is ineligible for any competitions conforming to MLAIC rules.

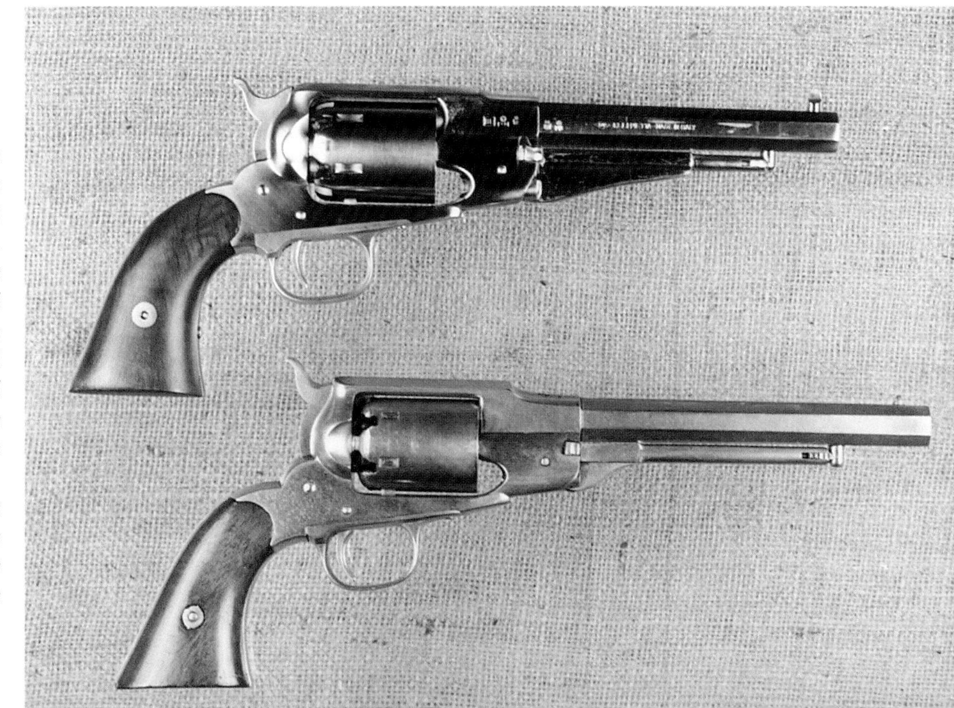

12. Two 36 Remingtons. The upper gun is the Pietta repro in stainless steel. Note the shortened barrel compared with the 44 illustrated in Plate 10. Below is the genuine article, a nickel plated original Beal's Remington in very good condition; from the serial number it appears to be one of the first to be made. Note the high spur on the hammer, the lack of relief where the barrel meets the cylinder, the much reduced web on the loading lever, and a driftable cone foresight.

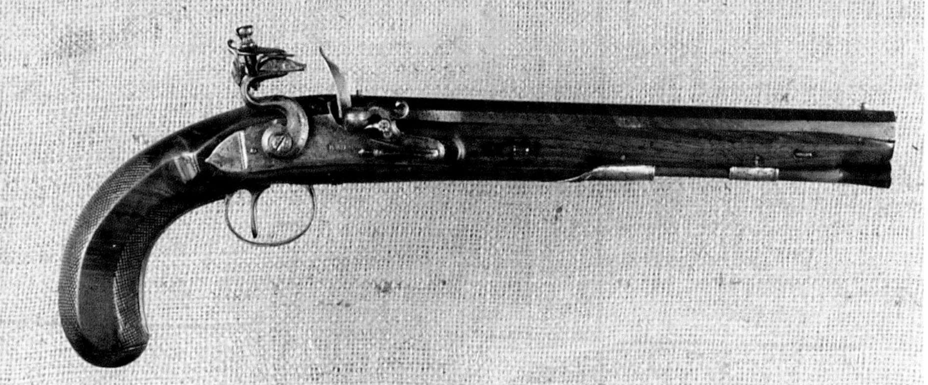

13. The author's 28 bore (.535in) Bass flintlock of about 1793. This is the epitome of the end of the century duelling pistol, with fast lock, roller on the frizzen spring and built-in 'pointability'.

14. The Nock. The silver fore-end on the half stock and gold rim and engraving on the barrel are typical of the duelling pistols produced by Henry Nock around 1800; this one is in 40 bore (.490in).

15. Another flint original, a Staudenmeyer with set trigger. John Henry Staudenmeyer had been apprenticed to John Manton, and was active in London at a number of addresses between 1799 and 1825. Note the similarity of the lock with the earlier Nock (Plate 20).

16. Pedersoli's Le Page flintlock in .45 calibre, the only Le Page smooth-bore calibre offered. It can also be supplied with a matching .44 rifled barrel. Those observant will see the simplified fore-end and the remodelled butt on the author's pistol.

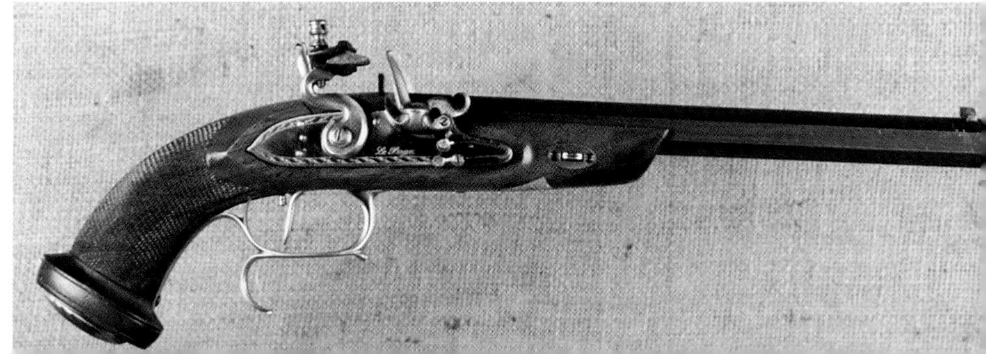

17. *A very old lock, probably of Italian or Balkan origin, dating from the 1730s. Note the parallel-sided pan, striated frizzen, no bridle and no link; no roller follower on the frizzen either; the tumbler and the link are more recent additions. The first true flintlock (with a vertical scear) has been attributed to Marin de Bourgeoys (Lisieux, Normandy) about 1610.*

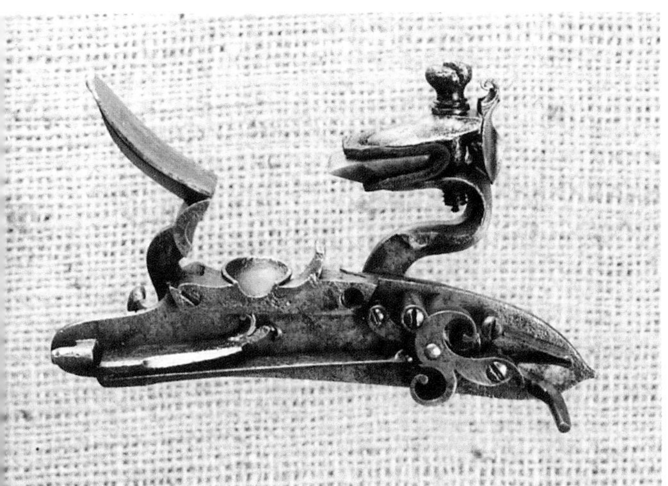

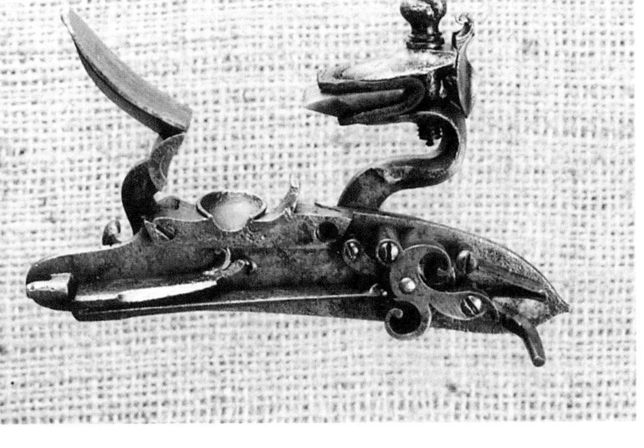

18. *By the mid 1700s basic lock design was well established. This one is from the Bass described in Chapter 5, finally put together between 1791 and 1794. Many parts could have come from a Twigg 20 years earlier or be used on a Probin 10 years later.*

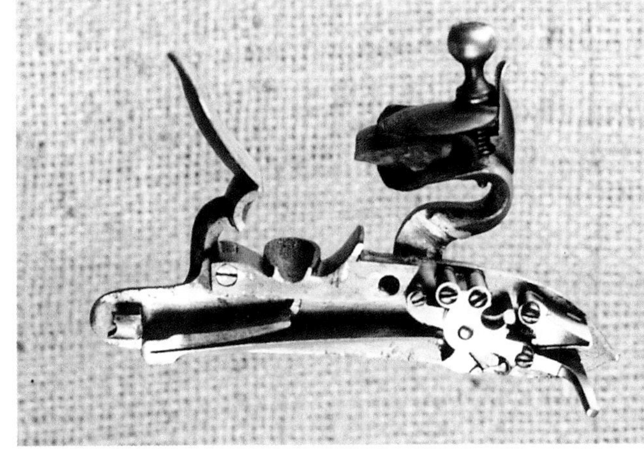

19. *The lock of the Staudenmeyer. The 'semi-rainproof' pan shape is getting narrower on this Staudenmeyer of the early 1800s, with less scrolling on the bridle, part of which has snapped off without affecting its functionality.*

20. *The lock of the Nock. This is of roughly the same vintage as the Staudenmeyer, although the Nock has an even deeper and narrower 'rainproof' pan. Someone had been trying to lower the original mainspring pressure; its replacement is shown here.*

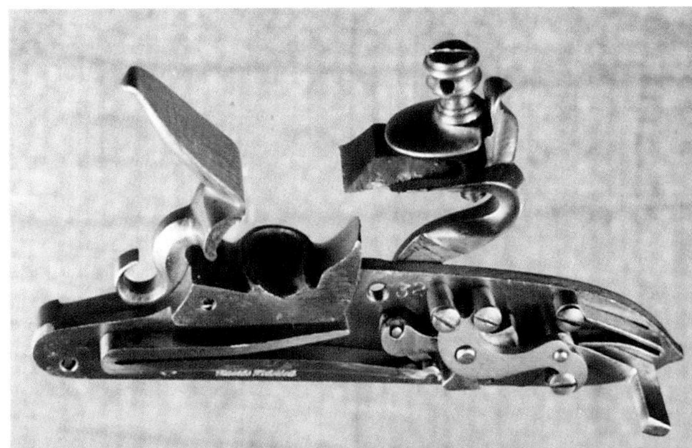

21. *The lock from the author's Le Page flintlock. Many parts are interchangeable with the percussion lock. Note that the pan is wide and shallow, not narrow and deep as in the Nock. The number of misfires in the pan I have is probably 1 in 30, usually caused because the flint has either lost its edge or worked loose.*

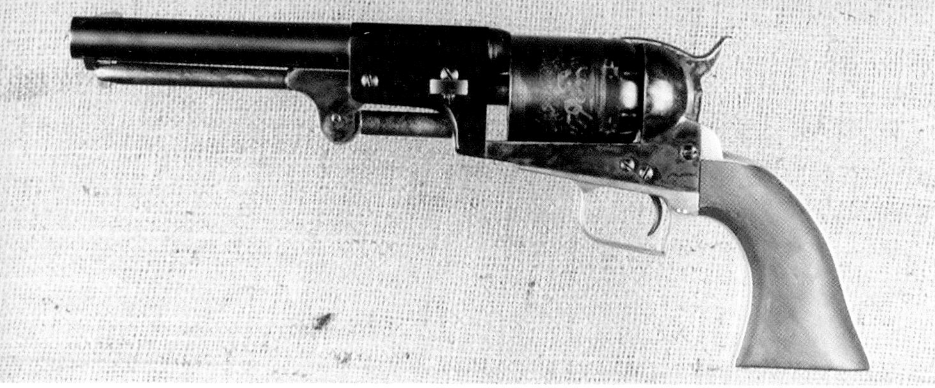

22. The Colt Dragoon in repro form. Big and hefty but probably not the best revolver for serious target shooting. Surprisingly, this model has only a minimal capacity for higher loads than the original Remington New Army. Was the original bigger?

23. The Rogers and Spencer in repro form. Note the quite different shape of the grip compared to the Remington, the high combe on the hammer (reminiscent of the original .36 Beal's Remington) and the quite different loading lever/rammer.

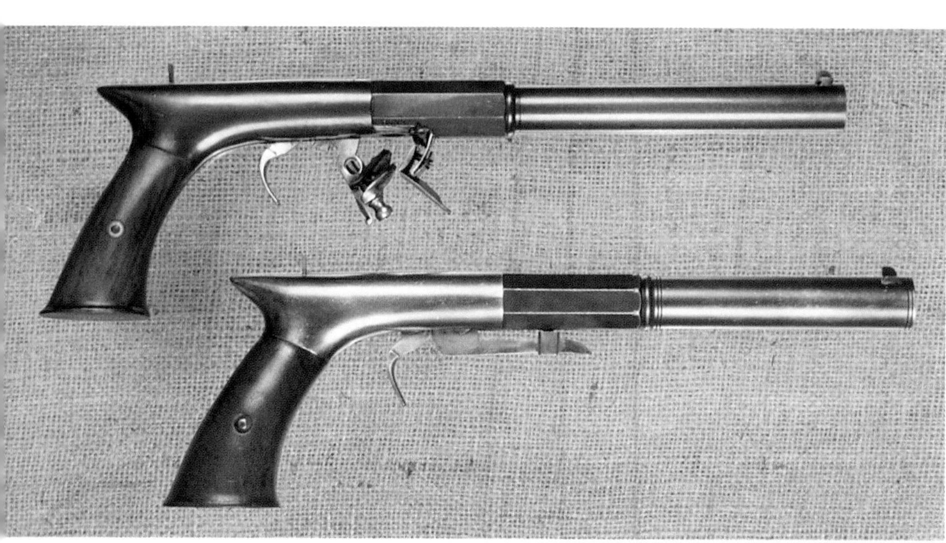

24. Jim Greathead's flint and percussion single-shots. These are based on the original boot pistols produced by the gunsmiths of Andersontown. These gunsmiths produced only percussion versions, so Greathead's work exhibits some imaginative thinking. The upper example is the flint version, which works despite the pan opening downwards.

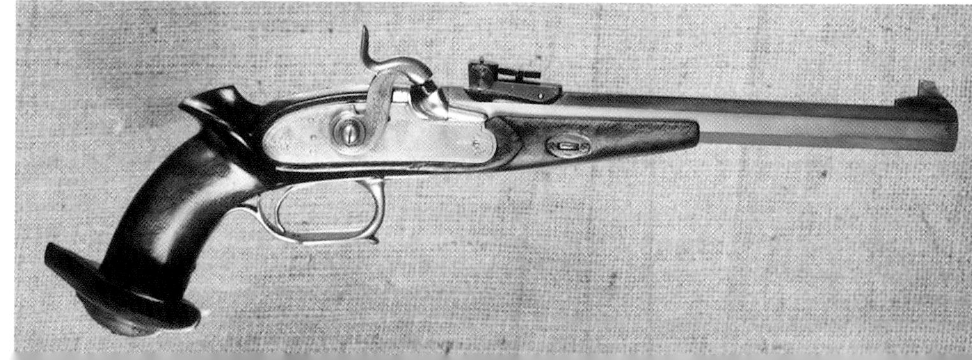

25. The author's 'free' pistol in .36 calibre. This clearly shows its Pedersoli origins. The .36 barrel, the same external size as the .44, allows the rear sight to be fitted close to the bore line.

26. The double-action only Bentley: an original candidate for the action ML and English pistol events? This gun dates from about 1857. It comes apart by driving out the wedge, in a similar way to the Colt single-action revolvers. The trigger pull, before it was modified, was dreadful. Joseph Bentley worked closely with the Webley family for many years.

27. A third model Tranter. Cocking the revolver with the middle finger and then releasing the hammer with the trigger finger takes some practice. This system is excellent for advancing target and similar disciplines, but remember that you have only five shots, typical of English revolvers. Note the similarity of the frame with the Adams below. Early Tranters were built to Adams's original 1851 patent.

28. The 52 bore Beaumont Adams and the 120 bore Adams; the British answer to the single-action Colts, 1851 style. Above is a 52 bore (.457in in the chamber, .451in in the bore), trigger cocking, five-shot Beaumont Adams, of about 1856; this one is fitted with a Kerr loading lever. Its little brother is another Adams, of perhaps three years earlier, an original five-shot, trigger cocking, 120 bore (.340in in the chamber, .331in in the bore). It is small enough to qualify for a 'pocket pistol'. The original Adams pistols were loaded with a ball with a spike on one side on to which was fitted a cardboard or leather wad. See *Chapter 6.*

29. For the pocket pistol events we have a brace of 35 bores, both of the traditional muzzle-loading variety. Many small pocket pistols were made with turn-off barrels, which may make life tedious for others during competitions. Note the back lock action on the one at the top. It is just possible to see the pips at the end of the barrels acting as foresights. These are fine for 10yd, provided that being there is as important as winning.

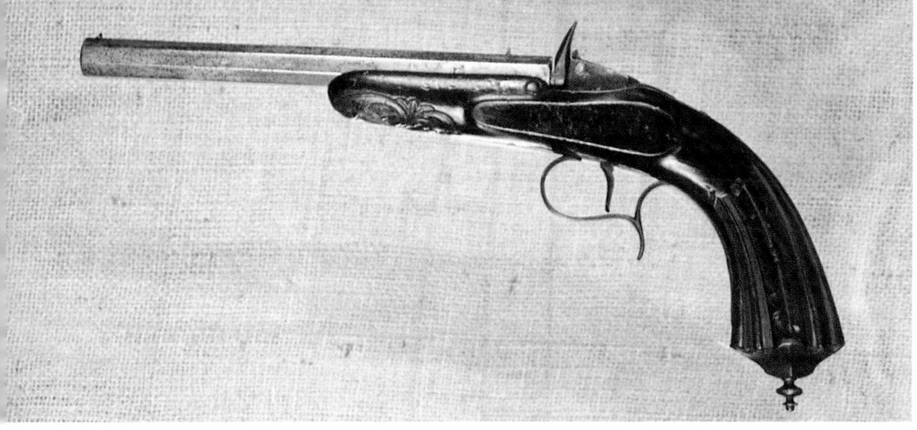

30. A typical gallery pistol; this example engraved E.P. Lefaucheur à Paris is in 120 bore (.342in). It groups well for a smooth-bore with 12 grains behind a .335in ball and a .010in patch. The large grip is particularly comfortable.

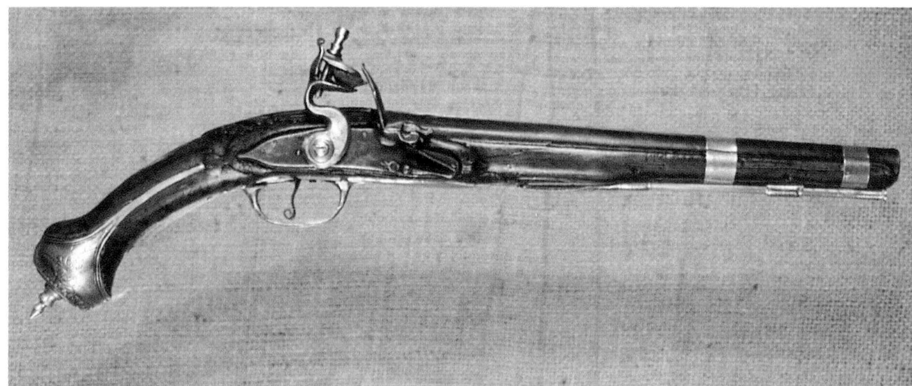

31. A 28 bore (.557in) Italian or Balkan pistol, dated by the Victoria & Albert Museum at about 1730. The original barrel bands may have been pierced silver or bound with silver wire and the false ramrod steel or wood. The rebuilt lock is shown in Plate 17. The owner was allowed a single shot with a much reduced load following the pistol's reconstruction before it was consigned to display only.

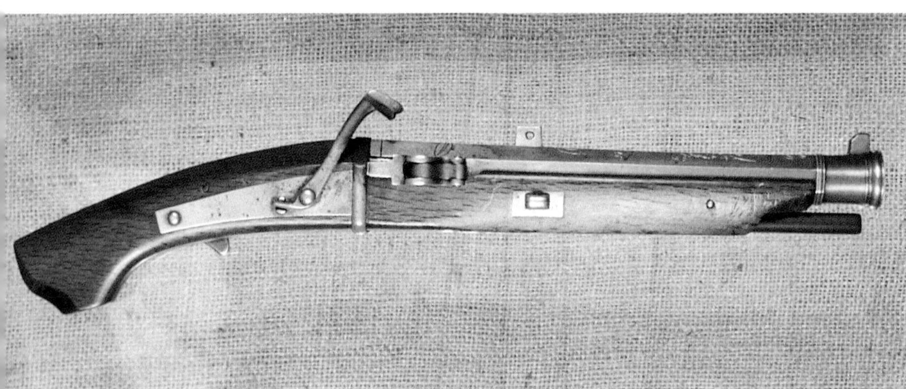

32. An original Japanese matchlock pistol in excellent condition. Compare it with the design of the repro shown in Fig.59, itself a direct copy of another original. Japan's self-imposed isolation until the mid 1800s restricted pistol development and manufacturing techniques, so there are no screws on the original. The repros follow this 'no screw' rule to the letter.

33. The 'ready for use' box putting everything to hand. See 'On the Range' in Chapter 3. The box holds nipple keys, pliers, ramrod, four rows of seven powder files, box of balls, caps, spare flints, flintlock pricker and powder trickler, knife and even an ice lolly stick. It also retains the essential piece of clean cloth hanging from the shooting table. The ever present scope and stand are omitted for clarity.

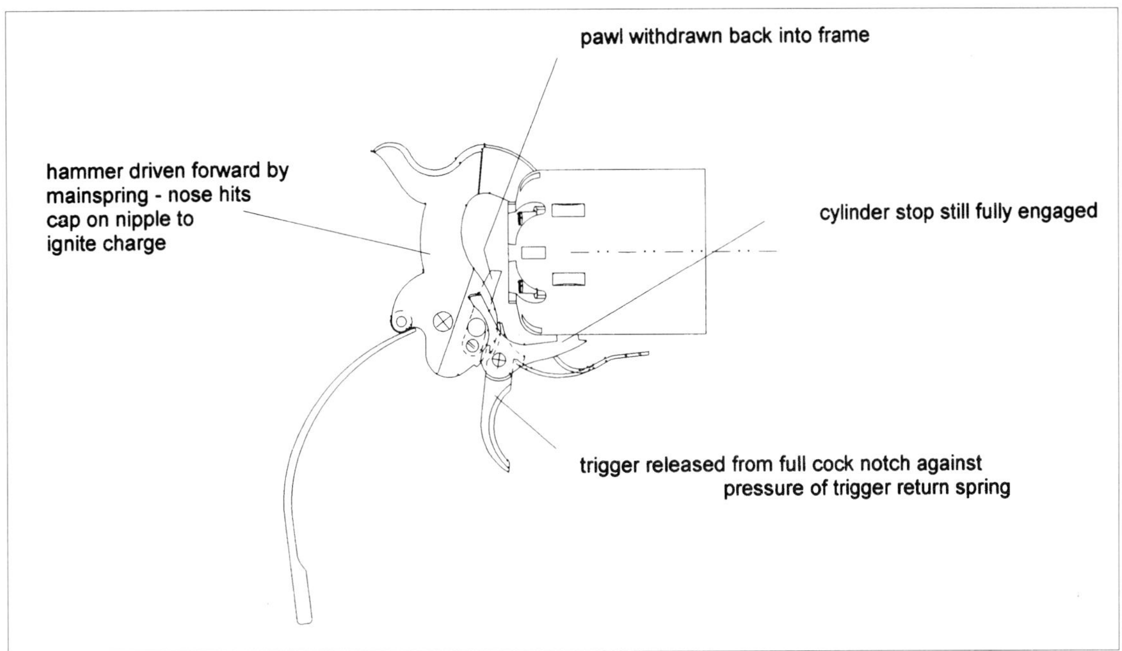

Fig. 32 The Remington lock mechanism – as fired.

lock the cylinder in place once the hammer starts to drop.[16]

At half cock, the pawl has already contacted and started to rotate the cylinder. This is why the correct dismantling procedure (see previous notes) is needed when removing the cylinder to protect the top surface of the pawl.

The Trigger

The back edge of the top of the trigger is held against the lower contours of the hammer and is kept in that position by the longer of the wings on the bifurcated trigger/cylinder stop return spring. As the hammer is drawn back, the top of the trigger drops over the half cock notch and, if pressure on the hammer is then released, the top of the trigger drops into this notch preventing any further forward rotation of the hammer. The half cock notch is (or at least should be) tapered and this taper prevents the tip of the trigger from bottoming in the half cock notch and damaging the top surface, which forms the scear.

To release the hammer it must be pulled back out of the half cock notch. Further rotation enables the back of the trigger, still being held against the bottom surface of the hammer, to drop into the full cock notch (or bent). The hammer is released by increasing the finger pressure on the trigger, which ultimately rotates about its pivot screw against both the pressure of the trigger return spring and the 'friction' of the bearing surface between the scear and the bent.

16. On early English revolvers, such as the Adams and the Tranter, the pawl remains firmly in contact with the ratchet to press the 'barrier' between the nipples against one side of the cylinder stop as the shot is fired (in Colts and Remingtons the cylinder stop drops into a recess in the cylinder wall). The mechanics of this system mean that the English revolver had to have an odd number of chambers, with five being the most practicable.

Controlling the Trigger Pressure

Many an original and most repros have trigger pressures of 5 to 10lb when new. This might be acceptable for their original purpose, but target shooters seek a crisp, light and repeatable trigger release or 'let off'. On the Remington and its clones this can be achieved quite easily. At least it can be quite easy if you do it correctly. Do it incorrectly and you have the sort of trigger pull needing a full two hands to release it or so light that you endanger everyone for miles around, with a ruined hammer and trigger into the bargain.

There are two things to be considered – trigger release pressure and 'creep'. Creep is that insidious problem of sliding the scear across the face of the bent in stages until, by design or chance, it drops the hammer. To get the release pressure right you have to get the correct angle of contact between the scear and the bent. Having done that, creep is removed by reducing the length of contact from front to back of this mating surface. Both are dealt with by good engineering practice, patience and a simple lapping jig, and not by dropping out the trigger on the firing point and stoning away with hope in your heart and a spare trigger or two when you get it wrong.

If you don't have precision grinding facilities or at least a new file and a keen eye, leave the bent on the hammer well alone. Settle for its imperfections and try to overcome the problem by working on the scear. It is much easier, much safer and, if you do spoil it, a replacement trigger is easily obtained and fitted. If this doesn't work you will have to start looking at the surface of the bent with a magnifying glass. If it has burrs on the lip or serrations across the surface use a file guide and ease them away with a good 'Swiss' file (Trying to straighten up the mating face with a hand held stone is asking for trouble). Make sure that the new surface is at right angles to the side of the hammer.

There is no possibility of reducing the trigger pressure by modifying the pressure exerted by the trigger return spring as we used to do on centre-fire revolvers since there is no coil spring to work on. All the work must be done by getting a good flat surface on the scear at the correct angle. This angle differs from pistol to pistol and is approached by degrees by lapping, cleaning, fitting and feeling until you have the trigger release pressure that suits you.

The trick is to make a simple tool to hold the trigger in exactly the same position every time you dismantle the lock-work. Then you relate the trigger to a sliding bar with a stone fixed to it. You mount this bar so that you can change the angle between the stone and the scear on the top of the trigger in a controlled way. The one I made, and have used on many a Remington and the occasional Colt, is made mainly of wood from the scrap box. It looks like the sketch in Fig. 33. If you use something like planed ramin from the wood shop for the slide and the fixed bar the whole assembly will stay square. The clamp is closed just enough to enable the slide to move backwards and forwards without any wobble. Make sure that the stone is square with the scear on the trigger before starting to lap. Also make sure that the screw holding the trigger to the trigger mounting plate is a good fit in the trigger bearing hole or you will not get a repeatable trigger position. Clamp the complete assembly into a vice or to a table top for convenience.

If the trigger pressure is too heavy, set the pin for the slide bar towards the top of the slide support. Screw the trigger to its mounting plate and rotate it until the top of the trigger forming the scear aligns as closely as possible to the surface of the stone. A gentle wipe with the stone will mark the surface sufficiently to do the final adjustment. Clamp the trigger in this position with the fixing screw. Then mould some quick-setting filled resin to one side of the trigger. This forms a reference position to which the trigger may be returned time after time. Wait until the resin dries and smooth off any surplus.

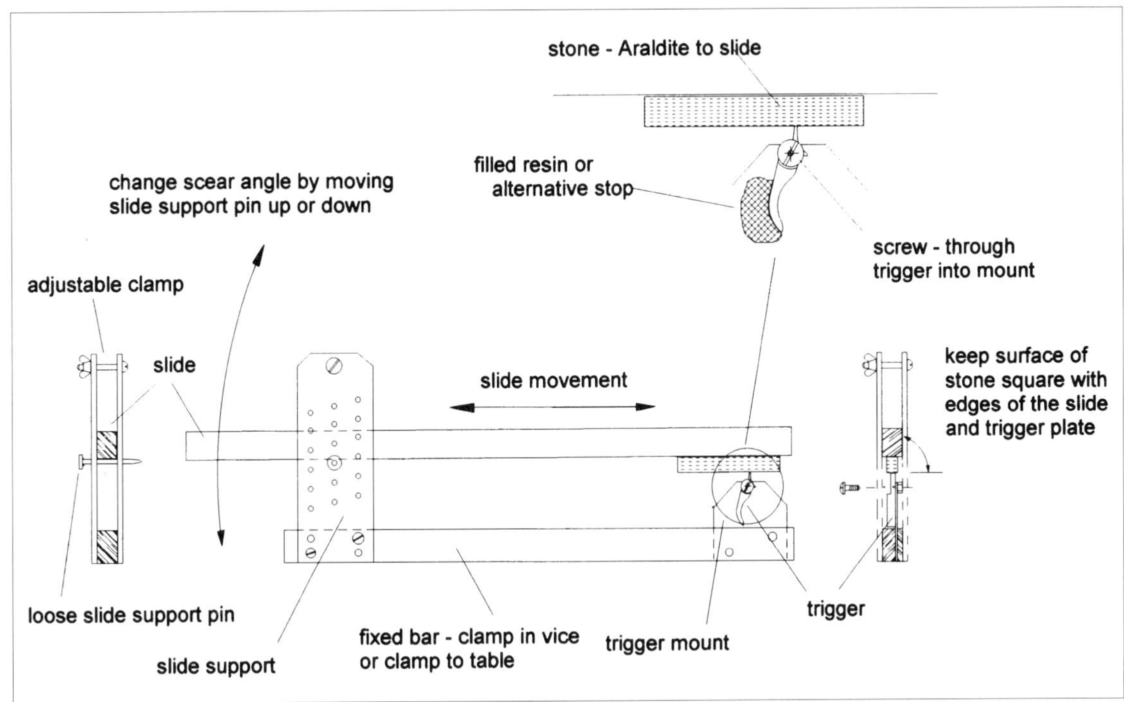

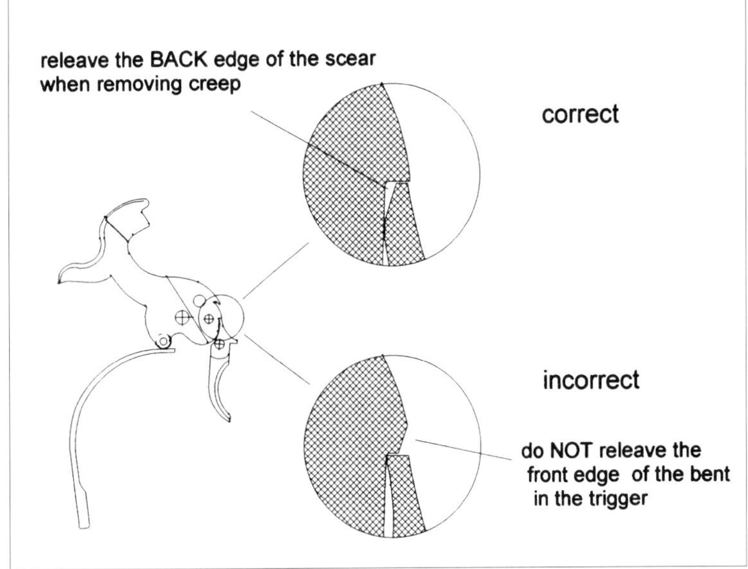

(Above) *Fig. 33 The Remington scear lapping guide.*

Fig. 34 Removing creep on the Remington.

Then slide the stone gently backwards and forwards; this will quickly produce a flat, shiny surface over the scear. Remove the trigger from the jig, clean and drop it back into the pistol. You can leave the flat bifurcated trigger return spring out for this exercise; just push the trigger forward as you thumb the hammer back – it saves a little time. Try the trigger release pressure. If it is too high, drop the locating pin in the slide support to the next level down: if it is too low or it doesn't support the hammer at all, move the locating pin upwards. Take the lock to pieces again, put the trigger back into the jig, lap the top surface, clean, reassemble and test as before. Work steadily and slowly in this way until the release pressure feels right for you. This can only be done, by the way, when the gun is presented in the firing position and actually dropping the hammer. Either put caps on the nipples or leave the cylinder out, allowing the hammer to drop on to its stop in the frame.

Remember to reset the trigger stop on the jig when starting to work on another revolver. Do not assume that you can use the same set up since both scear and bent will be at different angles when you start.

Once the trigger pressure is adjusted satisfactorily, you may be left with some creep. This is removed by stoning or filing the *back* edge of the scear away to reduce the amount of surface contact of the scear in the bent. Again, do this slowly and a little at a time until the 'feel' is right (*see* Fig. 34).

In removing the creep *do not be tempted to dress off the front of the bent on the hammer since it may seriously disturb the timing of the action.* If you do, you have a high possibility of the scear catching on the half cock notch as the hammer drops, resulting in light strikes and a badly damaged scear. On single-shot pistols, except those of very early vintage, there is a little swinging detent that lifts the scear over the half cock notch cut into the tumbler as the cock drops. The lock on the single shot Pedersoli, for example, fails miserably if you forget to put the detent back. Such detents are not fitted to revolvers, which rely on good profiling of the hammer and the scear getting out of the way of the half cock notch as the hammer drops.

ON THE RANGE

At last we have a well-prepared revolver and off we go to the range to try things out. Again, safety and preparation are paramount. Pistol, pre-loaded phials of powder, filler, caps, scope, grease and so on (not forgetting the lolly stick; *see* Appendix III). Before the competition starts, you should clear any oil from inside the barrel and from each chamber, and then take a few glances along the barrel to get familiar with the feel of the revolver, provided always that there is no one down range. In NRA competitions you need permission from the range officer to handle revolvers in this way.

All MLA-controlled details for 'deliberate' pistol competitions run for 30 minutes, with a further 30 minutes to clear the firing point and to allow for the next shooter to set up. This may seem long, but setting up for muzzle-loading tends to be time consuming, and a shooter needs time to settle down and relax before the detail starts. Remember that no practice cards on the day of competition are allowed, so this relaxation period is essential.

When the 30-minute detail starts, and not before, place a cap on every nipple and blow out any remaining oil from the inside of the nipples. From then on you have the rest of the 30 minutes for your fourteen shots: a fouling shot into the bank and thirteen on the target. This is more than enough time: generally revolver shooters are at least 5 minutes ahead of their neighbour shooting single-shot percussion, and the competitor on your left needs all the 30 minutes (and perhaps a few more) to get through the detail with his flintlock. So take time with loading, there is certainly no hurry.

A little time and motion study speeds up loading. Rest the heel of the butt of the half cocked revolver on the bench and support it about the cylinder with the left hand. You will be dropping the pre-weighed charge of black powder into each of the six chambers from individual phials, flipping the tops off into your 'ready for use' box as you go. So the rhythm is set up: powder, turn (putting the newly-charged chamber behind the barrel) count '1' – powder, turn, count '2' – powder, turn, count '3', and so on until you reach '6'. A little tap to settle the powder squarely in each chamber, then: filler, turn, count '1' – filler, turn, count '2'... until you reach '6' again. If you have double-charged one chamber the bright yellow filler will overflow and warn you. Likewise, if the filler disappears into the bowels of the chamber you have forgotten the powder. If you are using wads instead of filler you will have to invent your own mantra, especially if, as some people do, you seat the wad on top of the powder with the rammer before adding the ball.

To load the balls you can either leave the butt of the revolver on the bench, or copy many shooters in holding the revolver in the left hand across the chest, where it is a little easier to keep an eye on the head of the rammer. The rammer is first centred on the waiting ball and then pressed into the chamber with the loading lever. As before, it is: ball, press, check the depth, turn, count '1', ball, press, check the depth, count '2', turn – all the way up to '6'. Doing it in this sequence, rather than completing one chamber at a time, gives a better chance of getting a similar pressure on the ball – and hence the powder charge – in each chamber.

If you mis-load a chamber, finish loading the remaining chambers, then empty the faulty chamber completely and reload. You can drop the cylinder out of the frame to do this if you wish, then put it back to finish reloading. This is when you use the spare phial kept, not in the two rows of seven, but easily to hand. There is no penalty if you follow this procedure.

Still working on the face of the cylinder, it is: grease, rotate, count '1', and so on. Wipe off any excessive grease, both from the revolver and your hands, with the cloth hanging for this purpose from the edge of the shooting table. Then up the other way to cap, '1' to '6', as before, using your fingers or a cap dispenser, if you can get one to put caps onto the nipples of your revolver. Nipple dispensers are often a little too wide for a Remington, but you can often use a file to thin the ends of the cap dispenser so that they will fit properly. Go round each nipple, pressing the cap home with a clean lolly stick or the flat of a knife blade, making sure that the revolver is pointing down range as you do so. Loose caps seem inevitably to fall off nipples during a competition. If you do not have the correct size of caps you may have to squeeze them – making them slightly oval in section to increase their retention on the nipples.

Fun isn't it? The detail is 6 minutes old and you have not even fired your fouling shot. It is not for the muzzle-loader to slip quietly into the prone position, drop a round into his trusty .22 rifle, close the breach with the tip of the finger, and then release the shot with hardly a flicker of an eyebrow. *They* do not even have to have a bath when they have finished!

The way the detail is approached is important. There are some rules, rigorously enforced in MLA-run internationals, about loading the revolver. First, the chambers must be loaded with the cylinder in the gun. Taking the cylinder out and loading it on a separate press is not permitted[17] since this would be contrary to the 'spirit of the original' loading practices. Secondly, the revolver must be loaded and fired with a minimum of five shots at the first loading and a similar minimum at the second loading. This is to stop the shooter from treating his revolver as a single-shot pistol. The first of these shots may be placed into the bank, a fouling shot which is always recommended. Like

17. Provided always that a loading lever/rammer is normally fitted to the revolver. Some early revolvers had no such facilities – the early Adams is an example. A loading press (which has no advantage over loading the chamber in situ, despite press manufacturers' claims) may then be used. Supporting the complete revolver in a wooden rest or clamp rather than holding it in the hand is quite acceptable.

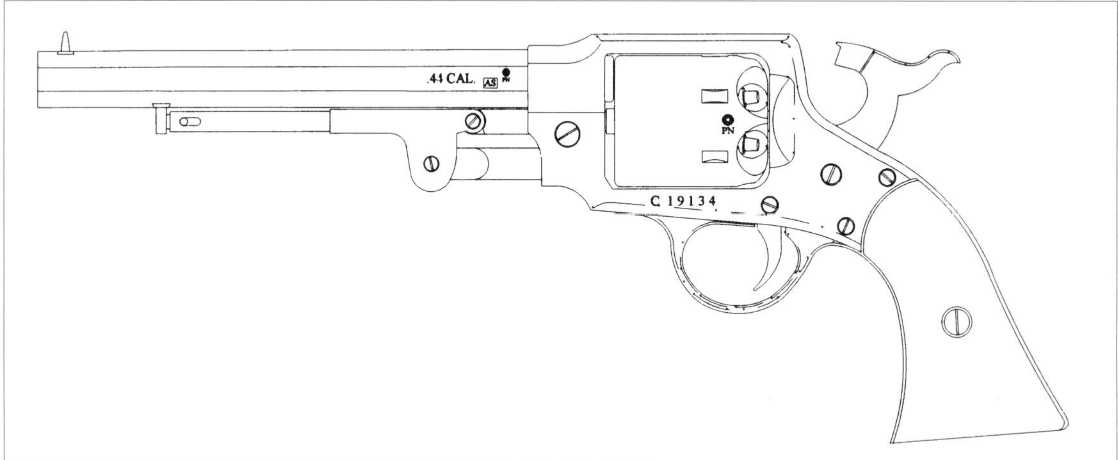

Fig. 35 The Rogers and Spencer 44 Revolver.

shooting the single shots, it is the closest you will get to a practice shot, and it is useful to remind yourself of the grip, sight picture and trigger release. Remember that you must inform any marker that you intend to fire a fouling shot before you start, otherwise your fourteenth shot may result in one of your highest scoring shots being discounted, even though you only have thirteen on the card.

Remember that in domestic competitions you will be shooting all thirteen shots into one diagram, whereas in most internationals you will be presented with a single target with two diagrams side by side and you have to put six on one diagram and seven on the other. Which diagram you shoot at first, the sequence you shoot them in (one shot on alternate diagrams if you feel so inclined and wish to put pressure on your marker) and which diagram you use for the six or the seven shots is up to you. Get your count wrong and you will lose one of the highest scoring shots on the diagram with eight on it.

There are ways of getting this count right when the diagrams are side by side. As previously stated, I favour a loading box (Plate 33) holding fourteen phials of powder in two rows of seven. For revolvers I load six chambers at the first loading from one of the rows and then put the fouling shot into the bank. I then shoot the remaining five into the left-hand diagram. Reload a further six chambers from the second row and put them all into the right-hand diagram. Reload the remaining two shots and put them into the left-hand diagram – making seven on the left and six on the right. This sequence ensures that you line yourself up with a new diagram following reloading each time, rather than changing diagrams part-way through the second cylinder. This sequence also allows for an error when you are shooting on your second diagram but accidentally put an additional shot on the first. By design, it was expecting a further couple of shots after the second diagram was completed.

However, this strategy fails completely on some ranges, such as Pforzheim in Germany, the scene of past world and European muzzle-loading championships. Here, the two diagrams are above each

18. You do not meet this problem with the single shots, since the patch wipes the barrel almost clean as the ball is forced down the barrel on to the powder.

other. The bottom diagram is shot first, a cord is pulled and the whole frame drops revealing the second diagram. The first drops largely out of sight. Here you plan to shoot six shots on your first diagram and the remaining seven on the second. If you shoot seven on the first diagram before you change diagrams nothing is lost. One shooter in either 'Mariette' or 'Colt' in the 1999 European championships put ten on the first diagram and three on the second, totally negating his efforts, irrespective of the fall of shot. Perhaps he did not know the rules. In any case, his coach had much to answer for.

As you shoot, the lubrication applied to each chamber melts and is blown in all directions by the flash from the adjacent chamber. This makes the grips on the revolver increasingly slippery as the detail goes on. It is better to stop shooting and wipe the grips with a clean cloth when this happens.

Although you shoot a fouling shot such that the first and subsequent competition shots have a similar degree of fouling in the barrel, some powder and lubrication combinations can create more fouling than may be desirable.[18] This is more of a problem with originals, where all but the best will have some form of pitting inside the barrel. These pits may cause a more rapid build up of fouling than normal. On my original Remington, for example, the first card is fine but shots start to fly halfway through a second card if the barrel has not been cleaned at the end of each thirteen-shot series. Now there is nothing in the rules for Mariette and Colt competitions to stop you from using a rod to clear excessive fouling from the barrel.[19] If you meet this problem, cleaning before loading the second cylinder may be appropriate. However, if you do this, use something like a nylon brush to remove the excess without scrubbing the barrel into a perfectly clean condition. If you make it too clean, you are back to the clean pistol you started with before shooting your fouling shot. Only you can decide whether or not your revolver will group better if left alone or cleaned halfway through your detail.

When you have finished, put the revolver at half cock, place it on the table in front of you with the muzzle pointing down range and sit down. Cleaning up and putting your equipment away while shooters on the adjacent firing points are still shooting is both disturbing and discourteous.

To be considered for the MLAGB team for the 'Mariette' a qualifying score of 92 or 93 used to be sufficient, but with the level of competition steadily rising, you now may need a 95 or more to make the team. When shooting an original for the 'Colt' the scores are probably a couple down on this. Berthod of France put up a 100 to claim the world record in Mariette in 1990, and only those in the high 90s are likely to make the rostrum in internationals these days. The Colt world record currently stands at 97, made by Bopp of Germany in 1989. So there is some space for you in the record books yet.

MAJ-GEN JOHN MONEY, *PARTIAL REORGANISATION OF THE BRITISH ARMY* (1799): 'AT SARATOGA THE FINEST ARMY IN THE WORLD .... LAID DOWN THEIR ARMS TO WHAT MR. RIGBY IN THE HOUSE OF COMMONS CALLED AN "UNDISCIPLINED RABBLE". BUT THEY WERE ALL WOODSMEN – THAT IS MARKSMEN.' BRITAIN MAY HAVE BEEN ABLE TO RAISE ITS OWN 'WOODSMEN' AT THE TIME FROM THE MANY RURAL WORKERS WHOSE SURVIVAL – UNDER STRICT PENALTY – DEPENDED ON THEIR SKILL WITH THE FLINTLOCK AND MANY A SURVIVING MATCHLOCK TO KEEP AT LEAST SOME FOOD ON THE TABLE. NOT NOW!

---

19. Unlike the MLAIC rules for military long arms such as muskets, which may not be cleaned during the competition. Did you know that they have to shoot without rear-sights, and still shoot in the 90s? In some NRA matches you may wipe out only between five-shot series.

THE ARMOURER'S TALE

If Geoffrey Chaucer had been writing at the end of the millennium, he would surely have included an armourer in that motley band who set off from Southwark to seek redemption at the tomb of St Thomas à Becket in Canterbury. So here is the tale the armourer would have told, translated into the more modern idiom of Nevill Coghill.

In Belgium, in the far-off past
A gunsmith strived and made to last
A pistol of the common sort,
Not built for sin, but honest sport,
And by the tenets of the day
He bored the chamber, come what may,
And took advantage, of a cartridge
Designed by his esteemed confrère,
The mighty armourer Flobert.

It may have been at least some weeks
Before through dusty window peeks
A man of middle age, it seems,
Indulging in his favourite dreams
Of taking to his bosom vast
A pistol that could take the task
Of beating his great rival Sid,
Who often on the Bourse outbid
The said LeClerk in daily business,
And let be said by honest witness,
As well as taking as his lot
The profit which was rightly got
By dealings of the baser kind,
As many in the markets find,
He took the prize so greatly sought
Which he, LeClerk, himself had bought
And presented to the gallery
Where oft he shot in rivalry
With others of his social clan
At balls and bells and candlelan.

A single glance, LeClerk was bitten.
It could be said he had been smitten
By the polished nickel frame
And the barrel of the same,
And soon the pistol's full amount
Was debited to his account,
And borne away to shoot his match
Without the usual ball and patch.

Around the galleries of Gant
And Brussels in the Rue Brabant,
The balls ejected from its barrel
Delighted those whose high apparel
Comprising, as the gravures show,
A high silk hat and glossy bow,
And in his hands that worthy fellow
Assured each one with mighty bellow,
He could at last be ever rid
Of the supremacy of Sid.
For whether shot at ball or disk
There never was the slightest risk
That, by the standards of the day,
His shots would ever go astray.
And much esteem it did achieve.
You never would at all believe
The loving care and great devotion
In scrubbing with a fairy potion
To rid of surplus particles
And other rust-promoting articles
That were applied to keep it clean
And make its nickel really gleam,
Whilst on the range that pistol bright
Put down the pompous Sid alright.
Until one day, we're sad to say,
That père LeClerk just passed away
From eating oysters out of season
Without much thought or any reason,
And in the Rue des Boucheries
(Where oft he ate charcuterie)
He lay apon the cobbles gasping
That his rival, should his passing
Become established, come what might,
Was to receive, in perfect right,
His pistol that shot true and sure
And keep it safe for evermore.
But in return he must resolve
To keep a promise and not absolve
To wed his daughter, strong and bold,
So engaging, he was told,
When smiling sweetly at the nation,
Around the back of Central Station.
Alas, despite all doctor's means,
LeClerk relapsed to Heaven's dreams

On learning of his rival's bid
To saddle him with Astrid,
Sid sought the lady at her work,
Which soon appeared to have a quirk,
And, being something rather shady,
It seems as if the 'foresaid lady
Was made of more than maiden's charms,
And often fell to stranger's arms.
The pistol then must take its chance.
Sid packed his bags without a glance
And legged it for another clime
Where his body could recline
Close to a range, with all at peace,
In rolling hills just north of Nice.

Left with nothing but her loves,
Sweet Astrid packed her father's gloves,
His long tailcoat and garter'd socks

Into a strong but airy box,
To which she added, to her shame,
The pistol in her father's name,
And to a cupboard, dark and damp
With nothing but a broken gamp,
Assigned the box, for ever more,
By closing fast the inner door,
And then for measure spent the season
In a spa – with detailed reason –
To engage a handsome beau
Who, on her marriage, would bestow
A life of honour and contentment,
Free from any past presentment.

Deep in the cupboard, 'mongst the socks,
The pistol slept inside its box,
And there it languished, year on year,
Until, in trembling and in fear,
Its barrel filled with ferric dust,
The house was cleared. It happened thus
That most was tipped into the bin
(Its state was such 'twas hardly sin),
Except, perchance, that pistol fair
Was kicked beneath a wicker chair,
Then gathered up without commotion
Well supported by the notion
That it would make financial sense
To sell it to a local fence,
And briefly, through this shady fella,
Support the purchase of some Stella.

So through the years and much abuse
Its only job was put to use,
By changing hands at modest prices
Between collectors, despite its vices.
At last the pistol, sad reflection,
Longing for some resurrection,
Fell perchance to loving hands
Within the sport in distant lands.

However, it was greatly feared
Of rumours of a group who steered
The form of pistols in that land,
Deciding which may then be banned
For public safety, so was said,
To protect old ladies then abed
(Whilst letting those with little conscience
Disdain the laws which craved a licence
For their sawn-off Purdeys fine
In support of major crime).
For in this way it made it easy
To garner votes from those of queasy
Disposition, knowing not
What futile laws the land had got,
And, in this mood of 'stuff the sport',
Where men of standing once had fought
In honest competition, had
In many an Olympiad
Gained honour for their country's team
And in their own land raised esteem
For their prowess with the gun
Oft handed down to father's son.
There rose at 'hest of government
A large and hidebound covenant
Which, in its depths, there were precepts
That, chambered in its present form,
The pistol could a mighty storm
Bring down upon both low or high
Any that should sell or buy,
Or back convert to some such form
That in their day had been the norm,
Including those that were intended
To be charged with spouts upended,
Ignited well by flint and frizzen,
Or get set off by power that's driven
From the brass percussion cap
With cock descending with a snap,
So, if it were to stay alive,
It need be hid from Section Five.

With risk and reason notwithstanding,
A plan was made for discrete handling
To hide its sins, the law defying,
Then make it safe from further prying.
And so within the dead of night,
With muffled lathe and shaded light,
Deft skills were worked with great effect
To rid that pistol derelict
Of defaults vast that, in the past,
Had ruined work once made to last.
The lap was spun in barrel's bore
Until it shone like suns galore,
And all the metal that was touched
With rusty pits was much o'er brushed
Until with fine and polished hues
The metal glist with ancient blues.
Whilst in the place of Flobert's cave
Appeared a nipple. What a knave!
Such was it finished, head to toe,
That examination could not show
The trauma that the gun had seen
Or rework there had ever been
Applied, in spite of laws and things,
Revealing new what future brings.

The old Flobert was twice turned round,
Azawi Trebolf now was found,
With rings of gold, like Paris tarts,
Engraved upon its upper parts,
Displayed for all in box sublime
Without a hint of any crime,
Nor hiding from the Law's advances
But happy now to take its chances,
Enjoying much a life rehatched
Its ball and patch and cap well matched
With fifteen grains of 'number one'.
And God bless all to kingdom-come.

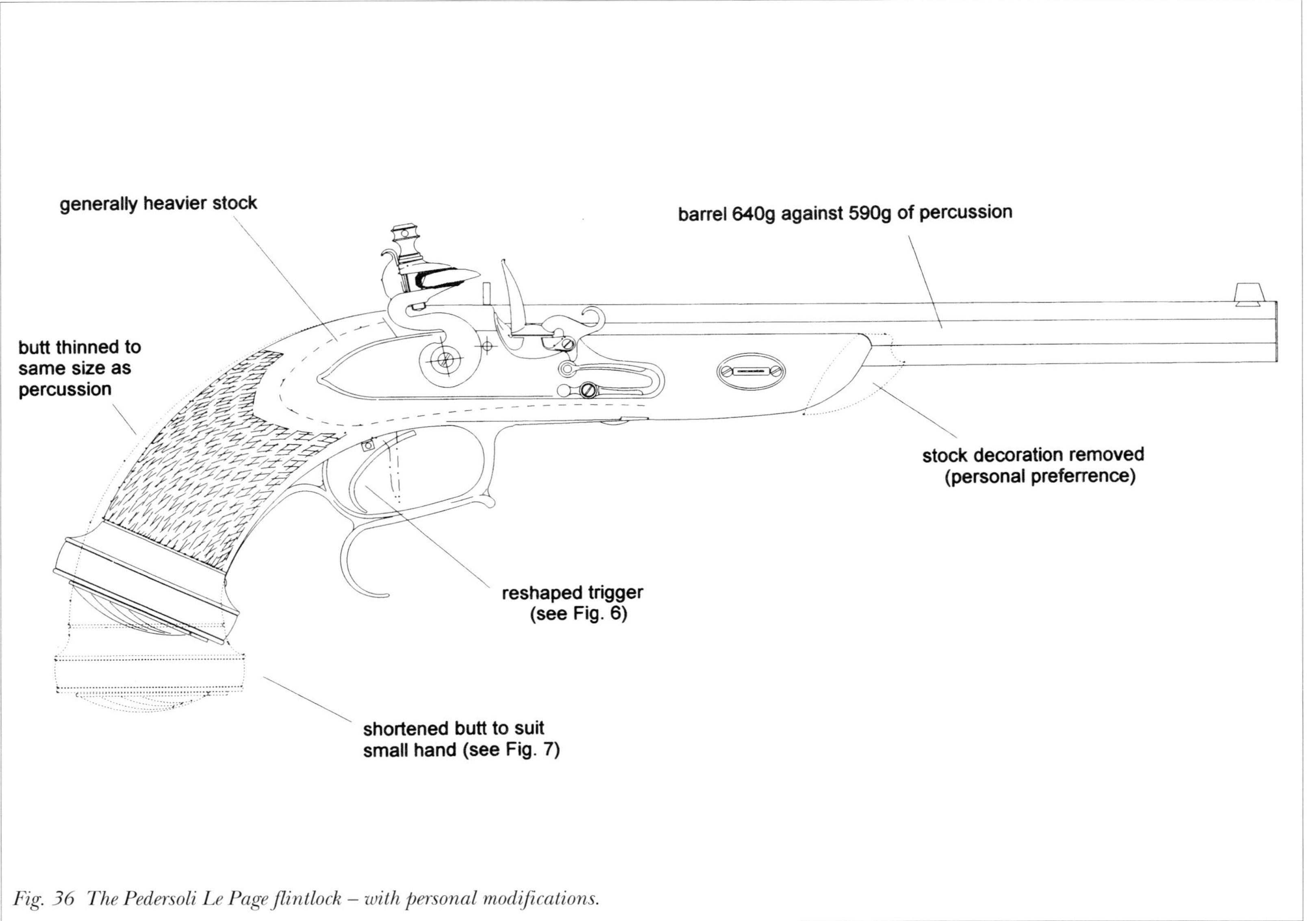

Fig. 36 The Pedersoli Le Page flintlock – with personal modifications.

4 And Then There Are Flintlocks

THE BACKGROUND

Flintlocks are fascinating, fickle and frustrating. If you are one of that rare breed who can identify with three-dimensional chess, then a flintlock should give you few problems. Any others should take up the flint with caution, garner any reserves of patience for the range, and hone their expletives. This said, the flintlock version of the Le Page, especially the rifled version, has many similarities with its percussion counterpart. However, flintlock competitions under MLAIC rules require the use of a smooth-bore barrel and this in itself provides some real differences. This requirement should not be confused with the intent that pistols should comply with contemporary manufacture. Rifled flintlock pistols were manufactured from their introduction in the sixteenth century until finally replaced by the percussion lock in the mid nineteenth. However, duelling with rifled flintlocks was considered unacceptable[1] so duelling pistols were nearly all smooth-bore, along with those made for military purposes.

Those familiar with flintlocks will tell you that preparation, cleaning and loading are much the same as with the percussion version, apart from the means of ignition, and in the case of the smooth-bore versions, the load. It is the little details that make the difference.

A LITTLE TWEAKING

The initial examination and maintenance of the flintlock Le Page (Plate 16) are much as with the percussion, although there are a couple of additional things that need attention. The first potential problem is the little roller that is fixed to the frizzen and runs over the cam at the end of the feather spring (*see* Fig. 40). It is this spring that keeps the frizzen either closed or fully open. This roller runs on a pin that is a push fit in its bearing. More than one person has found that this pin works loose and the roller drops out. On its third outing, and halfway through a team selection card, the pin on my new acquisition worked loose and the roller dropped out, to be buried somewhere in the grass in Wedgnock. It was easy enough to make another, but the match had finally to be abandoned, as the oft repeated claim (mainly from long arm shooters) that flintlocks do not really need a feather spring at all proved far from true on this occasion. The fault arose because the pin was peened over on the outside of the frizzen during manufacture, and, once loose, there was nothing to prevent it from falling out. I would recommend that, instead of waiting for the pin to come loose, you take the frizzen off and peen the back end of the pin slightly, which should resolve the problem for the foreseeable future. New deliveries of the flintlock examined in mid 1999 showed that Pedersoli had addressed

1. For a description of some high profile duels and the various rules under which they were carried out, see *A History of Shooting*, by Jaroslav Lugs (Spring Books, 1968). Some early percussion pistols were also made with smooth-bore barrels, presumably to comply with the same set of rules. Many other smooth-bore percussion pistols, especially those larger than 30 bore, turn out to be conversions from flintlocks.

this problem. However, you may well get an older version, either second-hand or off the shelf, and it will need to be checked. The second thing to remember is the rear sight, which must be assessed and if necessary reworked as shown (*see* Fig. 10).

As you become more familiar with the repro flintlock, you might consider tuning it a little to suit your own requirements. Fig. 36 shows the basic Le Page flintlock with the 'tweaking' that I have done to suit my preferences.

PREPARATION

With the Le Page flintlock, and many others of its type with a patent breech, there is a cleaning sequence that must be followed before dropping powder down the barrel. First, any oil in the barrel should be removed, just as in any other pistol. Next is to use a .22 or .32 brush with a patch to remove any oil from the patent breech. The final stage is to remove any oil behind the touch-hole. This is easier said than done when the barrel was last oiled after cleaning with a spray-type water-dispersant and lubricant such as WD-40, or over-oiled with a mop. If you leave a little oil in this 'hammer head' and then drop powder down the barrel, the oil is absorbed into the powder and it will never ignite. You can't rely on flashing the pan to clear this, as is done on the percussion versions. You really have to unscrew the touch-hole and clean the chamber behind with a piece of dry rag.

Examples of shooters with an oiled-up breech on a flintlock feeding a second lot of powder and ball down the barrel because they thought they had forgotten to load are legion. WD-40 dries leaving a wax-like film on the surface. When it dries this film builds up and can effectively stop the powder from getting close to the flash entering at the touch-hole. It really is safer to protect the barrel by spraying WD-40 on to a patch or mop and use that, rather than spraying it straight into the barrel, and avoid this problem. But if you do get caught with an oily or otherwise clogged breech, you have three options, depending on how well you are organized. The technique to try first is to slip the barrel out of the stock and unscrew the touch-hole. This is hollowed out from the back and is easier to clean if removed, rather than removing the blanking plug on the opposite side of the barrel. Clean as much of the oily powder out as possible, and then clean the powder out of the screw threads of both the barrel and the touch-hole. If you leave even the smallest amount of powder on the threads it is almost impossible to get the touch-hole to reseat to the correct depth, and then the barrel will not fit behind the lock. Trickle a little priming powder into the open breech from the priming flask, return the touch-

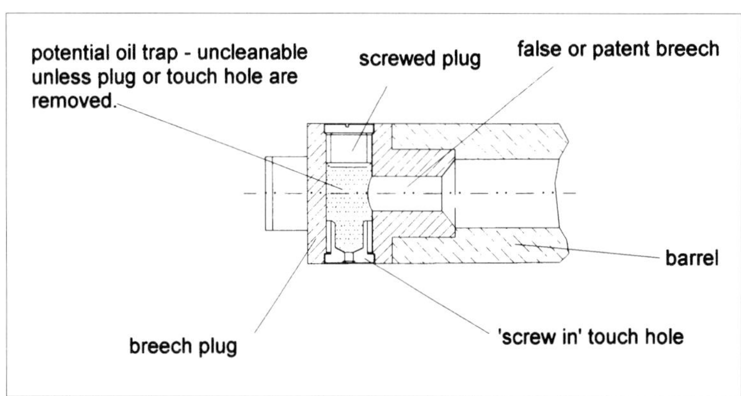

Fig. 37 The oiled-up breech on the Le Page flintlock.

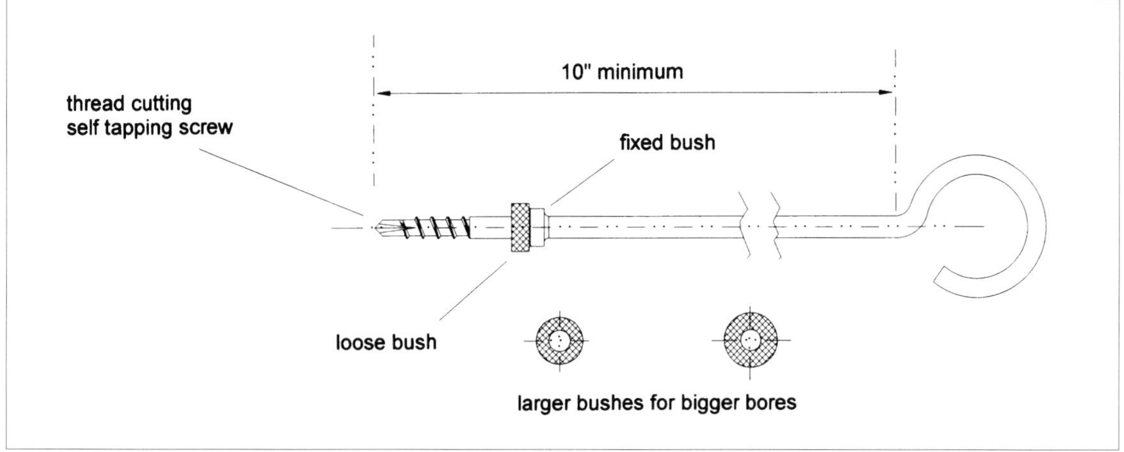

Fig. 38 The 'worm'.

hole, prime and try to blow the ball out. Do not forget to claim a misload from the marker *before* blowing out the charge.

If this fails to clear the pistol, you will either have to pull the ball using a screw-headed rod (or worm) typically as shown in Fig. 38, or blow it out with a blast of carbon dioxide. For this you need a little applied technology in the form of a Sparklet bulb and an adaptor to blast the CO_2 directly into the touch-hole. One commercial version is called a Silent Ball Discharger (Thompson/Center Arms). You need to buy the adaptor to use it on a flintlock, but it is a worthwhile investment. Be careful: it can pop the ball out all the way to the target on a good day. Don't forget to carry a couple of spare Sparklet bulbs – they will command a high price from your less well-equipped colleagues.

If you are faced with having to use the worm, do not try to use it without the bush. I use bushes of diameters related to the barrel diameters. These bushes prevent the screw from skidding off to the side where it can't cut into the ball. Screw the worm right through the ball, put a screwdriver through the ring, stand with a foot on each end of the screwdriver and pull steadily. This should release the ball. Use the patch puller (Fig. 16) to remove the patch if it does not come out with the ball. Clearing the ball and powder will give you a chance to clear the breech of oily powder and you can get back to the match, even if you have lost 5 minutes of the 30 allowed.[2]

With originals, with their gold or platinum touch holes permanently installed and no vent plug, the message is not to get oil in the patent breech in the first place.

LOADING AND THE LOAD

Convention dictates that the flintlock shooter will be using about twice the load of a fast powder in a smooth-bore flint compared with its rifled percussion counterpart. The increased velocity is deemed to compensate to some extent for the non-spinning ball. With 15 grains of TS2 or Swiss No.2 in the .44 percussion, you could expect to use

2. In official MLA-controlled matches, if you have a problem like this you have to solve it yourself. You are not allowed help from others.

about 30 grains of Swiss No.1 in the .45 smooth-bore.[3] Whichever powder you use, the smooth-bore flintlock is going to recoil to a much greater extent than its rifled cousins and the unwary will be given a sharp reminder with their first shot. My repro flintlock weighs 1.18kg, compared with the percussion at 0.98kg, the extra weight being useful in reducing the perceived recoil from the higher muzzle energy. However, this convention is not necessarily the right solution for you, a subject that will be addressed a little later.

A further 'problem' related to the flintlock is speed of ignition. The lock time for a flintlock can be quite perceptible, giving rise to all sorts of problems in keeping the pistol on aim. For this reason, use as fast a powder for the main charge as you can, and match this with an even faster priming powder.

THE BALL

It is accepted practice that the ball and its patch need to be a tight fit in the smooth-bore barrel to ensure repetitive accuracy. You will note shooters having to use a hammer on the starter to get the ball into the first few inches of the barrel, caused by the bore being a couple of thou tighter at the muzzle than at the breech.

Some of the older and more widely experienced flintlock shooters will argue for a 30 thou or thicker patch and a ball 15 thou or so under the true bore size for their .520in and above original pistols. This ruse is used to reduce the recoil from the heavier ball (the recoil is directly proportional to the *cube* of the ball diameter, all other things being equal). With a pistol of .500in and below you can approach the problem from the other direction, with a ball only 4 or 5 thou less than the bore with a 10 or 13 thou patch, which seems a better engineering solution. You can then work up the minimum load of No.1 to get the pistol to group, with many people using anything from 24 to 30 grains. This latter load, by the way, equates with Pedersoli's recommendations for their smooth-bore Le Page flintlock. However you decide to approach the ball to patch to bore combination in your newly acquired pistol, the need to talk to experienced flintlock shooters is paramount. Borrow balls until you find a combination that works for you. After that you are on your own.

THE FLINT

The flint needs to be hard, with a continuous sharp edge, which must be kept clean by wiping between shots. If it gets dirty it will tend to skid on the surface of the frizzen and create insufficient sparks to ignite the priming powder. Regular cleaning should also be applied to the surface of the frizzen, and for the same reason.

Never start a competition card with an old flint, even if it has been sparking well. While the best of flints will last for three or more cards before the edge goes, some will fail at the first strike. If you can't bear to throw apparently good flints away, put them in a separate tin for use during practice when the time taken to remove and set up a new flint does not matter so much.

The flint must be set in the jaws of the cock such that it first contacts the top 15 to 20 per cent of the frizzen. Flints generally have a flattish bottom, with a chisel edge at both ends. Normally the sharper edge is set to contact the frizzen, with the flat at the bottom. However, all flints differ in their size and shape, and occasionally you may need to put the flint in 'upside down' to get the correct contact with the frizzen.

3. You cannot normally buy a .36 flintlock repro since the minimum bore for original and repros under both MLAGB and IC rules is .43in. Many original flintlocks used in competition are in the .50 to .55in region.

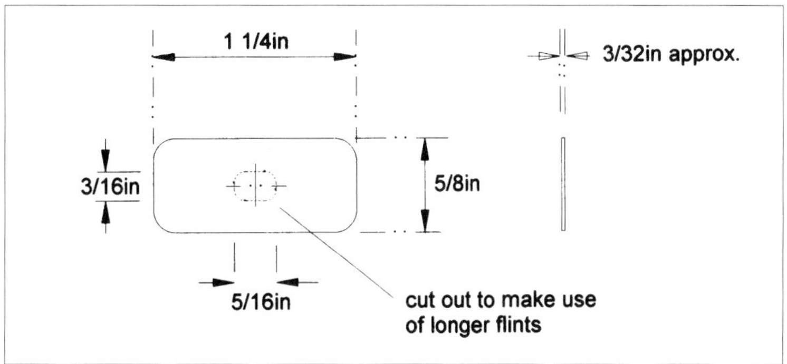

Fig. 39 The leather strip to hold the flint.

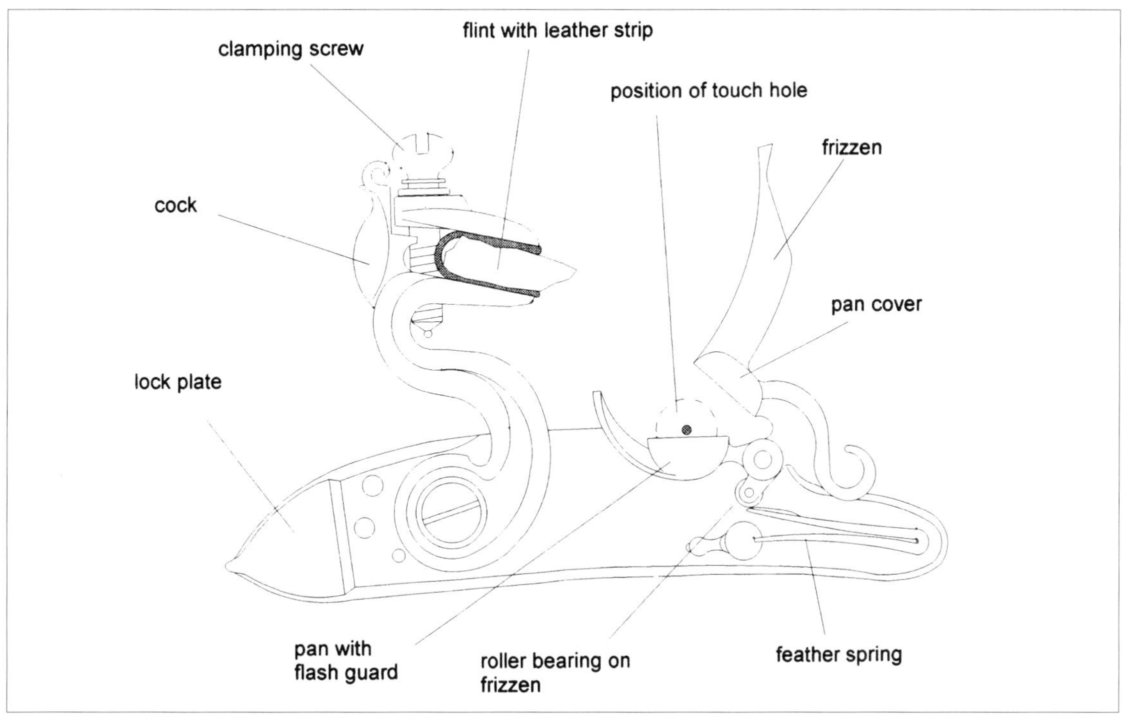

(Below) *Fig. 40 The lock of the flintlock.*

The flint is held in the jaws of the cock with a shaped strip of leather. Never use lead strip for this purpose as it 'flows' and the flint may quickly loosen. To get the flint adjustment right, you may need to cut a hole at the back of the leather, enabling the flint to be set right back against the clamping screw. Make sure that this strip is neither too thin nor too hard. If it is it will not take up the variations in the shape of the flint and will quickly work loose. Change the packing regularly. Oil and cleaning fluids quickly render the packing hard and unserviceable. With a thin flint, you may need to trim the packing a little to stop it from rubbing on the frizzen.

Be aware that to over-tighten the clamping screw may bend it. Normally you find this out halfway through a detail when you have to replace a flint. The only answer is a bigger screwdriver or lever until you can force the screw out to straighten it. This problem is often caused because the leather strip is too thin or too hard to grip the sharply curved upper surface of the flint to hold it securely.

Occasionally, a flint will just shatter completely, but more often you will find that a small part of the edge has fallen away. A quick look will soon show whether the edge has been rendered unusable. If the flint stops sparking but appears otherwise undamaged and has only 'lost its edge', try tapping *lightly* along the top of the edge of the flint with something like a screwdriver. This will often flake off very small amounts of flint along its edge sufficient to get off perhaps two or three extra shots, enabling you to finish your card without changing the flint.

When setting the flint in the jaws of the cock, it is absolutely imperative that its edge is parallel to the surface of the frizzen. The only way to do this accurately is to lower the flint on to the closed frizzen and hold the flint against it while the clamping screw is tightened. Finally, hold it up to the light to check that the flint didn't slide out of position at the last moment. If it is fitted on the skew, the flint will hit the frizzen on one of its corners and you will be lucky if you get a couple of shots away before the flint is rendered unusable.

Under no circumstances fit a new flint with any priming powder in the pan. If you let the cock slip from your fingers it will run down the frizzen and, with a new flint, will almost certainly set off the priming and the main charge. If you do need to replace a flint with the main charge still in the barrel, open the frizzen and blow or brush out the priming powder first, then slip the pricker (see later) into the touch hole.

Another thing to keep an eye on is that the cock is still holding the flint securely *after every shot.* As soon as it works a little loose it will swing out of line, and bang goes another flint. It only takes a second to check that the flint is secure between shots. Routine in loading is the key to effective flintlock useage.

While true flints are knapped from large nodules,[4] other materials are sometimes used. Agate is one and jasper another. Agates are cut from large blocks and machined to size. Jasper, although well known from earliest times, was never used as a 'flint', leaving agate as the only true alternative. There are also ceramic composite flints available, but these may have restrictions on their use in 'original' pistols. Generally, if flints work in your pistol, use them. Occasionally agate (or an equivalent) is the only material that will produce a spark with a pistol's combination of flint to frizzen angle of contact, frizzen hardness and the relative strength of the main and the feather spring. When they work they are fine, with an agate giving eighty or more shots before a replacement is needed. Being cut from a block, they are virtually identical in shape and size and are much less likely to move in the cock once properly clamped. Unfortunately, they are rather more expensive.

One point to watch is that the cock does not rotate so far as to allow the flint to hit the pan, when it will be rendered unusable. This is normally prevented by the flat on the inside face of the cock hitting the edge of the lock plate, preventing further rotation. Both the Nock and the Staudenmayer locks (Plates 19 and 20) had this problem. The usual solution is to soft solder a stop on to the inside face of the cock and filing to suit, stopping it from rotating too far.

THE FRIZZEN

As we have seen, the flint scrapes away at the surface of the frizzen every time it falls to produce the necessary sparks. In time, this

4. For a guide to knapping see *Gun Flints and How to Make Them*, by Gary Kelly (published by K Publishing, Gosport). Almost all the flints used in Britain must be made by the author's namesake, Tom Fuller.

action will wear away the surface of the frizzen and render it unfit for use. First indications are gouges which start to appear across the face of the frizzen where the flint first makes contact. This is followed by repeated attempts to fire before the priming is ignited, and flints breaking with relentless monotony. Before this problem becomes serious, remove the frizzen from the lock and carefully dress its surface by working in the downward direction (never across the frizzen) with 240 grade emery paper. Wrap the emery paper around a wooden former. Make sure that the surface of the frizzen remains flat. If this sort of work is not for you, your local gunsmith will do it for next to nothing.

To create a good spark, the surface of the frizzen needs to be really hard. This is normally achieved by through hardening, although in some instances case hardening may have been used. In the latter method, it is possible that you can eventually cut through this surface hardening; you will either need to replace the frizzen, have it case-hardened again or have it 'plated', a process in which a new surface is stuck on to the existing frizzen. The simplest alternative for the Le Page is to fit another frizzen – its cost will not break the bank. Finding a spare for an original Manton – now there is a retirement project for the committed shooter.

THE TOUCH-HOLE

The diameter of the touch-hole seems to vary from pistol to pistol. I have measured touch-holes on original flintlocks as low as 35 thou. In discussion with Pedersoli's representatives I was told that the diameter could be opened up to as much as 55 thou, depending upon on the main load and the priming combination. However, a recent replacement Le Page touch-hole was supplied at 60 thou,[5] so it seems as if they now exceed this limit themselves. If frequent flashes in the pan occur without igniting the main charge it is recommended that the size of the touch-hole should be examined. If it is on the small side, increase its size by no more than 5 thou at a time, provided always that you have eliminated other problems, such as a blocked touch-hole or patent breech.

PRIMING AND THE PRIMING POWDER

If you use a main charge percussion black powder such as TS2 in the pan, you could be faced with a problem or two. Even with a good set of sparks, the speed of burning in the open pan may be comparatively slow. This means that the essential pulse of red-hot gases necessary to force its way through the touch-hole to set off the main charge is slower than it could be. The result is a definite, click – wait for it – flash – wait for it – bang, by which time even the best of shooters will have lost their aim.

In a flintlock you must use the fastest powder available to you for both priming and main charge. In the UK at this moment this means Swiss No.1 for the main charge and an even finer grade for the priming in the pan, if you can obtain it. Fine grade black powder for priming is not universally obtainable,[6] although the MLAGB has recently started to stock a very fine grade of Swiss powder called 'ignition powder'. This has the consistency of

5. If the hole is allowed to become too large, perhaps due to gas erosion or too large a pricker, you will start to have problems with more than normal blow-back through the touch-hole and accuracy will start to suffer. I am told that this is more of a problem with long arms, with their higher breech pressures. Note that flintlock touch-hole sizes are normally larger than holes in percussion nipples, as the flame-edge pressure is much lower on the flintlock.

6. However, Swiss No.1, which is considerably faster than TS2, can often be used in the pan when anything faster is unobtainable. This is a stopgap and is not recommended for competition work.

dust and is generally best used as a 50/50 mixture with No.1. Finding a fast priming powder is essential, as the flintlock, albeit inherently slower than the percussion lock, can be speeded up remarkably by proper powder selection and application.

The second important point about the priming powder is how much and how it is placed in the pan. In the seventeenth century most pans were quite long with parallel sides (Plate 17), but the English developed the current lozenge-shaped pan early in the eighteenth. In this pan, the bulk of the priming powder is placed *away* from the touch-hole, with the intent that the charge burns towards the hole rather than *away* from it. Priming is carried out with the lock at half cock and never with the trigger 'set'.

Of prime consideration is ensuring that the touch-hole is quite clear of both priming and main charge powders, as well as fouling from the previous shot. If un-burned powder is blocking the touch-hole the essential pulse of red-hot gases from the priming cannot pass though into the main charge, as these grains of powder in the touch-hole will need to ignite and burn. In this case, ignition will be slower than it might be, or will not take place at all. To avoid this, a 'pricker' is used first to clear and then to fill the touch-hole during the loading of the main charge. The pricker is nothing more than a piece of bent wire, just smaller than the touch-hole itself. With long touch-holes, as in the author's original Nock, the use of a pricker makes the difference between reliable ignition and complete frustration. Attach a piece of brightly coloured tape to the pricker or you will never find it on the loading bench when you need it.

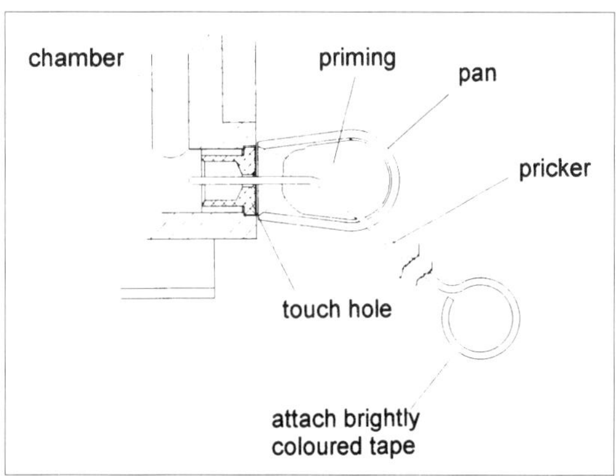

Fig. 41 The flintlock pricker.

If you fail to insert the pricker into the touch-hole before the main charge is loaded, you may find that the action of ramming the ball and its patch down the barrel blows some of the quite fine main charge powder out of the touch-hole. I first noticed this on a hot summers day in a period when the scores from my flintlock had dropped off alarmingly. I noticed that my arms were speckled with unburned powder, which could only have been carried by a jet of air from the touch-hole. This jet is produced by the tightly fitting ball and patch as it is driven down the smooth-bore barrel, which acts as a pump. I had previously noticed a few particles of powder around the pan but thought nothing of it, assuming that the amount displaced was insignificant. To test this, on my next shot I closed the frizzen before ramming the ball home, and, to my surprise, the loading action virtually filled the pan, which I subsequently measured as holding 6.5 grains.

Now a grain either way in a 30-grain load is not worth talking about, but if I were regularly losing up to 20 per cent of the main charge it was no wonder that my groups were widespread. Then I remembered that I had recently started to clear the touch-hole with the pricker after I had loaded the main charge, because a new pricker I had made kept falling out during the loading process. So back I went to the insertion of the pricker before loading, but now keeping it in its place by closing the frizzen on it, with an immediate improvement in my scores. Some trials took place in the clubhouse, showing that sometimes no powder was displaced through the touch-hole, while at other times from 3 to 5 grains were being lost. In reality my supposed 30-grain load was varying between 25 and 30 grains – not a good start for competitive pistol shooting.

I subsequently found that some single-shot originals actually relied on this phenomenon to prime the pan. Both John and Joseph Manton obtained patents[7] for this system, which totally ignores the advice given above on the use of a pricker. However, most duels would have been single-shot affairs, so a blocked touch-hole for a second shot would not have been noticed. Unfortunately, there are now remarkably few original Mantons with self-priming locks in existence.[8] There are, however, some beautiful repros of the Manton flintlocks by Hege. The top-of-the-range, all-engraved version has the John Manton self-priming pan as standard, and I am assured by Hege that they work consistently well. Their implementation forces a maximum of 1.5 grains of main charge powder into a narrow channel cut into what would normally be the pan, so that you can see that the amount of powder necessary for fast ignition may be quite small.

Now the above advice on the use of a pricker is given in good faith and is backed by the high percentage of the flintlock pistol shooters using this technique at the 1999 European and 2000 world championships. There is, however, a vociferous group within the muzzle-loading fraternity, particularly those who shoot long arms, who totally disagree with this principle. But they do all agree, however, that you must stop the charge from being blown out of the touch-hole during the loading process. They will recommend a piece of rag being held over the touch-hole, clamped into position with the closed frizzen. In muzzle-loading there is normally more than one way to do almost anything. In the end, it comes down to what actually works for you; you should then turn a partially deaf ear to any variations on a theme which may be aired in the clubhouse.

Priming powder is put into the pan after removing the pricker by using a powder dispenser, a device with a spring-loaded nozzle that will dispense the small volume needed. Pressing the nozzle into the open pan leaves the priming powder in the pan as the dispenser is withdrawn. You may need to give the nozzle a little tap on the side of the pan to release the complete charge since the finer the powder, the greater tendency it has to 'ball' and not flow freely. Rechecking that the lock is on half cock, spread the priming powder over the bottom of the pan by tapping with the non-nozzle end of the dispenser, keeping the powder *away* from the touch-hole.

The amount of powder needed is really quite small; filling the pan on the Le Page is both unnecessary and often counterproductive. Common powder dispensers will deliver about the right amount in a single throw. However, experience is really the only thing that will tell you what is right for your pistol. For instance, on the author's Nock with its so-called 'rain-proof' pan, the pan is both narrow and deep and the potential amount of powder that may be used is much smaller (Plate 20). Here I have almost to fill the pan to ensure first-time ignition of the main charge. This may be due in part to the greater length of the touch-hole from the pan to the patent breech[9] (nearly ¼in),

---

7. John's patent was No.2722, dated July 1803, while his brother Joseph's patent was granted in July 1815 (No.3942). Both depended on powder being blown into the pan through a hole and/or a channel in the closed frizzen and relied for ignition on the small quantity of powder thus transferred to the pan.

8. Source: D.H.L. Black, *Great British Gunmakers – The Mantons (1782 to 1879)* (Historical Firearms, 1993). Only three surviving self-priming Mantons are recorded by this highly respected source, none of them pistols. However, at least one MLAGB member is shooting an original Manton with a self-priming pan, so one should not believe everything in the books.

9. The 'patent breech' is, in fact, attributed to Henry Nock. His patent is dated in the mid 1790s. However, earlier French flintlocks with 'patent' breeches are reported.

as, in contrast to the Le Page, the back of the touch-hole is not opened out.

A colleague's Staudenmayer (Plates 15 and 19), with a similar pan shape, also works better with an almost filled pan. Note the use of platinum for the touch-hole on the Nock: it was cheaper than gold in those days.

LOWERING THE FRIZZEN ON TO THE PAN

This may seem a simple operation, but careful handing is required at this stage. On my Le Page, and using my normal ⅝in flints, the frizzen just makes contact with the flint when lowered if the pistol is on half cock, as it must be during the loading process. Hence, if the flint is not to be damaged, the lock must be placed on full cock before the frizzen is lowered to close the pan. Touch the trigger in this state, even when it is not 'set', and you have the pistol going off in your hands. It only has to happen once to remind you to keep the pistol pointing down the range at all times during the loading process, and a singed hand for a day or two reminds you to be more careful.

The safest technique is to hold the fore-end with the left hand (assuming that you are right-handed) and, with the pistol pointing down range, put the lock into the full cock position using the thumb and forefinger of the right hand. Only then lower the pan cover by holding the frizzen between the same two fingers. This keeps both sets of fingers well away from the trigger. The unsafe method is to place your right hand round the butt and thumb the cock back into position, since, sooner or later, a stray finger will find its way on to the trigger. If you let the cock slip with your fingers in the way you will slice a finger open with the falling flint.

IGNITION

You start with the lock at full cock. The frizzen has been lowered and this allows the attached pan cover to sit on the edges of the pan, stopping the loose priming powder from being tipped or blown out. Keep the pistol reasonably level or you may undo all the earlier good work and tip the priming powder back into the touch-hole (*see* Fig. 43).

Ignition is effected by the flint sliding down the frizzen, which scrapes off small pieces of steel that glow red hot from the transferred energy. They shower into the priming powder in the pan, which has started to be uncovered by the action of the flint sliding down the frizzen (*see* Fig. 44). These sparks ignite the priming charge in the pan, which flares in all directions, but is mainly directed by the shape of the pan towards the touch-hole, where the wave of red-hot gases

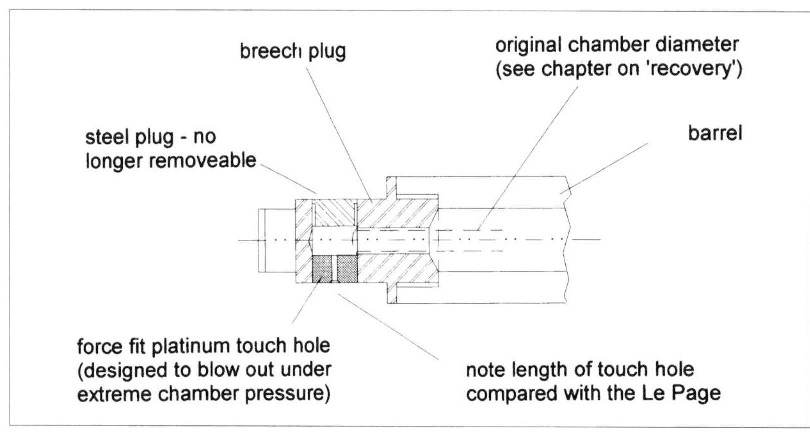

Fig. 42 The Nock and its patent breech.

forces its way through to ignite the main charge (*see* Fig. 45). The frizzen finally flies back into the fully open position by the impetus gained from being struck by the flint, and is held there by the roller on the frizzen going over-centre on a small projection on the feather spring. The cock is finally stopped by the step on its inside hitting the top edge of the lockplate. All this is going on while the shooter is trying to keep the pistol on aim (*see* Fig. 46). That is the theory; to get it to work consistently in practice requires the correct lock geometry[10] and dedication in the loading process.

SHOOTING

Having got this far, it is not unreasonable to present the pistol to the target and release the trigger. The technique is just as with the percussion pistols, with one or two provisos. First, you will find that the lock time, even in favourable conditions, will be perceptibly slower than with the percussion. This will mean that you must concentrate even more on holding on the point of aim.

Secondly, the recoil of the smooth-bore with its increased charge will be noticeably greater than with either the rifled flint or

Fig. 43 Flint ignition – first phase.

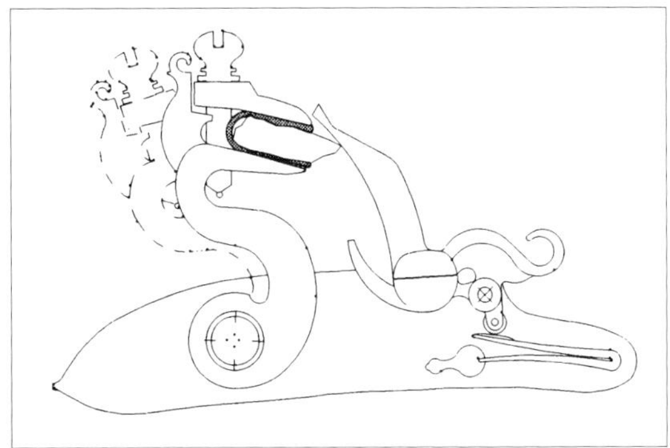

Fig. 44 Flint ignition – second phase.

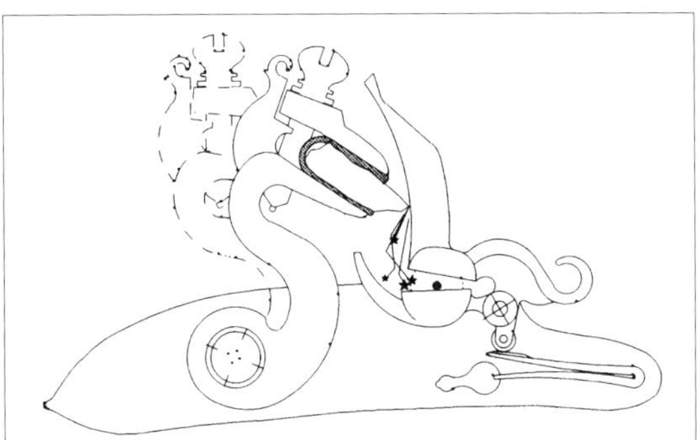

Fig. 45 Flint ignition – third phase.
(Right) *Fig. 46 Flint ignition – final phase.*

10. With the pistol unloaded and unprimed, and the frizzen closed, release the trigger while holding back the cock. Then let the flint slide slowly down the frizzen. The flint should contact the frizzen about a quarter of the way down. If the frizzen flies open before the flint is close to the bottom of the frizzen or the flint jams against the frizzen towards the bottom and will not go any further, then the geometry of the lock/flint combination is going to give trouble.

the percussion version, even with the increased weight of the pistol. You may well find that groups improve if you increase the strength of your grip. You can also apply clamping pressure through the little finger, which may counter the tendency for shots to go high. Many seasoned shooters use a glove to absorb some of the recoil, using a right-hand golf glove with its trigger finger cut off. It has much to recommend it.

Now, if the load you are using causes you to lose your grip on the pistol on discharge you will never be competitive. It is better to drop the load and put up with the theoretically larger group: your scores will improve considerably. Try shooting with a load as low as 21 grains for a couple of cards, increasing the load in 3-grain steps until your grip starts to fail. I have recently found that my Le Page will consistently give ten ring groups with only 24 grains of No.1, and I lose far fewer shots through uncontrolled recoil.

A potential 'problem' with the Le Page is that the butt of the flintlock is significantly larger than the percussion version. For those with small hands it may be worthwhile slimming down the butt to match the contours of the percussion. You will need to re-cut the chequering, but this is more a tedious than a difficult job if you have the right tools. Even those with larger hands may consider this modification for consistency of grip beneficial if they shoot both percussion and flint repros.

Warning: You are much more likely to experience a misfire on a flintlock than on a percussion pistol. If the powder in the pan flashes but the main charge fails to ignite, keep the pistol pointed down range while you clear any vestige of powder or other debris from the area of the pan with a toothbrush. Only when you are sure that a hang-fire will not occur, clean out the touch-hole with the pricker and reprime the pan. Matchlock shooters should be even more vigilant since glowing debris from the match can remain in the pan area for some time.

Once the technique of loading and releasing the shot has been mastered and a group of some respectability has been obtained, the fall of the shot must be centred on the target. Unlike with the percussion version, the only way to get vertical adjustment on the Le Page is by physically changing the height of the rear or the foresight. The Le Page flintlock requires just over 10 thou (actually 10.4 thou) of movement on the front or rear sights for every ring the shot must be moved on the PL7 target at 25m. Reducing the height of the front sight to raise the group (they are specifically made over high to allow this form of sight correction) may be done quite accurately if you use a vernier calliper between the top of the sight and the bottom of the barrel. There is obviously a limit to how much can be filed off. Alternatively, make a new but higher rear sight: it's only a piece of flat plate with a hole in it.

If you shoot with both rifled and smoothbore barrels, you have to get the rear sight at a reasonable height, and then work on the height of the foresights of the rifled and the smooth-bore barrel separately.

To lower the group you will have to file off the top of the rear sight, recutting the groove in the sight with a needle file or make a higher foresight. For lateral correction, the foresight can be tapped across in its slot, in the same way as with the percussion. With the spread of shot being markedly wider than with the rifled percussion, have two or three quite separate sessions shooting for groups before getting out the files.

How well will they shoot? Acceptable scores with a rifled flint need not be much lower than with the percussion, since with the same low charge it is a matter of good shooting technique rather than inherent accuracy. Scores in the mid 90s with the rifled version are quite feasible. The smoothbore flintlock is a different matter, with average scores well below the equivalent rifled percussion expectations. If you are going to have a chance of selection for the MLAGB international team you will need to be able to shoot close to 90 fairly constantly with the smooth-bore flint repro, with perhaps a couple of shots lower for originals.

At the time of writing, the world record for original flintlocks stands at 94 to Leonhard of Germany, while Giminez of France holds the repro record at 97[11], both records dating from 1987. That was a particularly notable year for pistol records, since four of the six MLAIC individual pistol records were still standing at the end of the century. There is no reason to suppose that originals in good condition are any less accurate than modern repros. The generally lower scores reflect the number of shooters in each class.

A FINAL NOTE ABOUT CLEANING

Cleaning for the flintlock follows the principles for the percussion, but remember that the pistol will be much dirtier than the percussion owing to the debris from the flashing pan. You cannot expect to remove this debris without dropping the lock out of the stock. My further recommendation is that the touch-hole and/or the blanking plug should be removed every time. A 0.32in brush is ideal for cleaning out the threads in the barrel once these plugs are removed. An alternative is to put the barrel into an oven after washing it out and drying it with patches in an attempt to exclude moisture from the cavity behind the touch-hole.

Following the earlier note about leaving oil in the breech, I strongly recommend that the barrel on the Le Page, or any other flintlock, is oiled with a sparsely lubricated patch rather a spray of WD-40 being directed straight into the barrel. A small drop of oil on the threads of the touch hole and blanking plug is a good idea before replacing them in the barrel. An alternative to oil is a couple of turns of PTFE (plumber's) tape around the threads. With original pistols, where the touch hole is a permanent fixture and the blanking plug is no longer removable, getting any excess of oil out is all the more difficult, so this point is especially important.

THE END GAME

Once you have the repro flint mastered, you can move on to the search for a suitable original. Shootable original flintlocks are few and far between, and, when you think that you have found the right one, sit down before you ask the price. With the growth of interest in the shooting of originals prices have climbed steeply, even for those requiring some reworking to get them into a safe and shootable condition. This is not an uncommon approach, with many an MLAGB member 'trading up' with the often unscheduled appearance of a more desirable pistol than the one in the shooting box. I decided to follow that route on both flintlock and percussion originals, as I describe in the next chapter.

The flintlock was without doubt the weapon of all time for the murderous activity of both the aristocracy and the nouveau riche of duelling. The matched pair was one thing, but form in the field was just as important. To quote one instructor in this dubious art : 'I cannot impress upon an individual too strongly the propriety of remaining perfectly Calm and Collected when hit: he must not allow himself to be alarumned or confused; but summoning up all his resolution, treat the matter coolly: and if he dies, to go off with as good a grace as possible.'

---

11. This was equalled at the Dutch Open at Luesden in 1999, so it can be done.

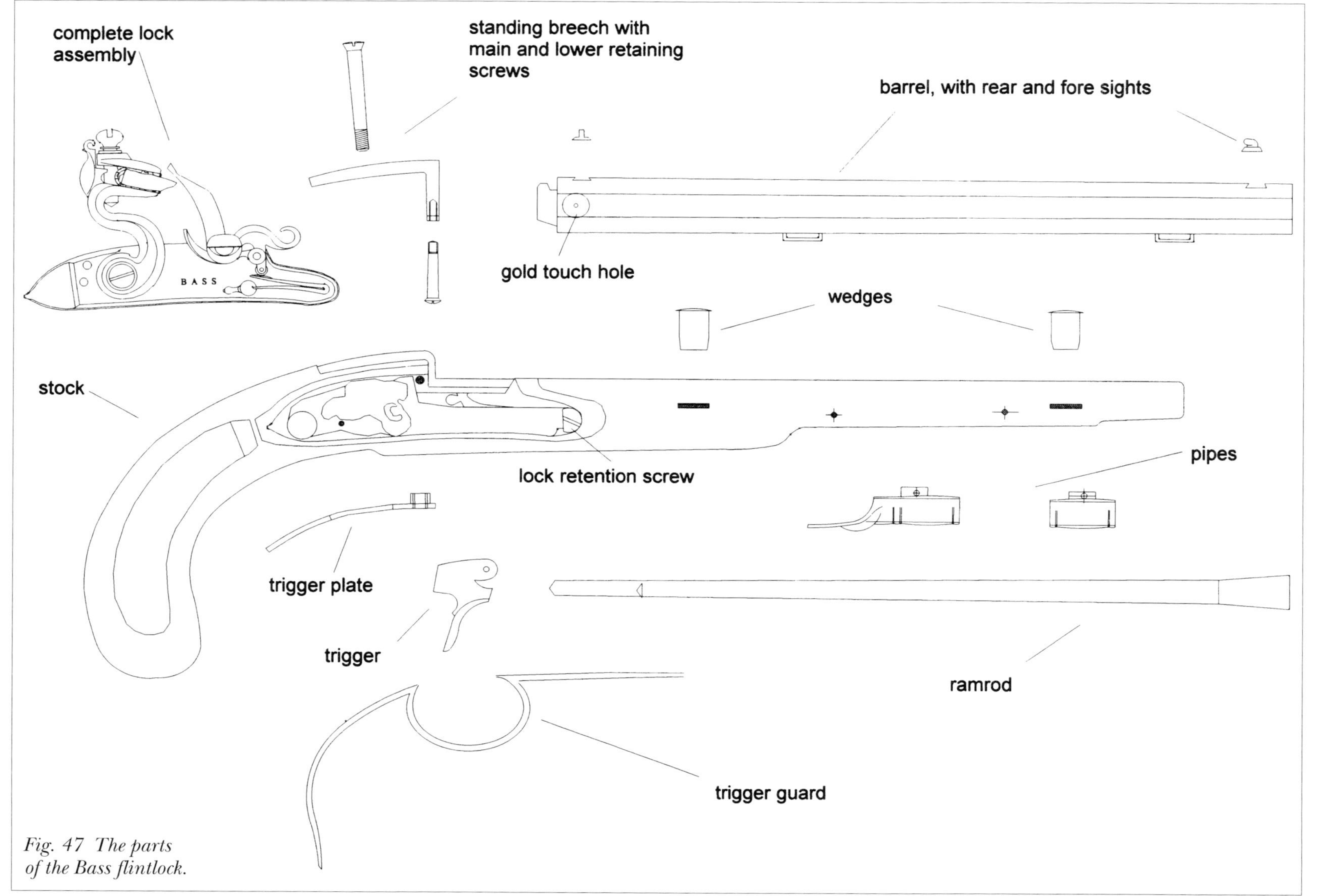

Fig. 47 The parts of the Bass flintlock.

5 Stories of Recovery

A DROP OF BASS

Once you have been caught by the 'original' bug, you are hooked for good. Many a devotee of the muzzle-loading disciplines starts searching the attic, attends car boot sales, and pays visits to elderly uncles in country retreats whom he has ignored for a decade in the hope of finding that elusive 'sleeper'. He gazes longingly at the Wallis and Wallis catalogues for 1971 and wishes that he had started searching earlier. In the last chapter I mentioned the lack of shootable originals. In reality, you can wait for years for the opportunity to buy any original at the right price. Finding the right flintlock is perhaps the most difficult of all, so that many a shooter will decide to take what he can get and work on it until something more favourable comes along. So this is the story of an original flintlock and its recovery from what was little more than a decorator to a fully functional target pistol. It started on the first of those freezing mornings – in the middle of August I might add – at the world championships at Wedgnock in 1998. A cursory glance at one of the trade stands grew into an invitation to handle, and from handling to inspection and from inspection to investment. And investment it is, since you are unlikely to lose your shirt when it comes to passing it on unless you have been sold a pup.

In these situations what you see is what you buy. Apart from the ability to drop a bore light down the barrel and check that the action is functioning there is not much that you can do about it until you get it home and strip it down. In this case, the barrel, with its gold touch-hole, was marked 'Bass – London', matching the 'Bass' on the lock plate. Getting out the relevant books[1] revealed that

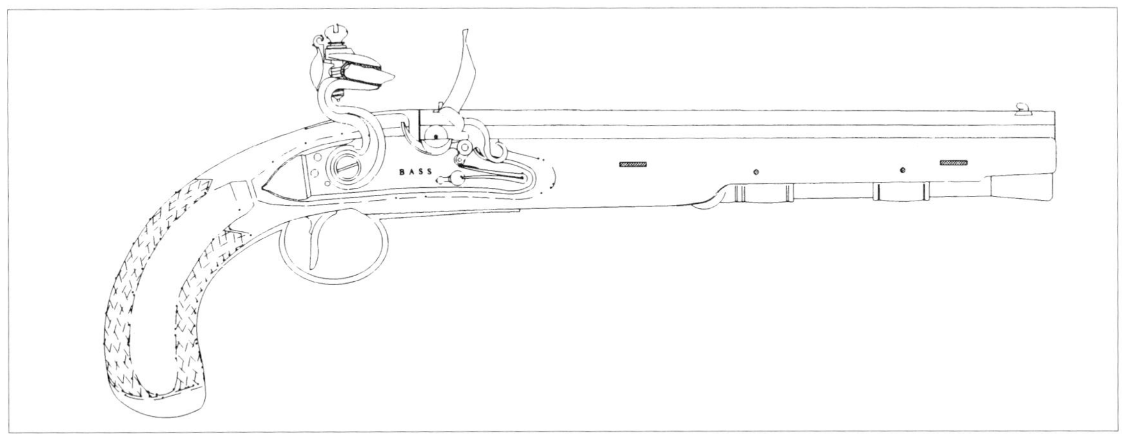

Fig. 48 The Bass flintlock.

1. *Great British Gunmakers, 1740–1790,* by Neale and Back, is a great starting point for the Twigg and Bass fraternity. This book is unfortunately out of print, with a good second-hand copy costing more than its original price of £75.

John Bass was in partnership with his uncle, the famous gun maker Twigg – also a John, at the time of the latter's death in 1790, and that Bass started to put his name alone on the guns the company continued to produce in 1791. Bass himself died in 1794, when all output from the company ceased. This closely dates the pistol's completion as 1791 to 1794. So I had a 200-year old pistol 'under recovery' (Plate 13).

In this case, what had been bought was a fully-stocked flintlock with a browned stub twist barrel with a bore somewhat in excess of ½in. It was fairly light, with a driftable steel rear sight and a bead foresight, which appeared to be all gold. The lock, without a set trigger, was fully functional. The frizzen had a small roller bearing mating with a ramp on the feather spring, which at least gave the possibility of a respectable lock time. The stock was covered by what looked like dark brown varnish and was finely chequered at the grip except over the flats on both sides. There were no escutcheons around the keys in the barrel and there was no mask or butt plate. A ramrod was present and of the right profile, but probably in too good a condition to have been the original.

My initial reaction was, of course, to fire it a few times to see what it felt like. Some 0.535in balls were 'borrowed' from one colleague and some 0.015in patches from another, and it was loaded with 36 grains of TS2, for no other reason than that I had some 18-grain loads for my rifled Le Page percussion available. Two things were immediately apparent. Although the bore light showed no particular problems on the trade stand, bells started ringing when a close-fitting ball was tapped down the barrel. It took the application of a sharp clip or two with the loading mallet on the ramrod once the ball was halfway down the barrel to get it seated on to the powder. Secondly, the trigger pull, which had not seemed unreasonable when held in the hand and released during its examination on the trade stand, felt like a ton and a half when the pistol was presented to the target.

Nevertheless, holes were scattered over the target at 25m. Half a dozen shots were enough to prove its functionality and to show the need for a leather glove at the next session. The thump from 36 grains in this comparatively light pistol started to bite into the palm of my hand. From this initial examination and short test, it was obvious that some serious work was needed, with the light weight being the only thing that could not, in theory, be fixed. Nothing ventured, nothing gained, and so the first action was to strip the pistol completely, clean the resulting parts and examine them carefully for any necessary recovery. Getting the pistol to pieces was a task in itself.

The barrel came off easily enough, the two barrel wedges sliding quite easily out of the woodwork, and the barrel was released from the normal hook at the breech. On the other hand, the main retaining screw between the standing breech and the trigger plate under the trigger guard was quite immovable, despite repeated applications of release oil. The final insult of immersing the parts in Coca-Cola (it often works) could not be used as the parts were still firmly embedded in the stock. Finally, I decided that it had to be drilled out from underneath. I used a 1/16in drill to start with, followed by one just large enough to clear the base of the screw threads. After drilling in about ¼in, the remaining threads parted, with the help of a sharp twist with a screwdriver.

The remnants of the screw had to be picked out of the boss on the trigger plate with the pointed end of a scriber. The screw, with its engraved top, and obviously the original, was put aside to have a piece grafted on to the bottom and threaded to suit. The trigger guard itself, with its distinctive pineapple finial, was released a little too easily, revealing that one of the wood screws retaining the trigger guard had been broken at some time in the past, leaving the tip buried deep in the stock. This had to be

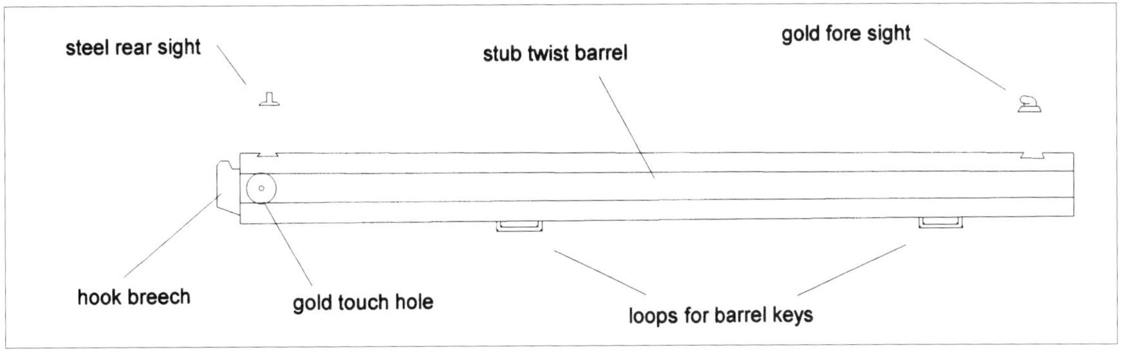

(Above) *Fig. 49 The Bass barrel and sights.*

Fig. 50 That corroded joint.

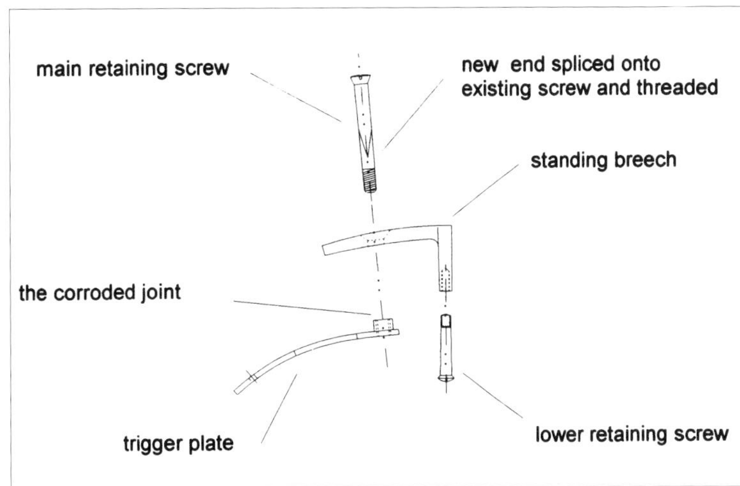

(Below) *Fig. 51 The pipes.*

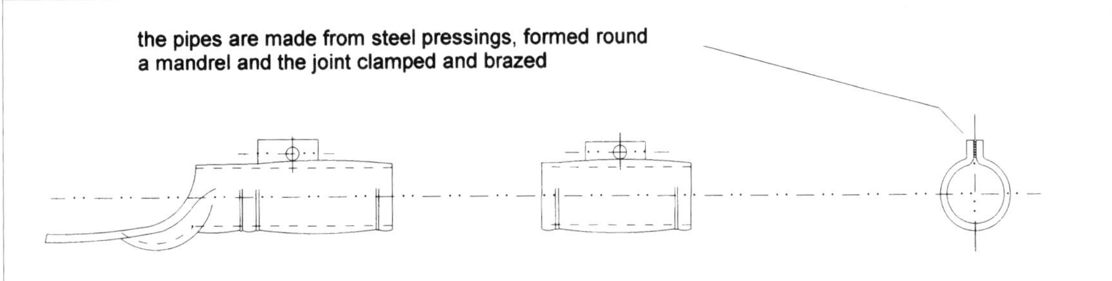

drilled out with a hollow drill (a one-off, made from the shaft of an old badminton racket) and the resulting oversize hole filled with a walnut plug. The biggest problems were the two pipes holding the ramrod, which were retained in position with pins driven through the sides of the fore end and which had never been out in their lives. But out they had to come, as the pipes were badly corroded and greatly in need of renovation. They finally responded to a thin, hollow-pointed pin punch, with the stock supported on a sandbag.

The removal of the tail pipe revealed some thin, brittle wooden sections, and I also noted numerous small surface cracks in the wood under the lock and trigger guard. Both these points were clear signs of a very dried-out stock, so the whole stock was wrapped in slightly damp tissue paper and a couple of layers of cling-film. After a week, the thin sections of wood had regained their springiness and most of the fine surface cracks under the trigger guard had closed up.

It was time to find out what lay beneath the layers of varnish that covered the stock, so a gentle scraping with a new Stanley knife blade in the direction of the grain began. Care was taken not to get down to the wood surface since this would have entailed a complete strip, fill and polish job, which would have destroyed the aged look of the pistol. It was also decided to leave the many small dents in the woodwork, which could probably have been lifted by steaming, for the same reason.

The job was finished with a general scrub with 0000s wire wool, to reveal the horrors beneath. These included a major repair at some time in the past just behind the lock,[2] where it looked as if the stock had been cracked wide open, and a number of wooden inserts where dents or gouges in the stock had been – not very expertly – repaired. How old these repairs were it would be difficult to say, but they were obviously not recent. There remained a couple of fine transverse cracks in the stock in the area of the standing breech and quite a bad split in the fore end, which had been held together by the pin to the forward pipe. Each crack was individually examined, with the ones in the direction of the grain being opened out and some old-fashioned glue forced in before the gap was closed and binding until the glue set. The transverse cracks were back-drilled with a thin drill, and super-glue forced into the cracks through these holes. This adhesive is ideal for the job since it is very 'thin', and is drawn into the narrowest of cracks. In this case it revealed their true extent, one crack being rather longer than originally anticipated.

The result of this work was a quite sound stock, which responded well to repeated applications of hand-rubbed shellac[3] and

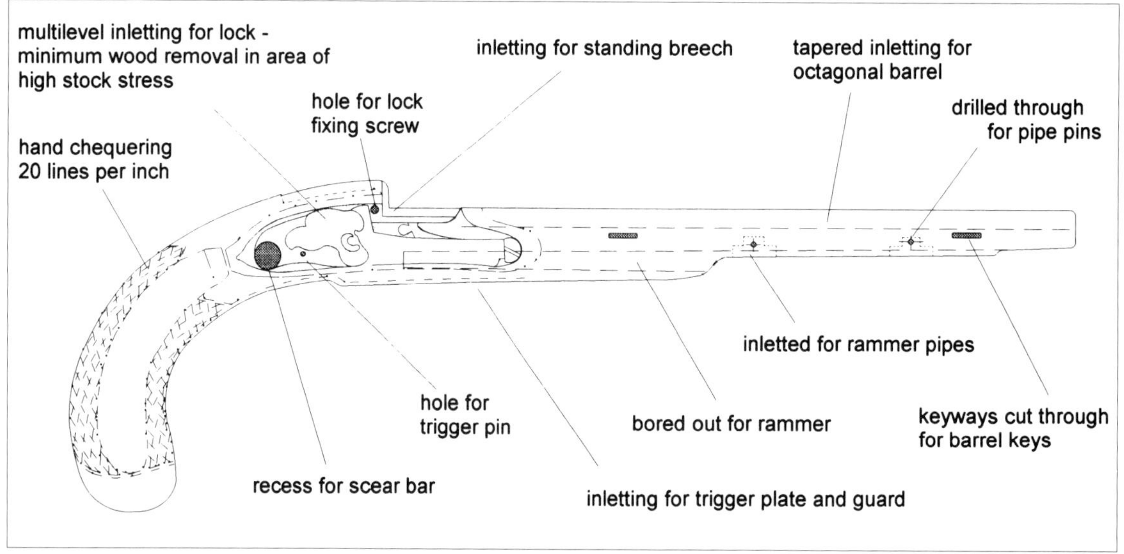

Fig. 52 The stock.

2. Early flintlock duellers, such as the Bass (being far too light for a military weapon), were apparently plagued by weakness in this area. It usually manifested itself when the gun was dropped to the floor butt first.

3. Boiled linseed oil is an alternative, producing a fine finish but taking, perhaps, somewhat longer to achieve.

wire wool. Eventually the vast majority of the surface pores had disappeared and the whole stock was covered with a thin, transparent skin that revealed the grain of the wood, and the old repairs as well if you cared to look for them. Fig. 52 shows the complexity of the pistol stock, a high proportion of which was done by hand in the late eighteenth century.

In between work on the stock there was the barrel to consider. On closer examination it revealed a common breech, that is, one in which there was no small chamber (patent breech) between the touch-hole and the main barrel. The bore, measuring 0.551in (about 28 bore[4]), looked quite good at the muzzle, but showed some particularly odd scratches along the line of the bore from the breech to the middle of the barrel. The underside also revealed signs of neglect and a lack of cleaning over a long period, with no browning and several patches of pitting. Nothing that could not be dealt with, however. Now removed from the stock, the underside of the barrel showed only the initial 'View' mark and, in front of it, the Gunmakers' Company proof mark, in the oval form with simplified crown that had been used in London since 1720.

Work on the bore started with repeated applications of a phosphor bronze brush, followed by well oiled 4-by-2. As this failed to make any real impression on the longitudinal striations at the lower end of the barrel, the decision was taken to lap the barrel to try to get these out. A suitable copper lap was fabricated and fed into the mouth of the barrel, lubricated with oil only. This revealed that the 'ball in the drain' feeling reported earlier had been no dream, as the lap stuck solid halfway down the barrel. Initial fears were that the barrel was deformed, but the problem was finally identified as a

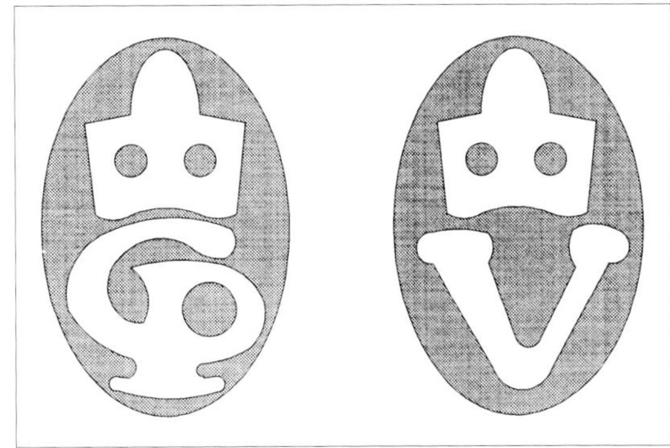

Fig. 53 The 1720 proof marks.

sleeve of hard rust, perhaps some 5 thou in thickness, which completely coated the bottom half of the barrel. Someone had obviously tried to clear this in the past, leaving the marks of a wire brush cut into the layer of rust to give the striations mentioned above. And was that rust hard! It was a good job that the pistol had really dried out, or there would have been no barrel left.

The rust was finally removed with a cleft dowel and emery cloth. Gradually the dowel reached the bottom of the barrel, bringing up rust and debris at each turn. And, as the dowel cut its way down, the oiled lap would struggle its way forward, until it would finally pass all the way down without too much difficulty. Then it was out with the fine grinding paste, easing the lap down in stages by hand, until it was possible to drive it with a low-speed, battery-powered drill. Slowly but slowly the rust-coloured sludge was replaced by a blacker mélange of oil, carborundum and iron, until most of the bore of the surface was a fine grey colour, revealing a couple of small areas of surface pitting, but nothing serious. The barrel was slightly tighter at the muzzle than at the breech, which is deemed the right thing for

4. Take one imperial pound of pure lead, cut it into twenty-eight equal pieces, roll one piece into a round ball and its diameter is '28 bore'. This process was established by royal decree since there were no dimensional standards, even from town to town, in England in the Middle Ages. Trying to get balls by mail order to fit your hackbut (however you spelled it) was consequently rather hit and miss. This system was in common use both in England and continental Europe by the 1540s.

a smooth-bore. With a well-cleaned bore, the oiled lap would slowly sink to the bottom of the barrel with a satisfying 'sloosh'. A final polish, more for the sake of appearance than for anything else, was achieved with some thickened Brasso in lieu of anything else on the shelf.

Some work on the exterior surface of the barrel was carried out and then it was put aside to be refinished by being lightly browned. I had no real qualms about refinishing the barrel since the existing browning already had that refinished look. On its completion, it had a nice transparent appearance from the very thin finish, revealing the quite coarse stub twist pattern; things were starting to fall into place.

The pipes holding the ramrod were identical in pattern to those used on pistols by Twigg and others as early as the 1780s, some of them being made in solid silver. The ferrous ones at least must have been standard gun-trade parts, as the identical style may be seen in illustrations of pistols well into the 1800s. Needless to say, since the pipes had never been removed before, the undersides were encrusted with dirt and rust, which had to be scraped off with the blade of a Stanley knife. This seems more effective and much less damaging than the use of a wire brush, as the pits in the surface can be cleared out, which only excessive brushing will achieve. An alternative to scraping is to soak parts for a week in WD-40 and then brush away the loosened rust with a bristle brush – I use an old Braun battery-driven toothbrush for this. Repeat ad nauseam; it's effective but takes ages. The exposed surfaces of the pipes had originally been polished, so, following a good deal of careful cleaning and recutting of contours with Swiss files, they were polished and finally sealed with a thin surface coating of picture varnish.

The lock was the only major item left to be tackled. It was almost identical to pistol locks by Twigg and others, such as Probin, dating from the 1770s, except that it had a hook at the front of the lock in place of the earlier second screw. There were two screws and a locking pin holding the beautifully scrolled bridle to the lock plate, whereas more modern bridles have three screws. There was some rust pitting on the back of the lock plate and a general cleaning of all the lock parts was clearly indicated (Plate 18).

A major problem was the cock itself, which was firmly rusted to the spigot on the tumbler. Immersion in release oil over an extended period failed to loosen it and trying to lever off the cock with a screwdriver from one side and then the other would damage both cock and lock plate, with no guarantee that it would be effective. So it was necessary to make a miniature hub puller[5] to assist in the process. It is a false economy not to make such single-use small tools since the potential damage to a 200-year-old lock is just not worth it. It worked first time, and the lock could be stripped and cleaned once the technique of compressing the mainspring – a little difficult because of the short upper arm – was mastered.

Apart from cleaning, an important task was to put an acceptable surface on the frizzen – also known in ages past as the 'hammer' or the 'steel' – since it was quite badly pitted down one side. A frizzen to work has to have a hard surface, and it is always uncertain whether machining the surface back to get rid of surface deformation will cut through any surface hardening. If it does, it will have to be rehardened or resurfaced as discussed in Chapter 4. I worked on the principle that the surface would have to be dressed back even if it were to be 'plated', so I went to work with a miniature grinder, trying to keep to the original

5. Made from a piece of steel tube peened over at one end to slip under the cock, with a central pressure screw acting through a tapped plate silver soldered across the top.

contour, and finished the surface off with 240 grade emery supported by a curved former. Trying the lock off the pistol showed a good shower of sparks, so it will be left in that condition unless and until more drastic action is proved necessary.

As previously mentioned, it was going to be necessary to work on the lock to reduce the trigger pressure to make it suitable for target use. The scear is only 40 thou wide, so any work on it would have to be carefully controlled. The seemingly obvious thing to do was to rework my Remington trigger lapping tool to support the Bass scear. However, when working on single-shot locks with swinging detents which lift the scear clear of the half cock notch as the cock falls, you have to beware of reshaping the scear so that it has a sharp edge, as you would normally do on a revolver. Because of the angles involved, this sharp edge may cut into the detent, especially if it is not as hard as it should be. Now my scear lapping tool generates a very sharp edge, so I had to use it with care, taking the sharp edge off the scear with a diamond file every time I removed it from the lapping jig. Once the correct trigger pressure was obtained, I slightly increased the radius on the tip of the scear to create the slight 'roll over' effect that I was looking for. With pistols fitted with a set trigger, this radius can be somewhat larger, as the shooter feels the creep only in the set trigger mechanism. With time on my side, a reasonably light and crisp release was obtained after an hour's work[6] and the pistol in its final state could be reassembled in its reworked glory.

The end of the matter? No, not really. There followed two months of increasing frustration at my normal distributor's failure to turn up with the required round ball mould. In the end Lee in the States responded magnificently to my faxed request for a .537 ball mould, which landed on my doorstep within five days and at less than the normal British price, even when insurance, carriage and freight were added.

With a 13 thou patch, the ball now slid without a hint of hesitation on to an initial load of 27 grains of No.1, and the first thirteen shots slotted into a 5in group (with a flyer or two) at the top of the target. So the lovely gold foresight had to be relegated to the safe and be replaced with a more mundane but functional one. I had just started the process of working up an acceptable load, ball and patch combination for competition use, when fate decided to take a hand. It took the form of a 40 bore (.490in) heavy flintlock from one of Bass's contemporaries, Henry Nock. At nearly twice the weight and shooting a 165 grain ball, against the 230 grains of the Bass, the Nock just had to be a better bet for competitive target shooting (Plate 14). So the Bass, after all the work done on it, will only be brought out for sport and demonstration, and not for serious competition.

THE NOCK-ON EFFECT

In the early 1790s Henry Nock was producing duelling pistols looking remarkably like the Bass, but before his own death in 1804 he was producing a different product entirely. In line with developments in the trade (probably spearheaded by Joseph Manton in the mid 1790s) he was producing a much heavier pistol with a set trigger, a much smaller bore with his own patent breech, a heavy rib under the half stocked barrel and escutcheons around the single barrel wedge as standard. As with any other pistol that comes the author's way, it was immediately taken to pieces for examination. Unlike the Bass, the stock was in excellent condition,

6. I cannot subscribe to the assertion that set triggers were invented only to reduce the time spent in getting a light, crisp release on a standard or common lock. It is just unsafe to have much less than a 500g trigger pressure with the relatively massive main lock springs fitted to flintlocks.

with no sign of brittleness in the wood nor softness through oil absorption.

The set trigger was a little harsh, but responded immediately to the stripping, cleaning and polishing of the moving parts. The lock itself seemed to function well outside the stock, but was difficult to set at full cock when fitted into the pistol. The problem was quickly traced to the scear bar fouling the top of the trigger before the lock was set, instead of having the necessary small gap. This is not an uncommon problem.[7] I first tried to resolve this by inserting a small packing piece under the rear of the set trigger assembly. A similar solution had been applied to a colleague's Le Page flint when the unmounted lock was returned from Pedersoli where it had been sent for repair. However, this still failed to give the necessary clearance on the Nock. The problem was resolved only by building up the top of the scear bar and then filing away the underside to obtain the necessary clearance.

The bore of the Damascus twist barrel had suffered from a lack of cleaning and protection in the past, resulting in areas of rust and debris towards the breech. While by no means in as bad a condition as the Bass, surface corrosion was still apparent even after a thorough brushing. So the lathe was uncovered once more, a new copper lap turned up and slotted, and the barrel quickly returned to a quite acceptable finish. There were one or two pits well down the barrel, but certainly having no effect on the pistol's potential accuracy. The only real trouble with small pits in an otherwise pristine barrel is getting them clean after firing.

Despite the pistol's now excellent appearance, early trials on the range were markedly disappointing. The priming in the pan repeatedly flashed only once in three or four strikes, and when it did ignite it failed repeatedly to set off the main charge. This indicated two separate problems. Striking the lock in a dark room indicated poor spark generation, in complete contrast to my trusty Le Page that spits sparks in all directions. The flints were new and the frizzen clean and nearly unworn, and the flint followed the contours of the frizzen from tip to heel without any hesitation. However, the pull required to put the lock into the full cock position was far lower than that on the Le Page, and the lack of ignition in the pan was deduced as being due to a weak mainspring. Closer examination of the lock indicated that the pistol had been through the hands of a target shooter at some time in its life, as he had set about lightening the mainspring. So a new and heftier spring was commissioned; the end result can be seen in Plate 20.[8]

Most Nock mainsprings were made with the curled end of the upper leaf bearing against the block supporting the flash pan, in common with the practice of contemporary gunsmiths. A few later models sported an unusual profile, as shown in Fig. 54. These are identical to some mainsprings produced by Forsythe's[9] company, who probably copied the idea. Presumably they were marginally cheaper to produce.

The second thing to tackle was the fundamental problem that the pistol would not 'go off': scarcely once in a dozen shots.

7. Some people will accept this situation as normal and 'set' the set trigger before the main lock. I consider this an unsafe practice and would never use any of my 'shootable' pistols in that condition.

8. A number of well-known flintlock shooters claim that both the main and the frizzen feather spring are far stronger than they need to be and thin them down. Others copy their actions without any real control over or clear objectives about what they hope to achieve. As mentioned previously, these springs on the Le Page are really quite heavy, but the lock is good at delivering fault-free ignition. In cases like this it is best to leave well alone.

9. The percussion 'scent bottle' curate. With Forsythe's original patent being supervised by James Watt of steam engine fame, and with James Purdy as his gunsmith, he had all the support he needed – except for that of the British Board of Ordnance. Shades of many a latter-day British inventor.

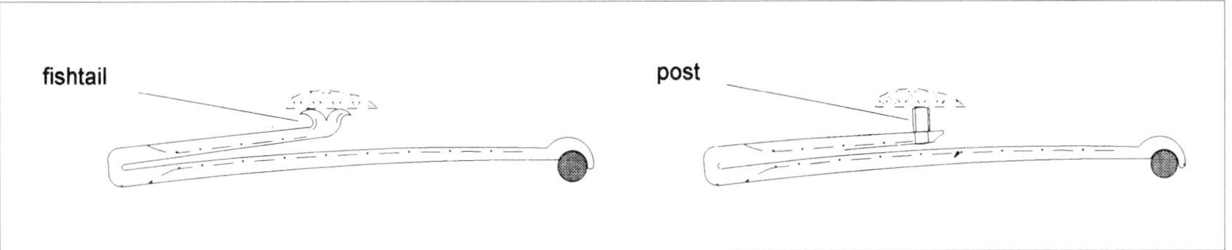

Fig. 54 Variations on the Nock mainsprings.

There was no oil in the chamber, the touch-hole (an easy 60 thou, just like the Pedersoli) was clear through into the chamber, and the chamber was clear of any rubbish, burned powder and old bits of 4-by-2. It took some weeks before I was able to solve it, a clear instance of the original and successful use of a pistol having been upset by modern technology. The technology in question was the drop tube. It appeared that pouring my best No.1 down the drop tube was no guarantee that it was getting behind the touch-hole. And here was the problem. The chamber diameter in the Nock was less than 3⁄16in in diameter against that of the Le Page of ¼in or more. The angled end of the drop tube settled into the lips of the Nock chamber, blocking the hole. A simple glass mock-up showed how the first grains of the charge would bridge the top of the chamber, preventing the remainder from dropping into the chamber and settling behind the touch-hole. This bridge persisted as the drop tube was withdrawn, however hard the ball was rammed down the barrel. Of course, this was giving the flash from the priming a major change of direction and nearly ½in of cold steel to negotiate before it found some friendly powder to ignite (*see* Fig. 42): not too useful when the other chap is standing ten paces away with a smile on his lips and a 28 bore Mortimer in his right hand.

What to do about it was the obvious question. Other Nock users in the MLAGB reported a ¼in diameter or larger chamber, and none reported ignition problems. So out came a long ¼in drill, and soon the problem was solved. The drop tube now sank to the bottom of the patent breech, with the first grains of the main charge dropping right behind the touch-hole. The rest of the chamber and the lower part of the barrel filled as normal as the drop tube was eased back up the barrel. A preliminary test with a few grains of No.1 and some tissue paper to keep it in place had an almost total success rate when the powder flashed in the pan. So that was that problem solved.

How did it go on the range? With the new mainspring fitted, the spark generation went straight back to what it should have been – bright, full and consistent. And with the main charge going off every time, coupled with the heavy barrel, it was a joy to look over those sights and put ball after ball into the black. So I had no excuses for not using it for the team trials the following week. Unfortunately, I had no option but to use the largest ball that I had which would fit inside the barrel, which ran out at about .458in. To get some sort of tight fit in the barrel I had to use two 13 thou patches and with only one practice session could raise only about 84 in the trials (the repro Le Page flint made up for it). It was only when I skimmed some .490 balls down to about .480 and used a 10 thou patch that things started to look promising. So I commissioned a .476 ball mould. With a 13 thou patch the pistol has become really competitive, grouping well within the 9 ring when the shot is released properly.

THE COCKED-UP KIRNER

The same day that I had all the parts to put the Nock back into operation, I was able to give my Kirner original percussion pistol its first proper trial. Having been frustrated by the Nock, the further frustration of the Kirner was unbelievable. It all started at the London Arms Fair, where I had already acquired the Nock. I must have been feeling flush at the time, as I became the owner of the Kirner – in about .44 calibre – within half an hour of purchasing the Nock. You can imagine the scene: you look at a pistol and tentatively handle it, only to find that it fits your hand like a glove. The bore is pristine, the lock crisp, the sights original. Then it becomes a battle of wits to prise the arm from the potential but apparently reluctant seller, who, for some reason, assumes you have unlimited funds at your disposal. It is not that I didn't need it (I had nothing to shoot in original Kuchenreuter) but to buy two originals in one day was likely to give any thinking man pause for reflection. But my old age pension had just gone up by £0.58 a week (less tax), so there was no real reason not to buy it, was there?

Now Kirner came from Budapest and produced some beautiful pistols, but was generally unknown to me, apart from a fleeting glance at a boxed pair in Paris. Even in Paris they were priced in US dollars, and anything in Paris priced in dollars is out of my price range. They were nestling beside the most beautiful boxed pair of original Le Page presentation pistols, the barrels an iridescent blue with gold inlay, at a mere $17,000. And that was in 1980.

You may imagine that my acquisition was not in this class. It was plain and undecorated, apart from some fine scrollwork on the lock plate and the muzzle end of the barrel, in common with most duelling-cum-target pistols of the day. It was marked as number '1' of a pair. Its simple lines were matched by a near perfect, dark blue, octagonal barrel and finely chequered, close-grained, light coloured, walnut stock. The rifling was clear cut and without any hint of corrosion. The foresight was an elegantly profiled pin head and driftable to take care of lateral group movements. The pinhead itself was really a little small by today's standards, but I certainly was not going to replace it. The rear sight was very low with just a hint of a V notch in it, and firmly locked into the standing breech with a small pin for a locking bolt. No opportunities for vertical sight adjustment there, unless a new rear sight blade were made and fitted. There was no set trigger. However, I was confident on examining the lock (it was taken apart on the stand) that the trigger pressure could be brought down to reasonable levels, just as I had done on the Bass. So interest was expressed and the price set at an entirely satisfactory level, at which I quickly wrote a cheque before the vendor changed his mind. You don't often get opportunities like that.

So I arrived at the range with the thought that at last I had an original which I could shoot from day one, without a protracted refinish and rebuild programme. It took but a single session to show how wrong I could be. The first shots printed into a neat group at 6 o'clock in the 6 ring, virtually point of aim, indicating that – as expected – a higher rear sight would need to be made. Despite the higher than desirable trigger pressure, the group was good, the sight pattern was good and the feel was good, all in all giving the impression that here was a pistol with which I could feel truly competitive. As always, interest on the range when a member is shooting a newly acquired original was high. A few shots were being fired by other shooters to see whether they agreed with my claims of having picked up a reasonable 'sleeper'. It was then that the cock fell into two pieces! Not fell off, but sheared cleanly, halfway up.

The joint between the two pieces was flat and smooth as if it had just been machined, but even Hungarian gunsmiths do not make cocks for percussion pistols in pieces and stick them together. An eyeglass revealed the problem: the scalloped rings of a typical fatigue fracture, starting from the bottom of one of the engraved lines cutting across the front edge of the cock. And that was the end of that particular shooting session. Not that it was much consolation, but I learned afterwards that this is not an uncommon problem, with more than one Wedgnock shooter indicating that it had happened to him as well.

The cock had, of course, to be replaced for shooting purposes, and I was lucky in finding a replacement that was similar in profile to the original. The original is now back in one piece, following a superb piece of silver–gold brazing in which there is some difficulty in seeing the joint. This will go into the safe, carefully labelled, along with the original rear sight, to go with the pistol when I 'trade up'. And now? I am pleased to report that the new rear sight is fitted, the trigger pressure is down to just under 500g, and, with 15 grains of TS2 behind a .440 ball and a 13 thou patch, it groups far better than I can hold it. If only I were 20 years younger!

FROM COWBOYS AND INDIANS TO A SHOOTABLE REMINGTON

At least the Kirner took little in the way of refinishing, which is more than can be said for another of the pistols on my recovery list, an original Remington New Army revolver in 451 calibre. I had mentioned earlier that you can make a shootable Remington from the most decrepit-looking object on the vendor's stall, provided that the inside of the barrel is good and the back of the cylinder forming the ratchet is reasonably untouched. I had the opportunity to purchase such an object (I will not describe it as a revolver in the state in which I bought it) at the 1996 world championships in Wedgnock.

To describe it as a wall hanger would probably be a little generous. The cylinder did not lock up at all and had not done so in all the years the children had been using it to play cowboys and indians. Because of the absence of the cylinder stop, the hammer had fallen at random on the back of the cylinder, peening the edges of the nipple cavities over, making dents in the back edge of the cylinder and generally closing up the tops of the nipples. Someone had tried to slot the original German silver cone foresight to accept a blade foresight and had broken off one side of the cone in the process. To cap it all, the whole of the frame had been wire-brushed to 'clean it up'. However, having borrowed a rod and wire brush from the next vendor on the block, the inside of the barrel was shown to be quite clean. And taking out the cylinder showed a cleaner and sharper ratchet than a 150-year old revolver might be expected to have. Moreover, the barrel, frame, cylinder and trigger guard were all marked with the same number, and the inspection marks on these parts also tallied. So nothing ventured, nothing gained, and the 'object' became mine.

By the end of the day it had been stripped into its component parts and the recovery process had begun. The replacement of the two (one on top of the other) broken, bifurcated trigger/cylinder stop springs by a single new one immediately resolved the cylinder stop problem. A complete set of new nipples had been purchased to replace the originals, which were put aside for recovery. All the original Remingtons on the vendors' stalls had been examined to get the right profile for the planned replacement foresight. The lock parts had been cleaned and inspected to find that they were quite undamaged, even the original pawl having the correct profile. About the only things that were under par were the wooden grips, where the surfaces were quite deeply grained as if they had been exposed to the weather for a month. This was a pity because

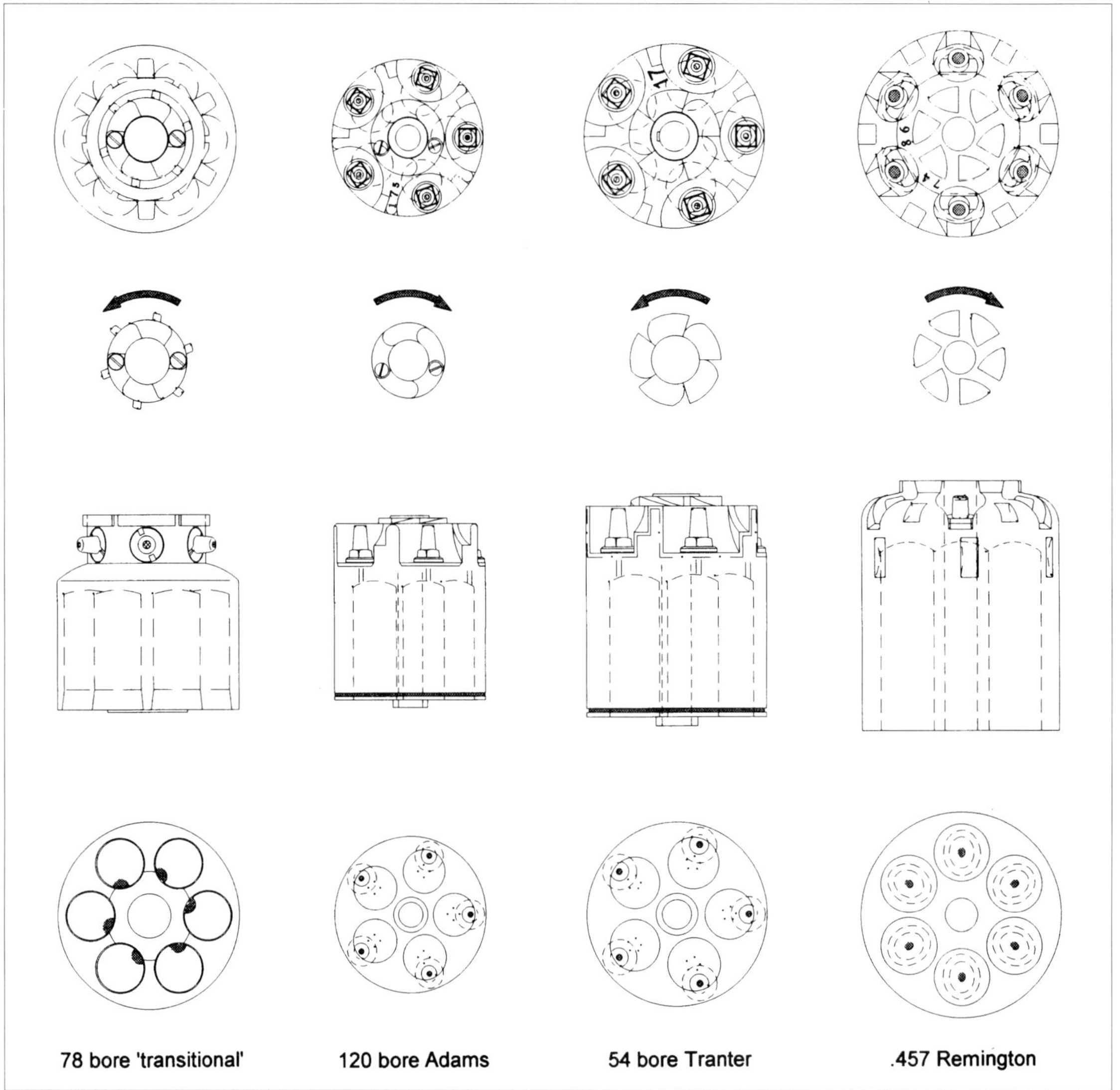

Fig. 55 Various percussion cylinders and their ratchets.

the inspector's markings on the butt,[10] which can be so informative about its origin, were faded and worn. All that remained was a degree of impatience for the end of the championships so that I could get to work on the frame and the cylinder.

The wire brushing of all the external surfaces was eventually counted as a benefit, since files and emery paper could be used to reprofile the back edge of the cylinder without having to worry about the retention of the original finish. A similar approach was

10. Even after taking the grip to a local store to use their ultraviolet bank-note checker they remained unreadable, so no match could be found against the list given in the Dixie Gun Works catalogue, my only reference on the subject.

taken on some dents in the frame and the barrel, which had been clamped in a vice without any form of soft jaws. The remains of the front sight were drifted out so that a replacement brass cone could be stuck on with super-glue. This temporary arrangement was in anticipation of having to make one of a different height once the fall of shot could be recorded on the gun's first visit to the range.

All that remained was to cover those bright wire-brush marks, which were the predominant feature of the finish. As I had no yet perfected my cold blueing treatment (*see* Appendix V), I discussed the situation with my gunsmith. He could have 're-blued' the gun, but, since the result of the chemical refinishing would be blacking and not blueing, I declined his invitation. I finally resolved to do this myself, using some oil of high oxygen content and a propane burner, a process that I had not used since I was worked briefly in a machine shop some forty years earlier. With the rigorously cleaned frame clamped in the vice, the flame was played over the lightly oiled metal until a fine, brownish-blue hue developed. With the different thicknesses of metal and consequently different surface temperatures, the whole surface finally displayed a variety of blues and browns merging one into the other, which gave the metalwork a rather worn, nineteenth-century appearance. A similar treatment to the cylinder, this time supported on a rod inserted into the cylinder bearing hole, finished the job.

We have already discussed the vicissitudes of Remingtons in Chapter 3. However, once you have dealt with their problems they have little to go wrong, provided that you clean them and keep a look out for broken springs and the odd unwanted burr. However, the comparative ease with which this example was brought back into shootable condition should not be taken as applicable to everything on the market. In this case, the end result is an original revolver put back into shooting condition meeting all the criteria of MLAIC rules at a cost of under £500. Other Remingtons I have seen on offer, exceeding this figure by 50 per cent, have been made up of replacement parts, with cylinders that do not match the frames, shot-out barrels and lock parts from repros that were never intended to fit an original.

AND FINALLY, THE POCKET REVOLVER

If you are going to shoot any of the pocket revolver competitions it is either a question of splashing out on an original, such as the author's 120 bore Adams, or picking up one of the many pocket repros on the market. Some time ago I was offered a little brass-framed, five-shot revolver at one of the Bisley trade shows. Although I had no real intention of shooting in this type of competition, the repro was offered at something like half the going rate because of some blueing problems on the barrel, so it seemed to be a cheap entree to the discipline (*see* Fig. 35).

The revolver in question was made by one of the Italian repro manufacturers, and was offered as a copy of the Remington 1863 five-shot pocket revolver in 31 calibre. I have no idea how accurate a copy it is since I have never seen an original, let alone had the opportunity to take one to pieces. I have no reason to doubt that it is as close to the original as other repros at the cheap end of the market. The Remington .31 looks, by the way, to be a scaled-down New Army without the trigger guard.

The revolver looked well enough when handled at the stand. It was only during its working-up period that a number of faults in the detail design and manufacture of the revolver made themselves apparent. My definition of a fault is something that prevents the revolver from working every time, or something that is likely to develop into a problem in the future. As I started to work up the revolver, a number of sometimes fundamental faults were brought to the fore, necessitating a rework programme that should not really have been necessary on a virtually new, commercial product, irrespective of its cost. Normally a revolver with these sorts of problem should be returned to the vendor, but, having the time and the interest, I normally like to sort out these teething problems myself.

The first problem to appear was poor cap ignition, primarily caused because my normal No.11 caps would only seat right at the top of the nipples. This was soon traced to their high degree of taper – the diameter of the nipples was good at the top but too big at the bottom. I had to drop the hammer on the same cap two or three times before it would go off. As I could not find another make of cap that was wider or shorter, I took all the nipples out, and having made a support to hold them, put them one by one into the lathe and filed the taper down so that the caps would go in all the way. A good test for a nipple is to put a touch of engineer's blue on the top of the nipple and push the cap down firmly. If it both retains the cap and marks the primer in the cap with the blue, the taper is about right.

A contributory problem with poor cap ignition was a very weak mainspring, which consisted of a rudimentary piece of flat spring steel. The .44 New Army has a properly tapered spring from its retention slot in the heel of the butt right up to the hammer follower. Unfortunately, the spring in this repro was so profiled that it was possible to lift the hammer nearly 3/32in from the cap before the follower met the slightest resistance from the mainspring. So the mainspring was taken out and bent a little straighter, which solved the problem at least temporarily. The long-term answer was to replace it with a properly profiled mainspring made, incidentally, from a worn-out diamond file. Small files tend to have just the right amount of carbon in them for flat spring manufacture.

The weak mainspring compounded with a hammer that only hit the cap right on the top edge rather than evenly across the cap, which is necessary to push it down squarely on to the top of the nipple. The profile of the nose of the hammer was round rather than flat, and looked decidedly unfinished. Although this may be what the original looked like, I dressed the face of the hammer so that it was flat, in the same way as the Remington New Army and its repros.

Yet a further problem with the hammer was that the nose was too wide to fit into the slots in the back of the cylinder between the nipples. These slots were originally used as a parking position for the hammer when the revolver was carried loaded – not that it would ever be carried loaded these days, on or off the range. Again, it was a simple matter of taking a few thou off the width of the nose of the hammer, but it was obvious that this had never been checked during manufacture.

In common with many a repro, the mainspring follower was quite solid in the hammer and would only turn when forced with a pair of snipe-nosed pliers. This had to be resolved by tapping out the pin holding the roller and reducing the diameter of the centre of the pin with some fine emery paper until the roller would spin freely.

Another pin that gave problems was the one acting as the pivot between the rammer and the loading lever. This was so loose that it worked itself out at least twice during its first visit to the range. It was necessary to push it back and then peen over the edges of the hole to stop this from happening again.

On taking the action to pieces, there were the normal collection of burrs on about everything, which is par for the course on this sort of low-value repro. The most serious was on the tip of the pawl since this had already started to degrade the ratchet on the back of the cylinder. Again, a deburr and polish job were required. Taking the action to pieces also showed that, at some time in its short life, it had been fired, and the action had neither been stripped for cleaning nor sprayed with WD-40. This had resulted in surface corrosion setting in on some of the bare metal parts of the action; it took a little work to get them clean again.

Once these problems had been identified and resolved, a smart little revolver which functioned reliably, shot after shot, was in my possession. On the range the revolver proved a little trickier to load than its big cousin, the 44 New Army. A revolver of this calibre only needs about 8 grains of TS2, although the chamber will actually hold about 11. This difference in load is not really worth worrying about, but as a trial I used 8 grains with a little filler. With the small chamber the filler needs to stop a little further down the chamber than on its larger counterpart since it has less space in which to be compressed. I used some .315 Hornady balls, which came as part of the deal, which seemed to fit neatly into the chambers. When dropping them into the mouth of the chamber you need to have the chamber close to the rammer; otherwise the ball fouls the frame as you rotate it.

At 10yd – the competition distance for this type of pocket revolver – shots printed about 8in high and 2in left from the point of aim. Unlike other target disciplines, these pocket revolvers are better set for point of aim since the likely target is the centre of the NRA DP1 (the updated 'Service Pistol' target). The rear sight was as on any other Remington, a V cut into the back of the top strap, and its small size precluded any chance of recutting the V to compensate for lateral movement. The foresight, a thin cone, was only 'attached' to the barrel as a push fit into a 90 thou diameter shallow hole – hardly a suitable mechanical solution to attach anything to the end of a gun barrel. A similar foresight could have been made with the necessary increase in height to bring the group down if the windage did not have to be considered as well. My shooting colleagues will tell you that I have enough trouble holding a group without the problems associated with 'holding off'. So off it went to the local gunsmith to have a tenon cut into the top of the barrel so that I could fit a new foresight of the right height and adjust the windage accordingly.

Once the new foresight had been fitted and adjusted for both windage and elevation, the revolver would hold 2in groups without much trouble at 10yd with a full load of 11 grains, more than adequate for this class of competition. A problem was the consistent appearance of a flier, normally about one in every five or six shots. Now there may have been a number of things wrong with the revolver as purchased, but the rifling in the barrel was cleanly cut and of good finish, and the chambers in the cylinder were aligned very well with the barrel – some cheap repros are a long way out. Coupled to this, the cylinder lock-up was really quite good and the trigger release was as crisp as you could ask for and no more than a pound, which is surprisingly low for revolvers made largely for the American market. So I must admit to these fliers being due to bad aiming and shot release. With its limiting 4in sight base and a grip requiring the little finger to curl under the heel of the grip, these revolvers are by no means easy to shoot accurately. I suppose it will come, as always, with plenty of practice.

This just leaves the pin fire revolver and the Lefaucheur (no – not Lefaucheux) gallery pistol, the Norfolk pocket pistol and a transitional pistol to work on in the dark evenings to come. No doubt one or two more will enter my collection as time goes on, all requiring a touch of loving care and the browning solution to bring them up to a safe and shootable condition. So there you have them, stories of recovery. Inspect, investigate, compare, research, clean, measure, test, deburr, refit, refinish and replace – all within the spirit of the original. But most of all, buyer beware!

THE AMERICAN TEAM CAPTAIN TO PISTOL RANGE OFFICERS DURING THE 1996 WORLD CHAMPIONSHIPS AT WEDGNOCK, 'YOU GUYS RUN A MEAN LINE!' TRANSLATORS BELIEVE THIS TO BE COMPLIMENTARY.

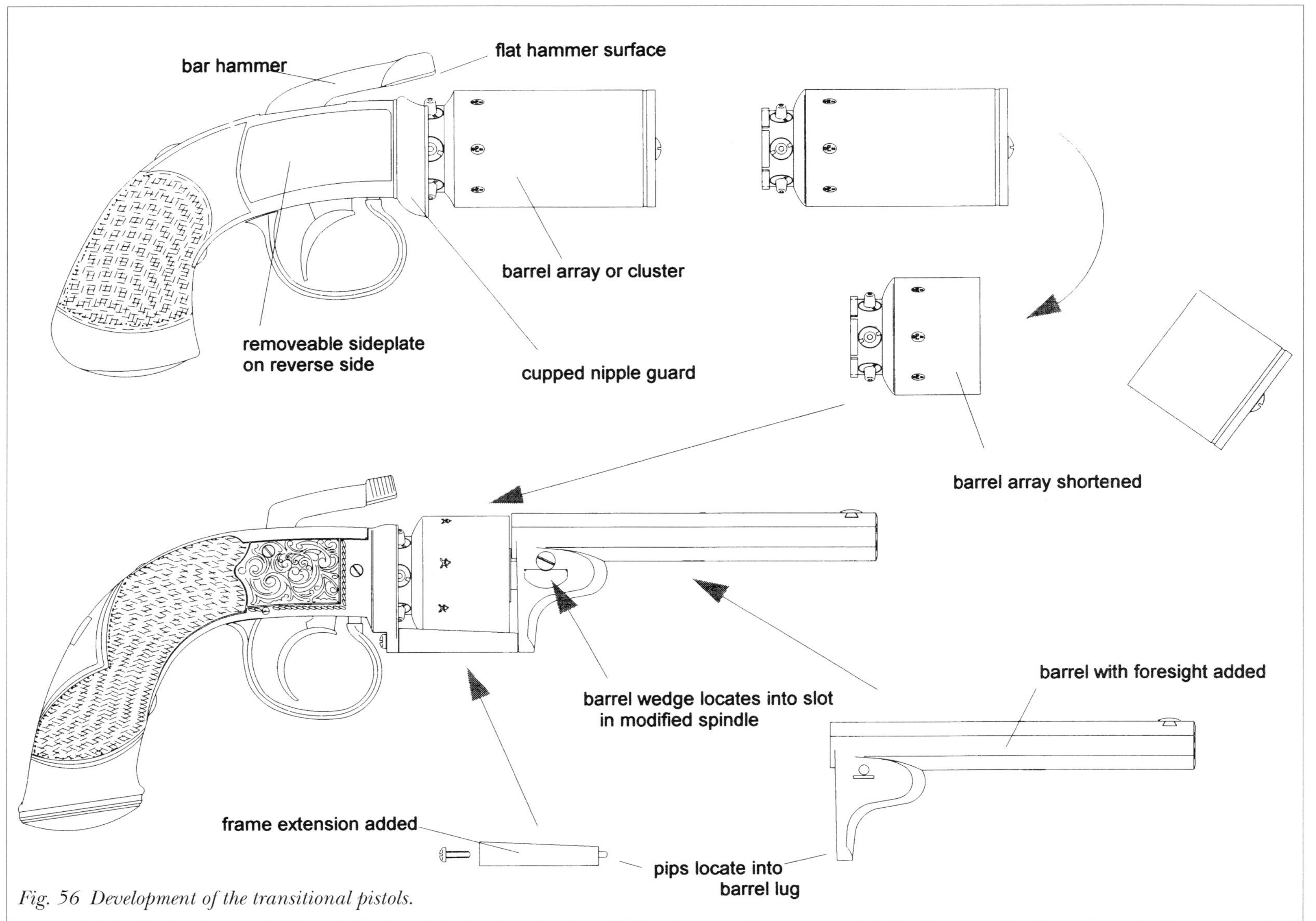

Fig. 56 Development of the transitional pistols.

6 Shooting the Odd Ball Through the Odd-balls

In the previous chapters we have concentrated on the pistols and revolvers which would often be shot under MLA and NRA match conditions. However, there is a great deal more to be had from shooting muzzle-loading pistols and revolvers than this might indicate. Competition is one thing, but just as rewarding is taking an antique pistol or revolver to pieces, finding out how the mechanism works, and finally taking it to the range and putting a few balls through it to test its accuracy and functionality.

In the United Kingdom you have to watch that you do not fall foul of the law when shooting 'antiques'. Genuine antiques may be held quite legally by anyone if they are not intended to be shot. For a short time after the passing of the Firearms (Amendment) Act in 1997 it was generally thought by the shooting community that if you had an antique and wanted to see what it felt like to fire it, all things being equal, that would not put you in trouble with the law. It was clear that if you wanted to shoot an 'antique' regularly, for instance, in MLA competitions, then the firearm had to be put on to the owner's firearms certificate. However, the current Home Office interpretation of the law clearly indicates that if you want to as much as discharge a single blank charge through an antique gun of any sort, that firearm must appear on someone's firearms certificate or shot gun licence.

Having clarified this, let us look at a few instances of pistols and revolvers made or modified for the sake of 'just doing it' and of 'originals' brought out of retirement to show their worth. We start with some pistols that are certainly not antiques, and fall outside the category of pistols that would be used in MLAIC-based competitions.

FREE PISTOLS

Earlier I commented that 'percussion single-shots' were as close as we shall now get to full-bore free pistols. Free percussion pistol is not currently a part of the MLAIC circuit, but it is fast being added to many muzzle-loading meetings, including some of those run by the MLAGB. One solution to obtaining a 'free' pistol is to modify something you can easily obtain which you know will shoot as straight as you can hold it.

So, with this in mind, I constructed a 'free pistol' from a 36 Le Page,[1] rebuilding the stock with thumb rest, palm shelf and so on (Plate 25). I fitted a set of click rear sights from my old Drulov .22in free pistol, which fortuitously 'fell off' just before it was submitted to the fiery furnace. The front sight originated from one of the set supplied with my Sako 22/32 target auto, which, of course, suffered the same fate. Now, modifying a wooden stock and a little metal profiling is one thing, but I am not equipped to cut dovetails in barrels to mount sights, so this task was assigned to my gunsmith. The position for the front sight was pretty obvious. The rear sight was placed originally in typical free pistol style

1. If you wonder why anyone would choose .36in as a bore diameter, it is exactly 100 bore.

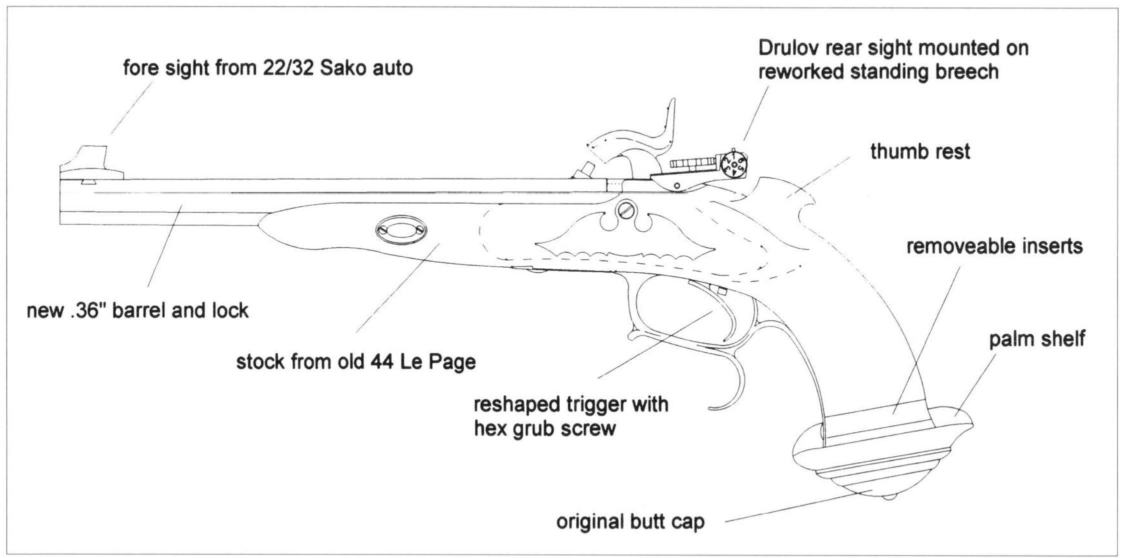

Fig. 57 Initial version of free pistol.

well to the rear of the lock (Fig. 57), where it was mounted on a reworked standing breech. I eventually opted for mounting the rear sight on the barrel forward of the nipple, however, as the accommodation in my ageing eyes failed to cope with this extended sight base.

The stock was no real problem, other than that I had decided to modify the one from the 44 percussion kit I started with some fifteen years ago. The pistol had seen some thousands of balls through it by this time, and a comparable number of cleaning and oiling sessions. As I cut into the stock to inlet pieces of walnut to make the thumb rest and palm shelf behind the breech, I was puzzled to see a dark stain slowly creeping up the new wood each morning. I suddenly realized that the new, dry wood was absorbing the oil which had seeped into the stock over the years, emphasizing my earlier comments about ensuring that the inside surfaces of the stock should be completely sealed with polyurethane or some similar varnish.

I wanted to keep the palm rest visually integrated with the stock rather than following the normal UIT practice of mounting it on an adjustable slide, keeping close to the spirit of the original, even on a free pistol. I provided for hand-size variations by enabling the fitting of different thicknesses of insert at the base of the stock just above the palm shelf. Two wood screws holding the palm shelf pass up through this insert and into the base of the stock, giving the pistol a fully integrated appearance.

The lock is, of course, slow when compared with a good .22 free pistol, and it is not helped by the set trigger mechanism not allowing a trigger stop to be fitted. I did indulge in some trigger bending, but finished by making another to my preferred profile by silver soldering a strip of steel to the base of the existing trigger and filing to suit.[2] Because this completely covered the

2. For details *see* Fig. 14. I was recently able to handle an old percussion Le Page with an almost identical curved trigger, which looked quite original. I wonder why they changed it? The curved trigger is no longer illustrated in the Pedersoli parts catalogue.

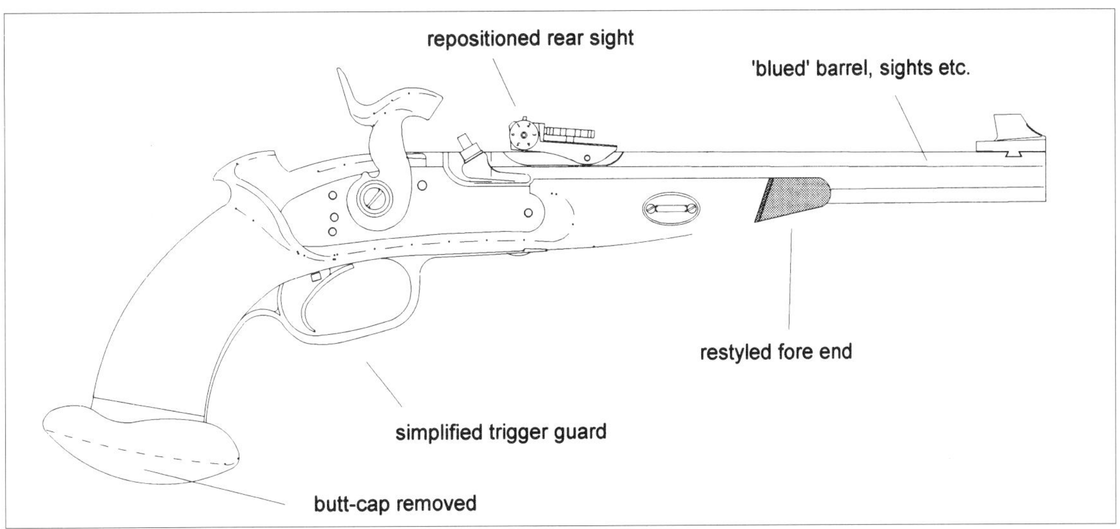

Fig. 58 The free pistol – the completed version.

set adjustment screw, a hole was drilled through the new trigger to give access to it. The set adjustment screw was replaced with a hex grub screw, not acceptable on the MLAIC version, but quite acceptable on a 'free' pistol. The trigger was also fitted with a side extension, since the reshaped trigger was so close to the rear of the trigger guard that it was difficult to get a finger behind it to set the trigger.

Having got the grip to my liking after several visits to the range, I completed the conversion by blueing the barrel (*see* Appendix V), removing the trigger spur and butt cap and adding a different coloured fore end to the stock. The result is that I have a visually attractive and superbly accurate pistol which just 'sits there' as a good free pistol should, and which will put shot after shot into the 10 ring on a good day.

I normally shoot 12 grains of Swiss No.2 in this pistol, as anything less risks the ball bottoming on the neck of the chamber without compressing the powder. However, I have tried using as little as 6 grains, topped up with a scoop of the filler I normally use in my revolvers. The perceived recoil with these reduced loads is quite negligible. The best I have shot with the normal load in competition is a 99,[3] and regularly put up a 94 or 95 at 25m indoors where the constant light and absence of wind are a great help. But however much I have tried, I have not been able to match these scores with loads below 10 grains. The group seems to open out slightly, keeping shots within a whisker of the 10 ring but giving no indication of putting five or six shots into the tight group that I can occasionally muster with the 12-grain load.[4]

By the way, do not be put off by the competitions for 'free' pistols in shooting programmes. You do not need any sort of 'special' to be truly competitive. With excellent barrels and a set trigger, any MLAIC

3. Nine consecutive tens followed by four consecutive nines. That elusive 'possible' with a muzzle-loading pistol, even with ten shots from thirteen, still eludes me.

4. However, some continental shooters have been observed using this technique with an unpatched ball in their smaller bore Kuchenreuter pistols, such as the .33 Hege. This may be because they are using a very light load that fails to fill the chamber (*see* Fig. 17).

compliant original or repro percussion single-shot will give a special more than a run for its money. Most of the meetings which list free pistol or revolver, be it percussion or flint, do so to give the shooter with a non-MLA-compliant pistol a competition that he or she may enter.

FREE FLINT

There are also competitions for 'free flint' at some meetings. Here is the chance to use the rifled Le Page flint in a competitive environment. Using Swiss No.1 with the otherwise identical load to that in the percussion Le Page, remarkably tight groups (for a flintlock, that is) are possible. Scores in the mid 90s, compared with the mid 80s for the smooth-bore, are common. Pedersoli will provide the Le Page with interchangeable rifled and smooth-bore barrels. Unfortunately, the flintlock barrel and lock are too large to fit into my percussion free pistol woodwork, although there is nothing to prevent a make-over for a flint in the same way that I treated the percussion Le Page. This modification could not be recommended if it were based on a smooth-bore flint, where the higher recoil will slam the unyielding stock into the shooter's hand and be too uncomfortable to shoot more than a few shots.

It is certainly more comfortable shooting all afternoon with the 44 rifled flintlock, since, even with a glove, the hand may take exception to too many consecutive shots with the 40 bore and larger smooth-bores. This makes the rifled flint an excellent introduction to shooting the flintlock for newcomers, who can acquire a smooth-bore barrel at a later date. In the United Kingdom you will require two slots on your firearms certificate to cover the additional barrel.

Another variant of the genre is the underhammer flint originally made by Jim Greathead (Plate 24). Greathead percussion underhammers are copies of the original Anderson boot pistols. There is no record of the gunsmiths of Anderson town producing an underhammer flintlock,[5] of which Greathead produced perhaps a half dozen. These pistols are bored under the .433 MLAIC limit and are also rifled, and, as such, may be shot only in the open flint competitions. Greathead used to shoot one of these pistols in open competition very effectively, turning up late on the last day and beating the field in devastating form. Unfortunately, the only sample I can regularly get my hands on suffers from ignition problems. This is nothing to do with the pan being upside down, but just a 'lack of sparks'. It also has a tendency to go through flints at an alarming rate. The problem has been identified as one of lock geometry and has gone back for rectification.

At the Cheshunt Club, where I do much of my shooting, the Flintlock Cup may be shot with either rifled or smooth-bore barrels. Compensation for the reduced accuracy of the smooth-bore is given by allowing eleven from thirteen shots to count, compared with the normal ten from thirteen for the rifled versions. Some open meetings give a bonus of seven or eight to the ten from thirteen shots for the smooth-bore. Either method seems to work out competitively in practice.

THE NEW AND THE OLD

With the surrender of all modern cartridge target pistols in the United Kingdom, attempts to fill the then defunct UIT target sector with small-bore, muzzle-loading pistols were launched. These were designed with all the advantages of a low bore line, did

5. Although an example by Calderwood of Philadelphia is on record. Several underhammer flintlock rifles are referenced in H.C. Logan's book on the underhammer (*The Pictorial History of the Underhammer Gun*, Arms & Armour Press, 1960).

not depend on the rotation of a heavy cock to set off the cap and were fitted with as crisp a trigger as one could wish for. They provided the (almost) complete answer to those who still hankered after the UIT precision single-shot events, and had neither the inclination nor the depth of pocket to travel to Zurich every weekend for practice. However, their availability has not galvanized any real demand from either the more traditional muzzle-loading or the disenfranchised cartridge-pistol shooters, and take-up can be counted in tens rather than hundreds. Nevertheless, these pistols, typified by the Westlake Phoenix, may still be obtained on demand. You may even be able to pick up a discarded Jurek, made in .38in calibre, if you felt so inclined – I know where No.1 is.

MATCHLOCK PISTOLS – THE TANZUTSU

What I believe will increase in popularity are matchlock pistols. Such pistols have been traditionally shot in the MLAIC's Pacific Zone, particularly by Japanese shooters who are only allowed to own matchlock weapons.[6] A number of European shooters had their interest stimulated at the 2000 world championships in Adelaide, where matchlock pistols were shot as a demonstration competition in both original and repro classes. The original class in this competition, the Tanzutsu ('short gun'), was won by the Japanese contingent, splendidly attired in traditional dress. The repro class was taken by the USA, with Australia in close attendance. I do not believe that there was a single entry from a European country.

The availability of original matchlock pistols must be several orders worse than of original flintlocks (*see* Plate 32), so that a demand for repros arose among European shooters. Some of those on offer seemed to have non-authentic features about them, and it was considered important to get repros which would meet the critical eyes of the scrutineers if the repro Tanzutsu ever became a recognized MLAIC match in its own right. So the author along with a band of like-minded MLAGB members, commissioned the British gunsmith Jim Alcock to make some match-quality repros that would meet in both construction and form the strict standards that the MLAIC could be expected to impose.

I believe that the matchlock pistol really arrived in the first half of the sixteenth century, well after black powder was first corned,[7] but with barrel making still in its infancy. The originals were very basic, where raising the long lever under the stock lowered the glowing match into the powder spread over the bottom of the pan. However, the principle of this new design strictly follows nineteenth-century Japanese matchlock practice, and replicates as closely as possible the bore size and barrel length, sighting arrangements and the 'snap lock' design shown in published data on the subject.

The prototype, close to the final version shown in Fig. 59, was submitted to the MLAIC scrutineer at the MLAGB international trials in November 2000 and was subsequently shot by a number of those present. The comparative ease with which team members slotted shots into the bull at 25m showed great promise. Half a dozen or more orders were placed, with delivery commencing in the middle of 2001. It would be interesting to see whether this section of the sport would take on greater prominence if someone like Pedersoli decided to enter the

6. Which, for some reason, seems to have no effect whatsoever on the high rate of gun-related crime in that country. Is there a lesson to be learned here?

7. The Earl of Warwick is reputed to have used the newfangled 'corned' powder at the battle of Barnet in 1471, the increased power apparently causing many balls to overshoot their mark. Other references indicate 1520 as a probable date for the introduction of corned black powder.

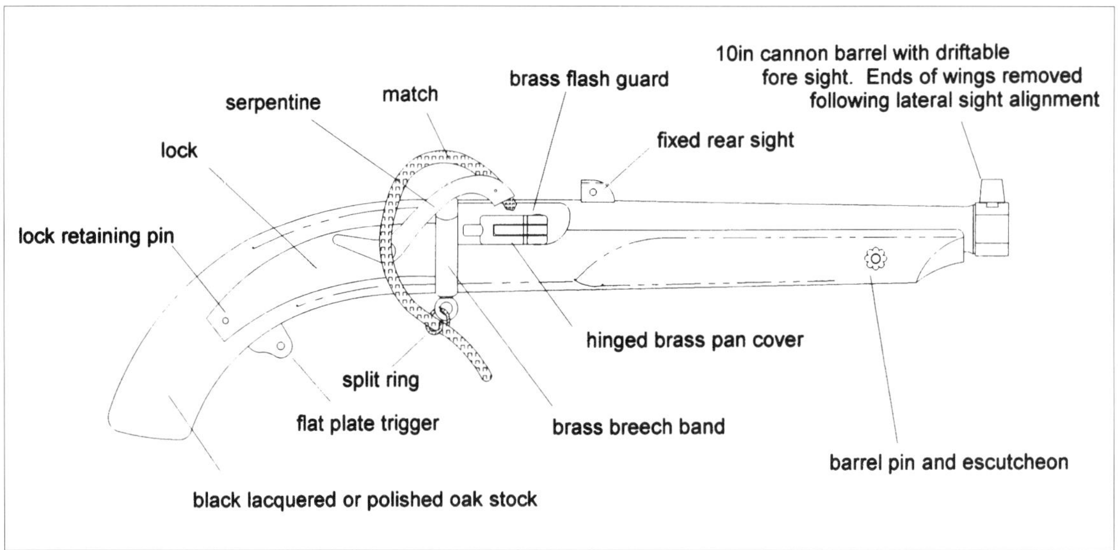

Fig. 59 The repro matchlock.

market. If so, it would certainly increase the interest in Europe in this branch of pistol shooting.

One of the things that has to be obtained before shooting a matchlock pistol for the first time is the 'match-cord'. By far the simplest solution is to buy this from any of the sources listed in the MLAGB journal *Black Powder*, where match-cord for the long arms shooters is offered. If you do, ensure that some samples are obtained first so that cord of the right diameter can be ordered. However, for the record, I decided to investigate its manufacture and obtained the necessary potassium nitrate (also known as nitre or saltpetre) from one of the chemical supply houses. I found out later that I could have bought some on my last visit to Wedgnock at half the price. In the distant past, the cord for match-cord was obtained as sash cord obtained from the local hardware shops. This was a round, woven (not twisted) cotton cord, available in several diameters and was just what was needed. However, nearly all modern sash cord has a large bunch of nylon fibres through the middle to strengthen it and these have to be drawn out before the cord is used. It is much better to extend your search to find some 100 per cent cotton cord, which needs to be woven in such a way that it will not unravel as the end is cut or burns down. Such loose ends enable too much air to get to the cord, which then splutters and sends sparks in all directions. These stray sparks could be extremely dangerous when the cord is slotted into the serpentine and the pan cover is folded back.

Some cord is coated with a thin layer of wax; if this is so the cord must first be boiled for 10 minutes with a little detergent in the water to leach out the wax which would otherwise stop the absorption of the nitrate. Having obtained some suitable cord, it is then immersed in a solution of the nitrate. I found that 110 to 120g of nitrate in 1 litre of water gave a cord which did not go out easily and did not burn too fast. The strength of the solution will need to be varied depending on the diameter and make-up of the cord that you select. Having given the cord plenty of time to absorb the solution, hang it up to dry in the airing cupboard for a couple of days.

When thoroughly dry, run the cord through your hands to remove surface nitrate; if you do not it will spit and splutter when lit, and that is the last thing you want from the safety point of view. Some people coat the finished match-cord with wallpaper paste or even slightly diluted PVA glue. This has the dual effect of preventing the match from sparking and the cord from splaying out too much when it hits the pan. Keep the finished cord in a freezer bag, and make sure that you label it with the source of the cord, the final strength of the nitrate solution and any dressing applied to the surface.

A good way to test match-cord, whether you make it yourself or after finding a vendor, is to stab the well lighted end into a very small pile of priming powder on a brick, when the powder should ignite almost instantly. If it does not, try increasing the amount of nitrate by 10 to 15g per litre and retest. Secondly, the match should stay alight without the end splaying out, and it should burn back to a glowing 'pyramid' before the match is required for the next shot. If the end splays out, the cord may have been over-boiled (this loosens the fibres and expands the diameter of the cord) or was not tightly woven enough in the first place. Tradition says that a match that burns about an inch a minute should be acceptable.

When the new pistol finally arrived its bore gauged out at .400in – equivalent to the Japanese 1.5 monme. Taking account of the available data on charges and ball weight against velocity in smooth-bore barrels, 20 grains of No.1 were selected for the initial trials. Experience and availability dictated the use of a 10 thou patch under a .395in ball, which felt right as the ball was driven down on to the powder. I have subsequently put the load up to 25grains, with a general reduction in group size.

Safety is everything, so before getting to the range it was essential to obtain a suitable perforated brass or similar metal pot in which to place the glowing end of the match when it was not actually slotted into the serpentine. This enables the match to be lit well behind the firing point so that it can be brought forward in safety. The glowing end of the match must be kept in this pot until the very last moment. This pot may be as simple as a small, round tin perforated to let the air in, with a fitted lid with a suitable slot in it through which the lighted edge of the match can be threaded. Some sand in the bottom of the tin to weigh it down will keep it stable on the shooting bench.

Before loading with ball, practise safe handling with a little powder in the pan, getting used to keeping the pistol pointed down range at all times as the match is inserted into the serpentine and the pan cover is folded back. Use this also to practise withdrawing the glowing match and closing the pan cover while still 'on aim'. This simulates the effect of a misfire in either the pan or a flash in the pan which does not ignite the main charge. *A late discharge of the pistol when withdrawing the match from the pan is a real possibility.*

Once the barrel has been charged – not forgetting the use of the pricker, the pan has been primed[8] and its cover closed, the glowing end of the match may be removed from the pot and pressed into the open clamp on the serpentine. The length of the projection of the match out of the serpentine will differ from pistol to pistol; the end should just reach of the bottom of the flash pan when lowered. A quick blow on the end

8. It is strongly recommended that the normal screwed end to the priming flask, quite satisfactory when used with the flintlock, is removed and the open end plugged with a cork. It is not unknown for a sliver of glowing match to remain in or about the pan following a misfire and to cause the priming flask to explode with disastrous consequences when the pan is reprimed. If this should happen, the cork will be blown out as the pressure starts to rise, resulting in a low pressure blast of flame – not nice, but preferable to an explosion.

to ensure a glowing match, and with the pistol pointing down range, take the approved grip before finally opening the pan cover with the free hand. In the real world the match may well have been locked into the serpentine with a sliver of bamboo, which was pushed through the clamp and into the match. In target shooting, with its reduced time from loading to firing, this pin is rarely necessary. When the main charge fires, it will often blow the match out of the serpentine. If it just drops to the ground it may not be too bad, but it may be blown some way, and the last thing you want to do is to shower the adjacent firing point with a swirling, glowing match. To avoid this, a ring should be fitted in front of the lock through which the match is threaded before its insertion into the serpentine. An open ring, as shown in Fig. 59, is much easier to use than an enclosed ring, since the loose end of the match may be clipped into place after the glowing end of the match has been inserted into the serpentine. With this sequence constantly in your mind, the safety of shooting the matchlock, always of some concern, should be assured.

On the matchlock the trigger pressure can be set quite low without a set trigger – never present on original Japanese matchlocks – since the coiled mainspring is much lighter than the average 'V' spring on either the percussion or the flintlock pistol. The design of the lock on this repro is a direct copy of an original, and has an internal coiled (as in clocks) mainspring with a compression coil scear spring, again as on the original. Tumbler and scear are of tempered steel, the lock plate and the serpentine being of cast brass. The lock plate is retained in the stock by the barrel band at the front and the simple expedient of a peg pushed through a hole in the back of the lock plate and into the stock. While fully in line with the original design, we shall have to see how this will stand up to the repeated firing which so differentiates a target pistol from its original intent.

Shooting the matchlock is similar to shooting the average flintlock, although the recoil with the .395in ball is much easier to handle. There is also less disturbance of the aim from the falling serpentine than you get with a flintlock since you do not have the thump of the flint on to the frizzen to contend with.

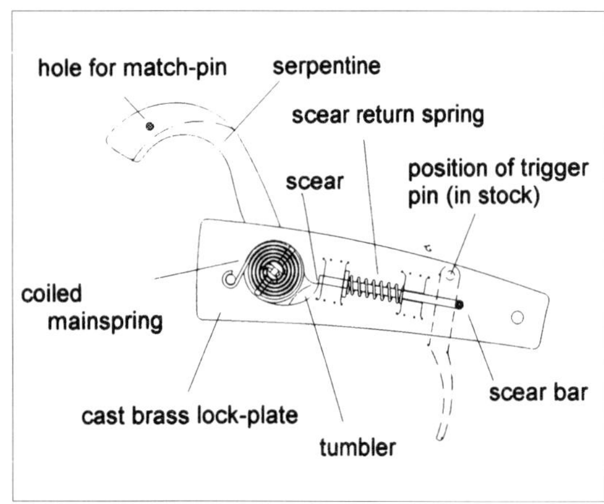

Fig. 60 Matchlock pistol lock.

THE LITTLE 'MUFF' PISTOLS

Having looked at some of the modern oddities, we now consider some of the many types of antique pistol that can be brought out of retirement. A good example to start with is the 'muff' pistol, of which there must have been hundreds of different makers, many with their own variants. They come in all sorts of size and shape, with both flintlock and percussion locks, invariably single-action (thumb cocking) and sometimes with two or even more barrels. Many of the barrels were about 40 bore, providing more than enough of a deterrent for any footpad when backed by 12 or so grains of coarse powder at a range of a few feet. Many were made very cheaply, while others have received all the loving care that only the best of the British and foreign gunmakers could provide. Whether ladies were in the habit of arming themselves by holding a small pistol out of sight in their muffs as they travelled throughout the land I cannot say. Many a 'gentleman' would keep one in his waistcoat pocket, however, and the size of these pistols is undoubtedly dictated by this mode of carry. Most of these little pistols had a very solid half cock notch which held the striking surface of the cock only just clear of the nipple. This allowed the pistol to be carried with a cap on the nipple, with the hollow in the face of the cock preventing the cap from being displaced.

Many of these little muff or pocket pistols come with 'turn off' barrels. One common version uses a ring key with a slot in it. The ring passes over the end of the barrel to engage a lug projecting from the underside near the breech. Turning the key unlocks the barrel from the breech, after which it may be unscrewed by hand. A second version uses a square key which engages slots cut into the bore of the barrel at the muzzle, providing the necessary torque to 'unstick' the barrel for reloading. In either case, the removal of the barrel reveals the small chamber leading to the touch-hole, with the open end shaped like a deep saucer. To load, the powder is trickled into the chamber until it half fills the 'saucer', the ball is balanced on the powder and the barrel replaced by hand. If you get the right amount of powder and the correct ball size (about 3 to 5 thou over the nominal bore size) the ball compresses the powder on one side and just cuts into the lip of the bore on the other, holding it in place. Too little powder and the ball is loose, leading to uneven or possibly dangerous burning of the charge. If the ball is too small, it will work its way down the barrel, with similar results.

On the little pistol shown in Fig. 61, engraved 'Norfolk – Bury St. Edmunds' on the lock plate,[9] the charge for loading as originally intended is about 9 grains, which drives a .490in ball fast enough for deterrent purposes. Some of these pistols, such as the Norfolk, have some sort of fixed sight or sights. It is not worth trying to get a group with sighted pistols when loaded in the traditional way since the foresight ends

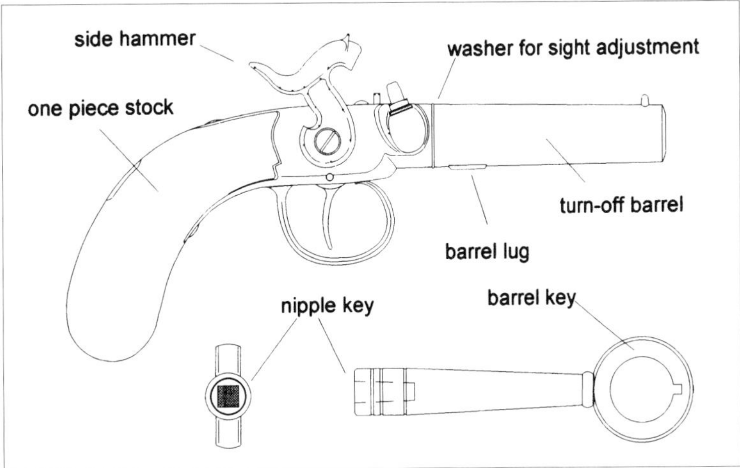

Fig. 61 The Norfolk pocket or 'muff' pistol; the combined barrel and nipple key are also shown.

9. When I initially requested that this antique pistol be added to my firearms certificate, the word 'Norfolk' I submitted came back as 'Norfolk Gun Co.', which is, I believe, a somewhat larger manufactory located somewhere in Virginia in the USA, a far cry from Bury St. Edmunds, England. At the same time my Kirner, clearly made in Budapest, came back with 'Kirner es Fija' on the certificate (I am told that 'Kirner es Fija' means something in Spanish that could mean 'completed by Kirner!).

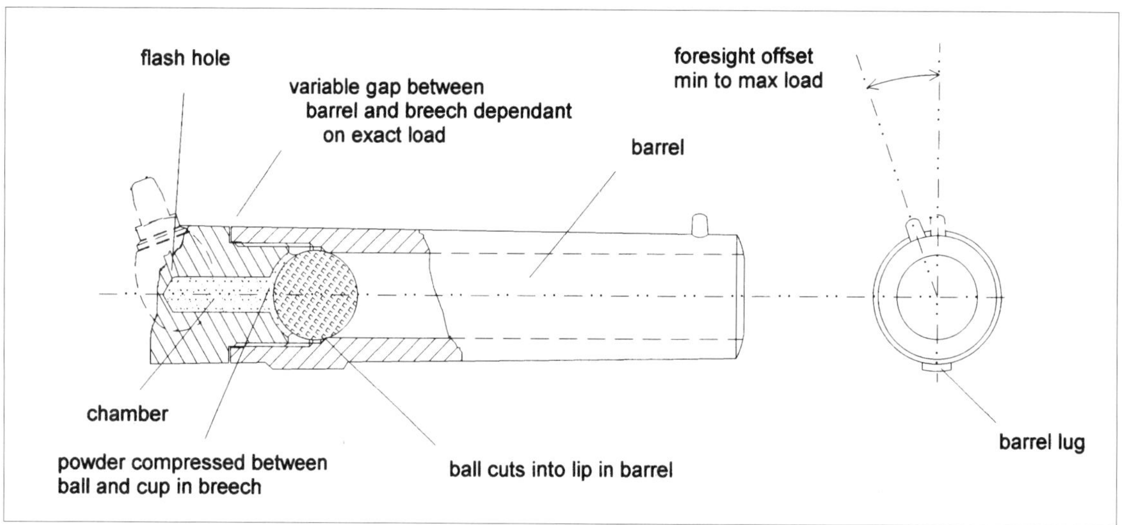

Fig. 62 The breech of the Norfolk muff pistol.

in different positions with quite small variations in the load (Fig. 62).

The best way to shoot these little pistols is to ignore the turn-off barrel until you come to cleaning it after shooting. Load the charge through the muzzle in the normal way, then load some semolina on top of the powder to fill the gap left by the missing ball. When working up this technique, make sure that the compressed semolina completely fills the bottom of the barrel. Then load with a patched ball. Using this technique, the foresight will stay in the same position during the detail. With an 8-grain load under a .470in ball and a 13 thou patch, I can occasionally get better than a 6in group at 10yd in a ten-shot series. Many pocket pistol competitions allow the shooter to place a white or black patch as appropriate on the target to act as the aiming point, since it is normally impossible to alter the sights as fitted to get the pistol to shoot into the centre of the target. This concession does not seem to be widely known by either competitors or range officers, so stand your ground on this point until proved wrong.

However, it should be quite possible to centre the group at least. If the group is off to the right, add a brass or copper shim washer between the breech and the barrel. This pushes the foresight to the right and the group to the left. The technique is to get a shim washer that pushes it over centre, and then lap off the breech end of the barrel to bring it back on line. If the pistol groups to the left, lap a little off the breech end of the barrel as before, but this time without the washer. For vertical sight adjustment you will have to work on the height of the front or the rear sight, as appropriate. If the front sight is raised too much, however, you may find difficulty in threading the barrel key over it.

THE 'PEPPERBOX'

What we now know as a 'pepperbox' was almost universally known in England before the 1850s as a 'revolver'. It was only with the advent of the Colt revolvers as promoted at the Great Exhibition at the Crystal Palace in 1851 that the word took on its present-day meaning. Prior to that date many of the pistols of this type were imported from Belgium, where the Liège gunmakers turned out enough to supply the continental market and the United Kingdom. Fig. 63 is fairly typical of the genre, only the Liège proof marks on the unfluted barrel array showing its origin. It is otherwise unmarked, and is even without engraving on the side plates. The bar hammer is mounted as standard off-centre to the right of the frame – it was easier to make the lock that way. The lock, as with almost all small pistols of this sort, can be cocked only by trigger cocking. These little pistols were designed entirely for self-defence and would not have been 'aimed' in any modern sense of the word. It is unusual to see such a pistol with a chequered, one-piece stock: most were made as separate plates secured by a screw passing from one side of the butt to the other, and were generally un-chequered. The butt shape is also a little unusual, they were usually lobed as on the Cooper described later.

There is not much to be gained in testing for the 'accuracy' of these pistols, which has always been somewhat irrelevant in their predominantly defensive mode. When you do take them to the range, you have to watch the size of the nipples. The ones on the pepperbox shown in Fig. 63 were just over 3.8mm at the start of the true taper on the nipples, compared with the 4.2mm on the Le Page percussion and the Norfolk pocket pistol. This is quite common for pistols of the period, with both my Adams 120 bore and the transitional pistol described later having the same cap size. The trouble with pepperboxes and transitional pistols alike is that there are generally no flash guards between the nipples. Squashing a No.11 cap down to hold on these smaller diameter nipples opens out the skirt of the cap. This allows a higher percentage of the 'flash' to shoot out of the skirt than happens with a well-fitting cap.[10] The adjacent cap, also being of loose fit with a splayed skirt, is ideally placed to be set off by this flash – just bearable on a pepperbox but much to be avoided on anything with a frame in front of the chambers. The only safe answer is either to find a source of small caps, not an easy task in the United Kingdom, or to make a new set of nipples to fit available caps.

Nevertheless, shooting such pistols at short range in reaction-type competitions can be great fun. As an example of this I

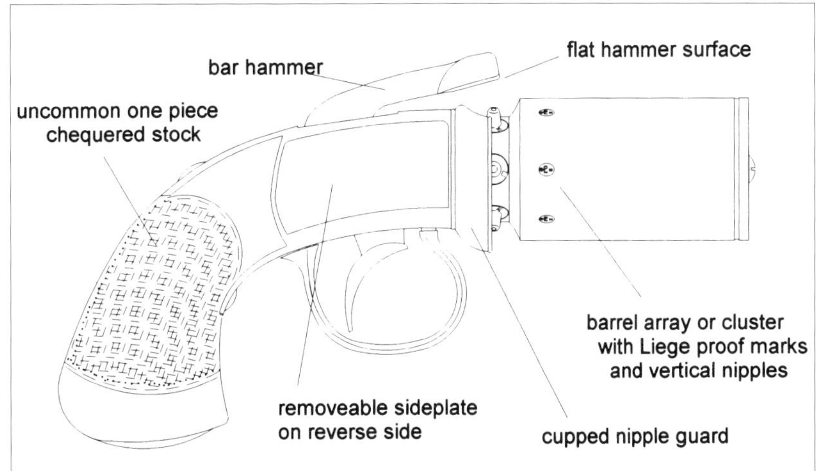

Fig. 63 An early Belgian pepperbox pistol.

10. I have a photograph of this happening, illuminated from the flash of the cap itself, taken on the transitional pistol. The cap does not normally break up until the main charge in the chamber is ignited.

investigated a later pepperbox, probably made in the 1850s – and of much better quality – marked 'J.R. Cooper Patentee'.[11] The only relevant patent issued to Cooper was for a pistol with nipples mounted parallel to the arbor, and was granted in 1840. Patents in Belgium by Mariette on the same subject had been issued in 1837, but had not been lodged in the United Kingdom. With flash guards between the chambers I felt I had a somewhat safer pistol to examine and shoot. The bore diameter was .390in ± a little, making it 80 bore. The 'chambers' in the barrel array (also called the barrel cluster) were straight bored and had none of the usual tapering at the muzzle intended to ease the loading of the ball.

The locks on Cooper's pepperboxes are of the trigger cocking type, but are unusual in that they are basically 'underhammers', some of which were also made by Mariette. The pistol itself has a couple of doubtful attributes. First, there is no rebound on the hammer, so that the trigger has to be pulled to lift the hammer from the nipples[12] to turn the barrel array when putting on the caps, a problem common to all pepperboxes and transitional pistols. This also means that, unless you are aware the problem, the hammer permanently rests on a cap on the nipple unless the array is rotated so that the hammer rests on the flash guard between each chamber. On this pistol there is a small and not very obvious notch cut into the underside of the safety catch to locate around the flash guard, which resolves this problem. With the hammer resting on a cap, it is theoretically possible to set off the cap with a forward blow to the ring hammer. I tried this on several occasions but failed to get a cap to discharge.

The second problem with this pistol is one of ergonomics. The stock is quite comfortable and the hand drops naturally into position with the trigger well located. The angle for drawing the trigger back is quite natural. The problem is that the back of the ring trigger hits the middle finger well before the hammer latch on the trigger can press on the frame to release the hammer. The stock has to be gripped quite low down – with the little finger under the grip – for the trigger to go back to the hammer release position. I think that this could cause a problem for someone under pressure or unfamiliar with the pistol.

Like any pepperbox, the barrel array has no equivalent to a later revolver's cylinder stop; it is not needed since there is no alignment problem between the 'chamber' and the 'barrel'. The barrel array is prevented from spinning uncontrollably by a spring fixed to the arbor.[13] This spring bears on the inside of the array's central bearing and acts as a brake. It is also prevented from rotating in one direction by the pawl being in constant contact with the ratchet on the end of the array. This pawl is not withdrawn into the frame as in Remington and later revolvers. The array revolves anti-clockwise from the rear.

To get at the lock mechanism the grips are removed, followed by the left-hand side plate. Undo the small screw going up through the frame near the rear of the trigger, which goes up into a boss on the inside of the side plate. The side plate may then be lifted off by sliding the projection on the

11. It is interesting to note that all the sources state that the side plates for Cooper's pepperboxes were marked 'J.R. Cooper's Patent', although the pepperbox examined and that shown in Taylerson's classic book on the subject are marked as above.

12. The face of the bar hammer on pepperboxes and transitional pistols is flat, that is, there is no 'cup' which drops over the cap before it is set off by the falling hammer. This means that much more debris is blown about as the back pressure from the main charge breaks up the cap. As always, wear glasses when shooting.

13. The word 'arbor' is comparatively modern. In the mid nineteenth century it was known as the 'spindle'.

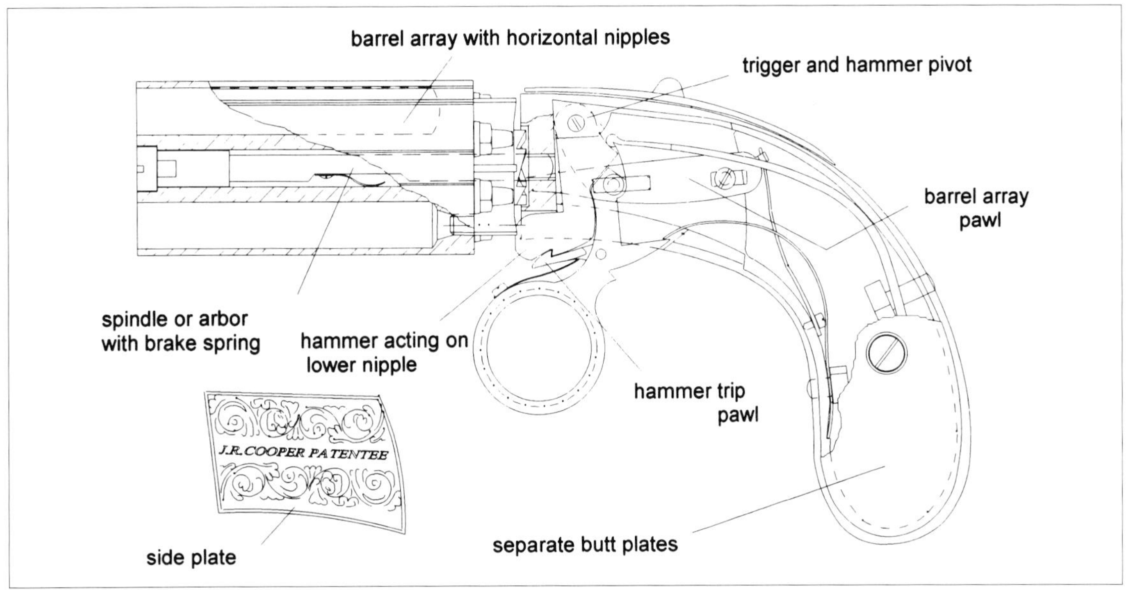

Fig. 64 Sectioned view of the Cooper pepperbox, with engraved side-plate.

front of the side plate out of its locating hole in the front plate.

Both the trigger and the hammer share a common pivot pin, situated at the top of the frame. As the ring trigger is pulled backwards, the hammer pawl pulls the hammer back against both the pressure of the mainspring and the somewhat lighter trigger return spring. At the same time a pin on the 'inside' of the trigger pushes up the barrel array pawl, which is kept in a forward position against the ratchet on the back of the array by its own light spring. As the trigger is rotated, it reaches a point where the hammer pawl comes into contact with the underside of the frame. When the trigger is further rotated, this pawl is forced out of engagement with the notch in the hammer (the bent), which falls under the influence of the mainspring.[14]

The rearward travel of the trigger is finally stopped by the flat on the rear of the trigger hitting the bottom of the frame. At that point, the trigger return spring is acting on the tip of the rear trigger projection and the free end of this spring is quite clear of the surface on which it was originally pressing. On the example examined, this spring is a little weak and has only just sufficient pressure to push the trigger forward against the resistance of reseating the barrel pawl on the ratchet and reseating the hammer pawl for the next shot. The trigger pull is quite smooth although a little heavy, but not unduly so considering the personal protection function of the pistol.

I put some dozen shots through it, much downloaded in deference to the owner. I used a .380in ball and a 13 thou patch over 11 grains of Swiss No.2. In real life, the pistol would have been loaded with an unpatched, tight-fitting ball tapped into the mouth of the chamber and driven on to the powder by forcing the ball down with

14. This type of lock mechanism is normally attributed to M. Mariette, and it has been asserted that Cooper re-engineered the much earlier Mariette 'revolvers' with their separate turn-off barrels.

the arbor. The nipples are, as on the previously described pepperbox, quite small, but with the flash guards in place, I used squashed down CCI No.10s for the caps. The falling hammer set these off in 95 per cent of the cases. The force exerted by the hammer could have been increased by adjusting the hammer mainspring retention screw, but, since the pistol was not mine, I chose to leave it as it was. The pistol would originally have been loaded with anything up to 20 grains of powder. Even with the reduced load, it seemed surprisingly loud in the enclosed range, occasioned by the short barrels. Twenty grains would have frightened off an aggressor, even if the shots went wide.

Shooting single-handed at a PAA target at 7yd, a group of twelve shots about 6in wide and 24in deep was achieved. This predominately vertical group was caused by the complete absence of sights, with the rotation of the barrel array giving little chance of an aimed shot. Pepperboxes made for G. & J. Deane in the 1850s did have a foresight fitted above each chamber. I tried making some temporary foresights by sticking pieces of paper on to the barrel array and trimming them to size, but, as they were rotating all the time the trigger was being pulled, no real improvement in the group resulted. Range discipline prevented me from firing a few shots two-handed from the waist, which was the probable method of discharge if the pepperbox were ever fired in anger.

THE 'TRANSITIONAL' REVOLVER

The form of the 'transitional' pistol was well defined by J.N. George in his book *English Pistols and Revolvers*, published in the mid twentieth century. His definition was for a pistol of small calibre with a bar hammer, self-cocking (trigger cocking), predominantly of Birmingham manufacture, with lock cases and mechanisms of the form of pepperboxes from which they were derived, with vertical nipples without flash guards, and the barrel attached to the frame as a separate entity.

The unnamed model in my possession certainly falls within this description, sporting six chambers in a cylinder with vertical nipples. The 5in barrel has nine grooves with a very slow right-hand twist in a barrel measuring out at .406in (about 70 bore). The lock work is similar to that of the pepperbox described above, except that a 'cylinder stop', comprising a simple sliding bar attached to the trigger, is pushed forward through the frame to engage with what is best termed 'the spokes of a cartwheel'. These 'spokes' may be seen quite clearly in Fig. 65. They are actually made as projections on the outside of the removable ring, the face of which provides the ratchet for engagement with the cylinder pawl.

Before the 1850s both pepperboxes and early Colt 'revolvers' were quite rare in the United Kingdom, and it was really the revolvers shown at the 1851 Great Exhibition that aroused interest in revolving-cylinder, fixed-barrel pistols. In response to the sudden demand created particularly by the Colt exhibits, and to get round some of Colt's patents (the last of which did not expire until 1864), the Birmingham gun trade produced their own version of the revolver. Utilizing many of the existing parts and tooling for pepperbox manufacture,[15] they cut down the length of the barrel array, fixed an extension on the front of the frame and fixed a barrel to this frame by the simple expedient of putting a bolt through the cylinder 'spindle' or arbor (*see* Fig. 56).

15. These tools would have been used for both pepperbox and transitional revolver manufacture for another seven years or so. Pepperboxes did not really come into their own in England until the 1850s, when many thousands went through the Birmingham proof house.

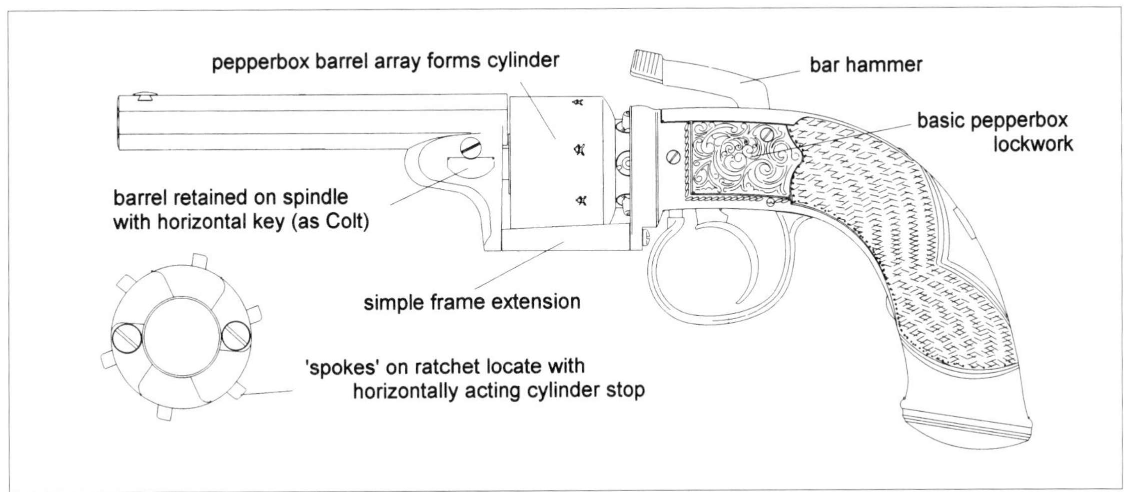

Fig. 65 The 'transitional' revolver and the cylinder ratchet.

This 'simple extension of current manufacturing practice' produces some oddities of design. In my example, the bar hammer is offset to the right, as one would expect, enabling the shooter to align the top of the barrel with the small German-silver foresight. Unlike some better quality examples, there is no rear sight. As the nipple has to be aligned with the hammer at the point of ignition, it forces the cylinder into a particular position with reference to the frame at the point of discharge. If, as in this case, the nipples are mounted exactly between the chambers, it pushes the chamber to be fired somewhat to the left of the centre of the frame. The barrel has to line up with this chamber. This leaves the cylinder arbor somewhere between the centre line of the barrel and the hammer. Transferring this design to my computer-aided design system, I sympathized with the original designer who must have been highly adept to get the timing of the lock mechanism right.

A second manufacturing oddity was thrown up during the redrawing exercise, which related to the rather short cylinder. This will take a maximum of 11 grains of powder, which is not much behind a ball about .400in in diameter. It appeared that, if the cylinder were any longer, you could not get a drill down the chamber at the correct angle to get the flash hole to connect the back edge of the chamber with the cavity beneath the nipple.

Another problem concerned the nipples, which, while being of the standard diameter for the age, were very short with a very small skirt diameter. These skirts were slotted on their periphery to allow a two-pronged screwdriver to unscrew the nipples. A further problem with the nipples was their fine and very shallow, non-standard screw thread, which made the manufacture of a new set of nipples for safe shooting a rather more expensive activity than had originally been indicated.

Another interesting point was that, without any real experience of producing revolving-cylinder arms in the 1850s, it was assumed that it was necessary to prevent 'gas leakage' between the fired chamber and the barrel itself. This led to attempts to provide 'gas sealing' between the cylinder and the barrel. On my example it is activated by a plunger which presses against the rear face of the cylinder, sliding the cylinder along its arbor so that its front face is pressed against the rear face of the barrel. The plunger projects through the front face of the frame and is pushed forward by a flat spring housed in the lock cavity itself. This attempt at gas sealing must not be confused with that detailed in Lang's patent, which forced a cone on the front of each chamber into the forcing cone of the barrel. Lang's mechanism is complicated by the fact that the cylinder must be moved rearwards to withdraw the cylinder from the forcing cone before the cylinder can start to be rotated.

I was able to give this revolver an initial test with a few of the original-sized caps. Using the full 11 grains that the chambers allowed and quite a tightly fitting ball tapped in with a soft mallet, useful groups at 10yd could be achieved, despite the lack of a rear sight. However, the typical open-frame construction allowed the barrel to 'wobble' on its arbor, which was obviously counterproductive. This problem was eventually traced to the poor fit of the arbor into the lug below the barrel, and not to an ill-fitting wedge, as is often the case in open-frame Colt revolvers. So the revolver went back into the safe until time permitted some reworking to resolve the problem. All in all, I thought this a pleasant revolver to handle, the finely chequered stock – complete with silver escutcheon – and the fairly light and smooth trigger cocking mechanism making it much more than a conversation piece.

THE ADAMS 120 BORE REVOLVER

Adams brought out his solid-framed revolvers at about the time of the Great Exhibition, where they were shown with little fanfare. Colt, of course, made a great thing of the Exhibition. Adams intended to bring out three different sizes, the largest of 54 bore, then an 80 bore and finally a 120 bore, which did not see the light of day until perhaps 1853. It looks just like a scaled-down version of its larger brothers. In these revolvers, the number of chambers is dictated by the combined flash-guard cum cylinder stop. With the chamber to be fired located at 12 o'clock, you have to have an odd number of chambers since the cylinder stop is located in the frame directly opposite the active chamber.

It is interesting to examine an extract from the case-lid label for an 'Adams Revolving Pistol' of 1851, marketed by Smith, Elder and Co., of London (*see* box below). Similar loading instructions would have applied to the 120-bore Adams trigger cocking revolver.

Note that, in these necessarily brief instructions, there is no mention of the

Extract from a Case-Lid Label for an 1851 'Adams Revolving Pistol'

1st. First explode a Cap on each Nipple to clear them from any accumulation of oil or other deposit, to ensure certainty of fire.

2nd. Pull the trigger into the position of the dotted Trigger [as illustrated on the label]; this will draw the hammer back; then press in the Stop Spring with the thumb and hold it there, while allowing the hammer to return to its position of rest. The Chambers will now revolve freely. Put the powder into each of the Chambers with a flask, then press the Wadded Ball *close down upon the powder* – the wad next the powder, put on the Caps, and loading is complete.

To Fire, pull the Trigger five times in succession.

To take out the Chambers press in the Stop Spring, and draw the Spindle towards the Muzzle, when the Chambers may be readily removed.

To disengage the Stop Spring, pull the trigger.

Keep the Spindle clean, and oiled occasionally.

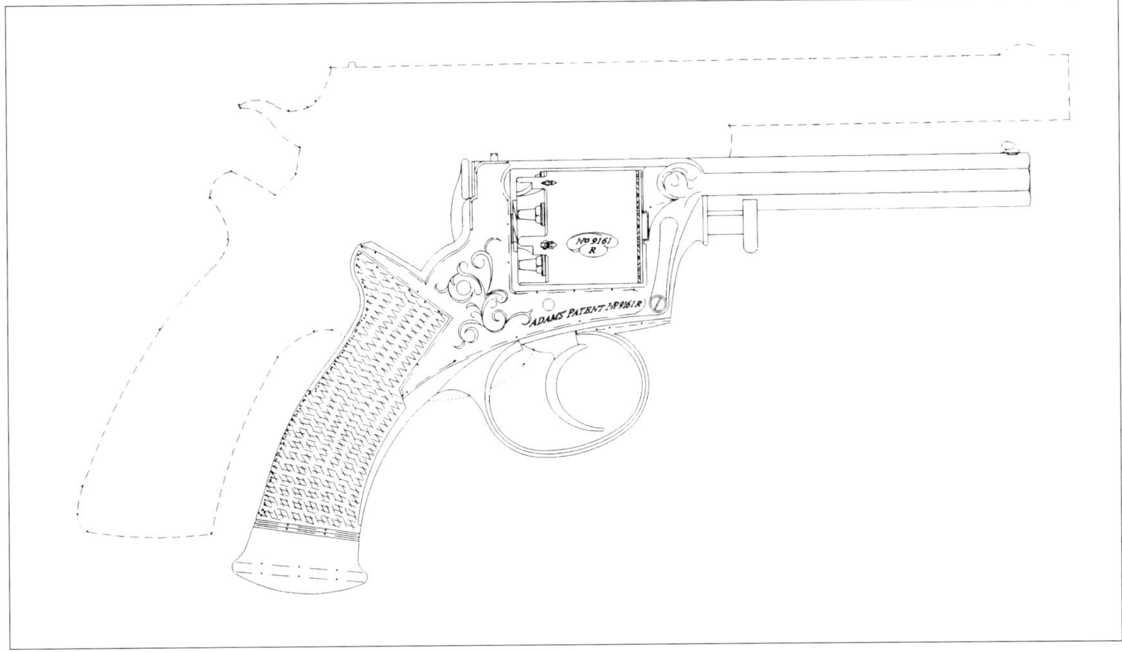

Fig. 66 The Adams 120 bore; the shadow shows the relative size of the 54 bore Beaumont Adams.

load of powder to be employed, indicating the use of a flask with spout provided in the fitted box, as well as the provision of the 'wadded balls' and caps. There is no mention of cleaning after shooting nor the effects of discharging the corrosive caps of the period and leaving the revolver loaded but uncleaned over a considerable period. There are also two 'stop springs' – one to hold the hammer out of engagement with the cylinder and the second to release the cylinder arbor or spindle.

I had acquired the Adams specifically to shoot in 'pocket pistol' as well as the MLAGB's Crimea Cup competition. It was in excellent condition, although probably subject to refinishing at some time. The only real problem was the perennial one of finding quantities of the correct sized caps to fit on the small nipples. The obvious answer was, once again, to make a complete set of new nipples. An easy enough job, except that the threads in the nipple seatings in the cylinder were 5/16in × 32 tpi, while those on the nipples themselves were 5/16in × 28 tpi. Obviously not the original nipples, and thus no wonder one of them would not sit properly on its seat. The new set, designed to fit No.11 caps, was soon completed.

Of course, I did not have a ball mould of the right size. The chambers 'miked out' at .340in, indicating that I would need a .342in ball if I were to use modern loading techniques, that is, without a wadded ball. To check the size, and to calm my impatience, I skimmed down some 350 balls I had acquired by the simple expedient of forcing them through a steel die with a .342in hole in it. Fig. 66 shows the method of die making I used. This shaves a thin ring of lead off the ball – rather like that of ramming a ball into the unchamfered chamber of a Ruger Old Army – and requires a great deal less pressure than trying to swage it through a tapered die. Without a suitable press at the time, I forced the ball through the die between the jaws of the garage vice. You end with a ball with

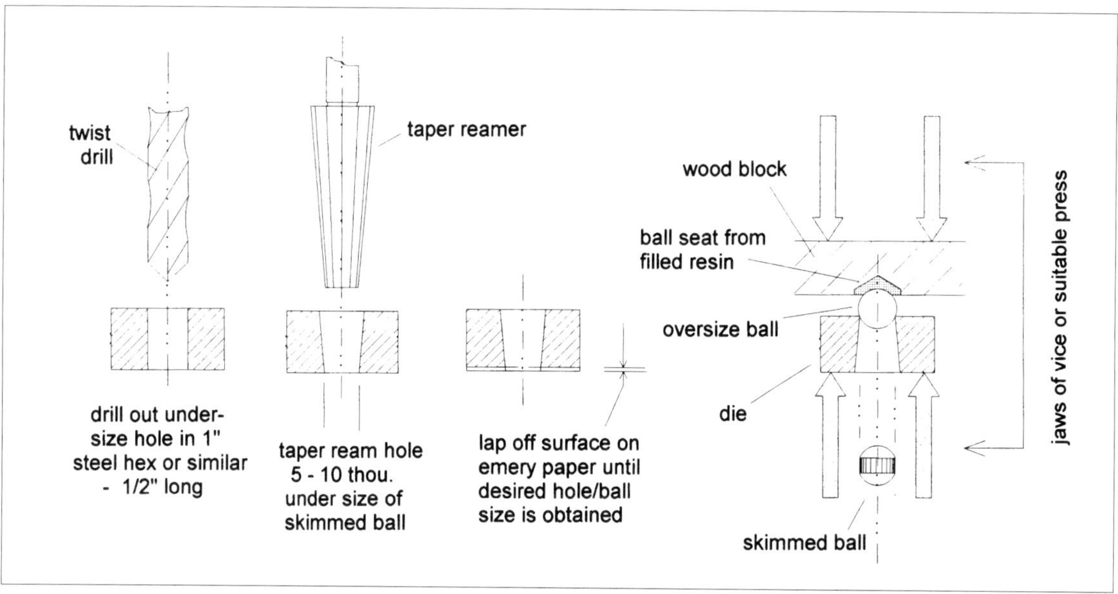

Fig. 67 Skimming balls down to size.

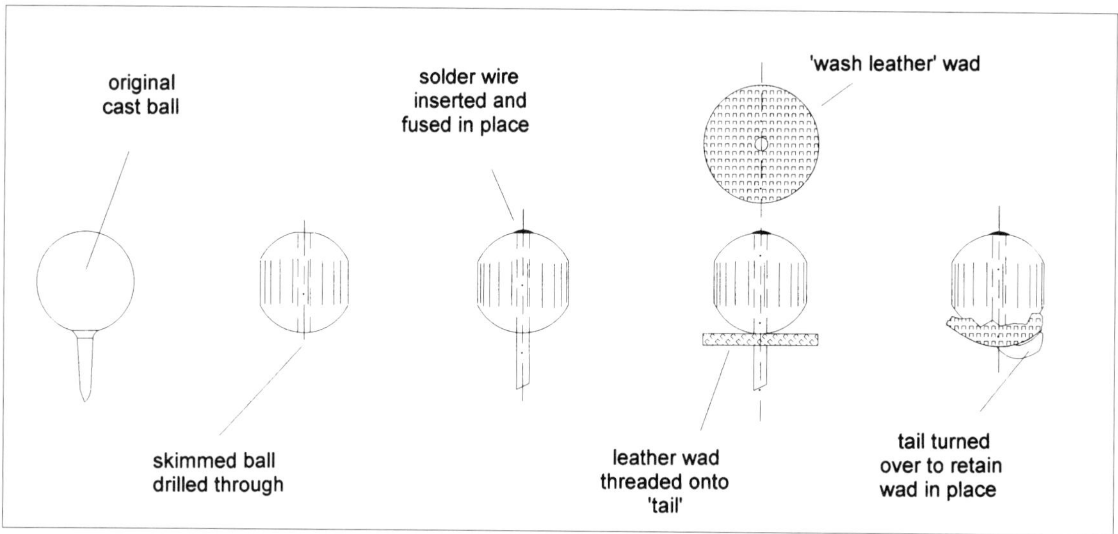

Fig. 68 Making the wadded balls.

cylindrical sides, which is what the ball looks like after having been pressed into the chamber of a revolver, although you do not normally see it.

These skimmed balls loaded easily over 13 grains of TS2 and gave a tight group at 10yd, despite the trigger cocking only mechanism. I also tried a lower charge, making up the volume difference with semolina, but the results were not so good and I quickly reverted to full loads for the remainder of the day. The Adams action was smooth, and at least as good as the reworked S&W586 I used when shooting PP1 in the past. These trials indicated that the ball size selected was about right, and so a .342in mould was ordered. I used the time waiting for the mould to arrive to make a simple loading press, since the 120 bore Adams, designed for a wadded ball, had no fitted rammer.

The key question now was how would it perform with a wadded ball. With no original wadded balls to go by, I had to rely on the information in Chamberlain's *The Adams Revolver* (Barrie & Jenkins Ltd, 1976). The balls are shown as being cast with a short, tapered 'tail', over which is threaded the wad, which is retained in place by bending the tail back over the wad. I had no intention of ordering a second mould so that I could modify it to cast such balls for the quantity I required for the trial. Instead I made another skimming die, this time of .340in diameter, so that the resultant balls would slip more easily into the chambers under finger pressure. The 'tails' were added by drilling a hole through these balls and threading short lengths of 12 SWG solder wire through them, sealing them in place with a hot soldering iron. The wads themselves were originally made of leather and so I made a few from the off-cuts from the material I generally use to make my leather flint clamps. These felt too thick, so I made some more with some so-called 'chamois leather'. These new wads looked and felt much better. You have to get exactly the right diameter for these wads, since, when they are folded round the back of the ball, they have to provide sufficient retention for it in the chamber. If you do not get the size right they shake loose as the adjacent chambers are fired. On the other hand, they must not be so large as to wrap around the periphery of the ball, which prevents its insertion into the chamber. The wadded balls do not look particularly neat when made in this way, mainly due to the wrinkles in the wad when the tail is turned over to keep them in place. There is not much you can do about that unless you try to preform them into a cup shape when wet, an exercise I did not try. They actually closed round the ball very well when pressed into the chambers, and retained the ball in place to the extent that I could not move them unless I gave the cylinder quite a smart tap on a wooden table.

On the range these wadded balls certainly failed to give the excellent groups that the conventionally loaded chambers gave at 10yd, opening out the group by some 50 per cent. For the pistol's original intention, such a group is irrelevant, since it was well within a 6in-ring at normal pistol ranges. It was at 25m that the real effect of the offset tail and wad could be seen. The 4.5in, three-groove barrel had problems in keeping more than three shots out of five of the wadded balls on the normal PL7 card. So there is no doubt that any competition shooting will be done using normal loading techniques and the press.

GALLERY PISTOLS AND THE 4MM *ZIMMER-PISTOLEN*

There must be many types of pistol and revolver that I have failed to mention, let alone tried to obtain and test. However, no summary like this ought to ignore the gallery or saloon pistols, since without doubt they formed the link between the personal defensive arm and the sport of 'target shooting'. The variations on these pistols are bewildering, being large and small, rifled and smooth-bore, cheap and cheerful, and of the most magnificent workmanship. The first of these examined here is a typical French product, marked 'E.P. Lefaucheur à Paris'. Of 120 bore, it sports a smooth-bore barrel of over 8in in length, fitted with a barleycorn front sight and 'U' rear sight. It is furnished with quite a large fluted grip and is well balanced.

This pistol was complete and in its original form when purchased, but it has to be said that it was in a poor state. The outside of the barrel was covered in a thin, hard layer of rust and the stock was covered in what looked like thick varnish that had been nibbled at by a hungry mouse. Nevertheless, the lock did not require much work, but the inside of the barrel had to be subjected to a thorough rust removal and refinishing process. This is one advantage of the smooth-bore barrel: you can do a lot of work on it without spoiling the pistol in any way. If the bore size is increased a little it does not really matter – all you need is a slightly larger ball or a thicker patch. The nipple was a little loose in the breech owing to corroded threads, so the breech was tapped out a larger size and a new nipple turned up to match. The barrel, by the way, was the first I reblued as described in Appendix V.

The bore was a little above its original .339in owing to the refinishing process it had been through, and I initially settled for a .330in ball and an 18-thou patch because of their availability, but finished testing with a .335in ball and a 10-thou patch. On first testing this pistol it shot very wide (examination showed that the bore was in no way concentric with the outside of the barrel) at the test distance of 10yd. However, once the sights had been corrected it shot like a dream, with a 2in by 1in group, despite some excessive creep on the trigger. At first it seemed very tolerant of the load at this range, with the group – well within the 9 ring – hardly changing between 6 and 12 grains. It was only when I went up to 15 grains that the group really tightened up, with almost every shot dropping into the bull at 10yd. Lightening the trigger pull and removing the creep has further improved its grouping capabilities.

Such pistols as the Lefaucheur were made as 'indoor' target pistols and were shot extensively in the galleries which started up in London, Paris and other major cities throughout Europe in the mid to late nineteenth century. The facility set up by the gunmakers Gastinne-Renette at 39 Avenue D'Antin in Paris in 1835 was typical. Originally built for duelling practice, it widened its scope to become an all-comers target-shooting establishment as duelling fell into disrepute. The gallery was rebuilt at the turn of the century, incorporating a number of individual shooting booths, each having a shooting position without a table for the shooter but with one for the personalized loader, telescope and all. The luxurious vaulting on the ceiling and marquetry-decorated wall-panelling make our present ranges look spartan. Contemporary lithographs of these ranges show bewhiskered gentlemen in tail coats and tall hats shooting at a variety of targets: silhouettes for duelling, together with cards, candles, animal outlines and the forerunners of our present roundel targets, at distances from 15 to 25yd. Early shooting stances, originally designed to protect the body in duelling, would hardly be put forward today as suitable for shooting, with their exaggerated, bent elbows, bringing the rear sights within 20in of their aiming eye. This is not to say that this technique was not effective in its day. As late as 1930 the Pistol Championship of the World, held in Antwerp, was won by M. Revilliod de Budè of Geneva, using an even more exaggerated version of this stance. It must be said that the stock on his pistol seems to have been especially adapted to enable the hand to take a firm grip, but how he could see either the sights or the target evades me.

Bore sizes for gallery or saloon pistols varied considerably, perhaps the smallest commonly found being the 4mm saloon pistols, often of German origin (hence the designation *Zimmer-Pistolen*). Remember that the current air pistol standard of .177in is 4.5mm. I was lucky enough to be able to examine some original pistols, all with bores varying between 4.0 and 4.1mm diameter. Some had quite pronounced rifling, and much deeper than on current air pistols. Some of these pistols are very

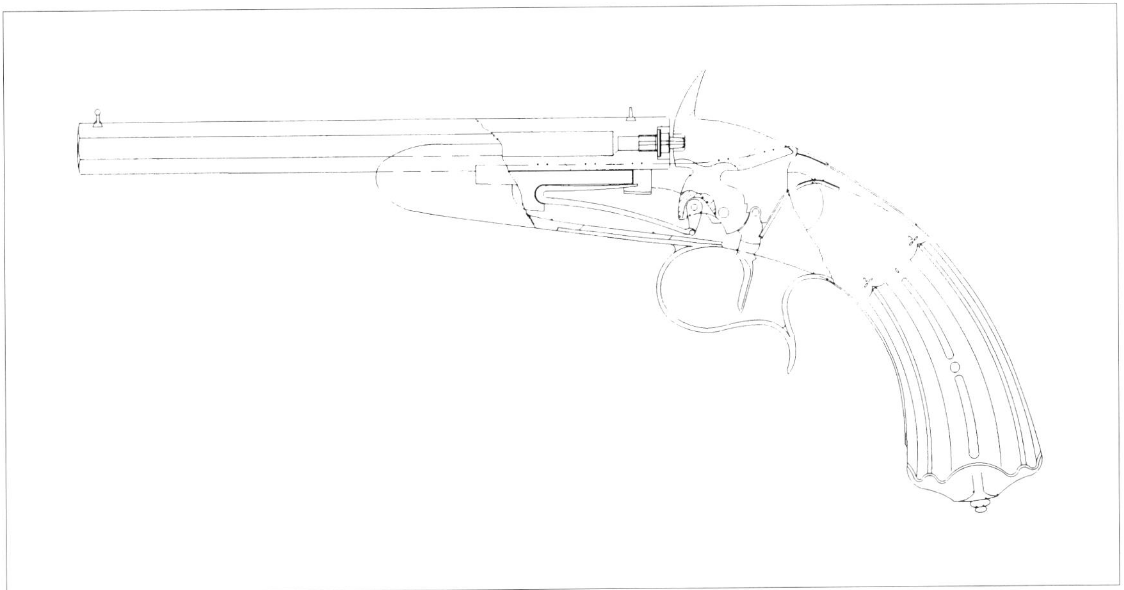

Fig. 69 The Lefaucheur in section.

basic, with the nipple screwed into the end of the breech in line with the centre line of the barrel, the lock being single-action with no half cock, and many with no stock in front of the breech; in fact, the original zip gun. Pistols similar to these originals are available from Pedersoli and others.

With a 4mm bore (about .155in, or not much more than ⅛in), the use of a loading funnel is not practicable. The thing to do is to use the original technique of a little brass cup on the end of a piece of ⅛in steel rod. The cup is filled with powder, the barrel – muzzle to the floor – is lowered over it, and then the complete assembly is turned upside down. This enables the loading cup to be withdrawn, leaving the powder at the breech end of the barrel. To try to load these pistols with a patch under the ball is tricky, and they were commonly used with a fairly tight ball and no patch. Balls were originally available from 4.00 up to 4.10mm in close steps, essential to get the best available seal without a patch. To shoot them you will have to make up a new set of loading equipment, including the loading cup and a much thinner starter and ramrod. The load for shooting these at 10 or 15yd is ridiculously small, with 3 grains being as much as you would normally require. You even feel that the primer might do the job on its own, which it certainly can, as Flobert illustrated in his original gallery pistols using his unique metallic cased BB (bulleted breech-cap) cartridges.

At the other end of the scale I once negotiated for a true German *Zimmer-Pistole* in 4mm calibre, beautifully made but suffering from ennui and in dire need of a makeover. This pistol, made by Wacher, who came from Memingen to the west of Munich, was complete with a set trigger and what looked like the fixings for a shoulder stock. A real piece of craftsmanship when compared with the average saloon pistol made for use in the public galleries, of which a representative model by Pedersoli, shown in Fig. 70, is typical.

These percussion gallery pistols developed into rim fire cartridge pistols in the 1850s and 1860s, following the invention of the Flobert BB cartridge in 1845. Many

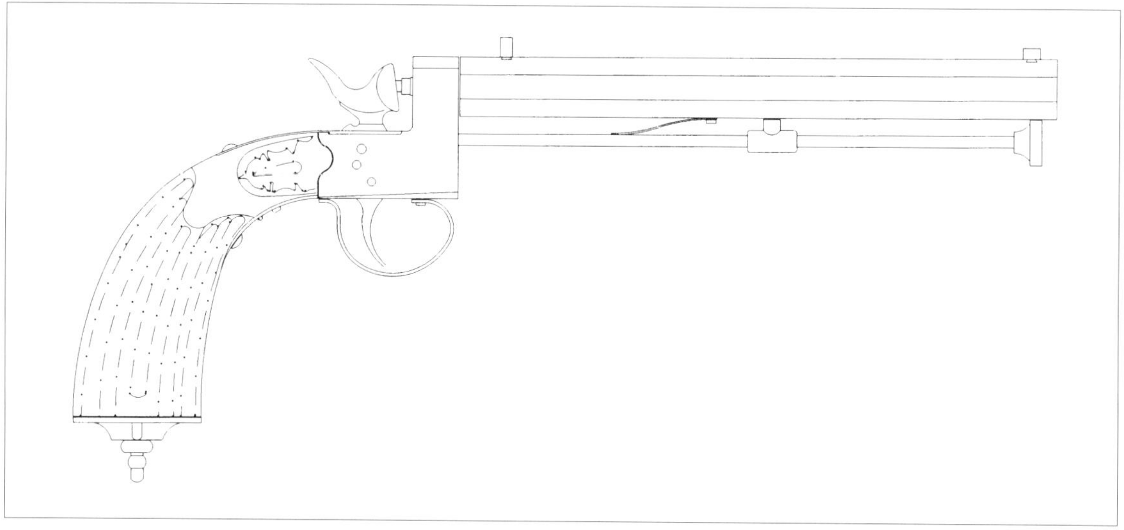

Fig. 70 A typical saloon pistol, this one is a Pedersoli copy of a Belgian original.

manufacturers adopted the rim fire breech-loading system using the 5.5, the 6.0 and even the 9mm Flobert cartridge. The 4 mm percussions were remade using the 4mm rim fire. These minute cartridges come in three 'lengths', the smallest so small that you cannot really imagine any powder in it at all. Most of these 4mm cartridges were made in Germany. These early rim fire pistols produced in their turn a host of more modern, single-shot pistols. You only have to look at the development of the early muzzle-loading gallery pistols, through the beautifully made breech loaders of Max Fischer, to the very basic Stevens and the well finished in-line Smith & Wessons; they culminated in the Webley single-shot .22s and the same pistol chambered for the .32 Smith & Wesson. By the way, Flobert rim fire cartridges have not as yet found their way on to the obsolete cartridge list, so that pistols chambered for them are proscribed under current British firearms legislation.

THE END – OR IS IT?

So that is it: muzzle-loading pistols and revolvers, from the sophisticated to the sublime, with some additional information and advice in the appendices which follow. Those who find discrepancies here will be listened to with care and humility, in accordance with what I consider should be the ethos of the sport. And as for the shooters, the final quotation will, I am sure, ring many a bell.

NEVERTHELESS, I AM SENSIBLE, THERE IS NO BECOMING SHOOTER BY BOOK. YOU MAY FIND HERE THE RULES AND PROPER DIRECTION FOR THAT END, BUT PRACTICE ALONE CAN MAKE YOU MASTERS. BARE THEORY MAY AS SOON STAMP A GENERAL AS A MARKSMAN. NO – YOU MUST SWEAT AND BE COLD, MUST SWEAT AGAIN AND BE COLD AGAIN, BEFORE YOU CAN ARRIVE AT ANY DEGREE OF PERFECTION IN THIS ART. I HAVE FURNISHED YOU WITH ALL NECESSARY TOOLS OF THE TRADE, BUT IT IS TIME AND EXPERIENCE THAT MUST FINISH AND ACCOMPLISH THE WORKMAN. AND EVEN AFTER SEVEN YEARS INDUSTRY, YOU WILL FIND BUT TOO MANY OCCASIONS TO PROVE YOU STILL DEFICIENT AND IMPERFECT.

EXTRACT FROM THE APOLOGIA TO *PTERYPLEGIA: OR THE ART OF SHOOTING* BY A.B. MARKLAND (ST JOSEPH'S COLLEGE, OXFORD, 1727).

Appendix I

The Le Page Set Trigger

INTRODUCTION

The functioning of the set trigger on the Le Page is typical of modern, single set triggers. Originals having the trigger set screw positioned behind the trigger pivot screw tend to work in the same way.

When a muzzle-loading pistol with a set trigger is not 'set', it functions in exactly the same way as one without a set trigger at all. As the main lock is put on full cock, it is held in position by the scear that engages in the bent, an indentation in the tumbler that is attached directly to the cock itself. To release the main lock, the trigger is rotated until its upper edge comes into contact with the scear bar, a projection at right angles to the scear itself. Further pressure on the trigger rotates the scear about its pivot screw, which releases the scear from the bent, and allows the tumbler – and hence the cock – to fall under the pressure of the mainspring.

The problem here is that the necessarily heavy mainspring exerts considerable pressure at the interface between the scear and the bent. With no set trigger, this interface has to be profiled and polished with extreme care to get the trigger pressure down to an acceptable level for target use. It is often difficult to get a safe set-up with a trigger pressure much less than 500g under these conditions. The object of the set trigger is to release the cock by replacing the uncomfortably high pressure on the trigger by the energy released from a separate spring.

FUNCTIONALITY

If the set trigger is not 'set' (Fig. 71), the backward pressure on the *trigger* (words in italics denote the Pedersoli parts description) pushes the top of the trigger against the main scear bar and eventually trips the main lock. The other parts of the set trigger mechanism are not activated, other than the quite light *set trigger spring* which pushes the trigger into its forward position via the *set trigger ratchet.*

When the trigger is set (Fig. 72), the top surface of the trigger is held 2 to 3mm away from the main scear bar. When the set trigger is released (Fig. 73) the trigger flies back under the pressure of the *set trigger loading spring* acting through the *lever*, clipping the main scear bar quite sharply and dislodging the main scear, which releases the cock as before.[1] Let us see how it does this.

The set trigger has its own scear and bent, the scear being placed at the end of the lever, with the bent being formed as part of the ratchet. Note that the bent is placed directly over the ratchet pivot screw, which is important in keeping release pressures low. As the trigger is pushed forward to set the trigger, the lever is pushed down by the top edge of the channel in the trigger against the quite heavy pressure of the set trigger loading spring. The lever rotates about the same pivot screw as the trigger itself. The curved end of the lever pushes the ratchet back until it falls below the bent, when the light set trigger spring pushes the

1. The mechanisms of modern set triggers are considerably more complicated, with a separate 'fly' releasing the main scear, and where the trigger hardly moves at all during release. On repro muzzle-loaders, the set trigger mechanism has to conform to traditional techniques.

bent over the top of the scear, and the trigger is 'set' with an audible click.

To release the set, pressure is applied to the trigger, allowing the tip of the *set trigger adjustment screw* to push against the underside of the ratchet and slide the bent off the scear as it rotates about its own pivot screw. This allows the trigger to be forced upwards by the loading spring, which is exerting pressure on the other end of the lever, which itself pushes against the top of the trigger channel.

ADJUSTMENT

Both the trigger release pressure and any associated creep are adjusted by the adjustment screw fitted just behind the trigger. As this is screwed in, it pushes up the ratchet which, in turn, pushes the bent closer and closer to the edge of the scear and both the trigger release pressure and the creep drop away together. If it is screwed in too far, it will release the set completely. This is one reason why you never adjust the set trigger with a loaded pistol in your hand. The possibility of causing injury to yourself or others is quite real.

TYPICAL PROBLEMS

The normal problem with setting the trigger is caused by the tip of the adjustment screw not being geometrically round. If you cannot set the trigger light enough for your liking, or it goes from 'creep-creep-creep' to 'let off' after hardly touching the setting screw, persuade someone with a miniature lathe to round the tip of the screw carefully to a polished dome shape. Alternatively, get the supplier to send you another one. The second problem is the scear to bent interface, both parts of which have to be flat, polished and without even the smallest of grooves across them. If the 'let-off' is rough it takes but a few minutes to take the lock to pieces, lap the mating surfaces flat, and reassemble.

Note that the adjustment screw is retained in place by the somewhat crude method of distorting the threaded mating hole in the trigger to form an interference fit with the screw. If the adjustment screw is frequently 'adjusted', the screw threads will wear and the screw will work either in or out under the repeated shock of firing the pistol. And that will change your carefully set trigger pressure, with the trigger either not holding at all or the pressure climbing higher and higher with every shot. So, once you have the trigger set to your liking, degrease the set trigger mechanism completely and apply Screwloc or something similar to the set adjustment screw to keep it in place. Do not forget to re-lubricate the lock after the Screwloc has set.

It is not unknown for the main trigger release pressure to be too high for the energy provided by the set trigger to dislodge the main scear. This often occurs when parts of the main lock, such as the mainspring or the tumbler, have been replaced from stock and the new assembly has not been tested in a pistol before being returned to its rightful owner. If this appears to be a problem, the first thing to do is to ensure that the screw retaining the heavy set trigger loading spring is fully home. The last half turn can make a surprising difference to the energy provided by the set trigger mechanism. If this fails, you have no option, other than returning the complete pistol to the supplier, to work on the main scear to bent interface to reduce the release pressure. You probably only need to polish the tip of the scear with an oily strip of fine emery paper (1200 grit or more), supported by a strip of flat metal.

OTHER SET TRIGGER TYPES

Set triggers with the set screw in front of the trigger, such as the author's Nock flintlock, work in a similar way. The main difference is that the lever and the ratchet are oriented 'back to front' compared with the Le

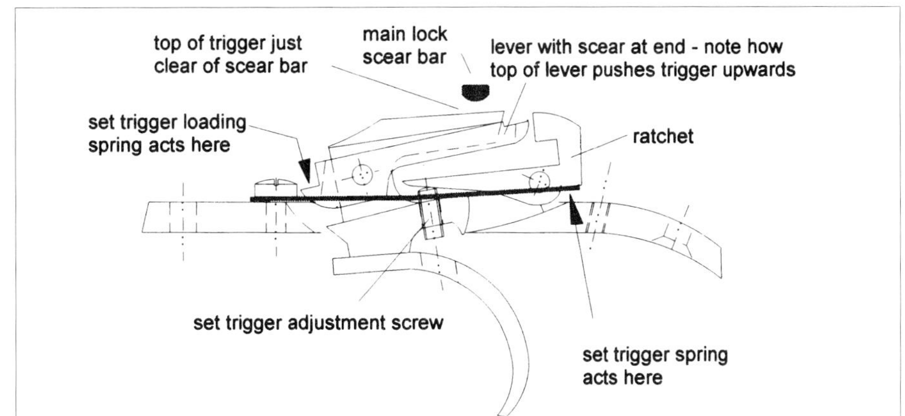

Fig. 71 Le Page set trigger – unset.

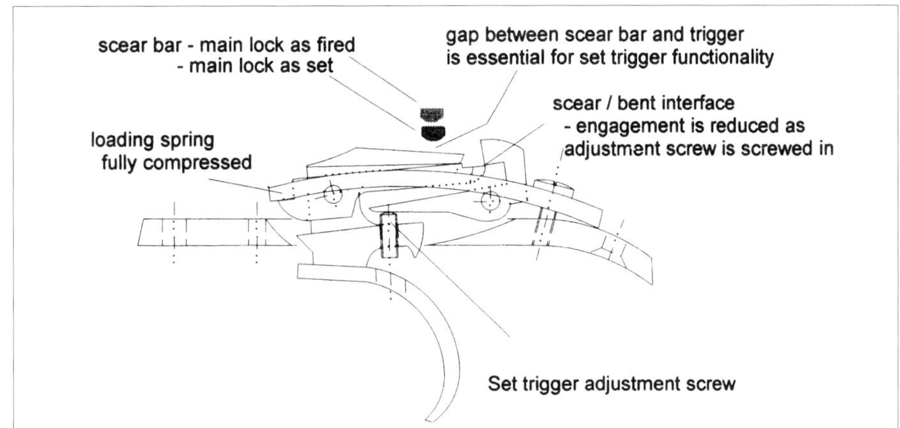

Fig. 72 Le Page set trigger – set.

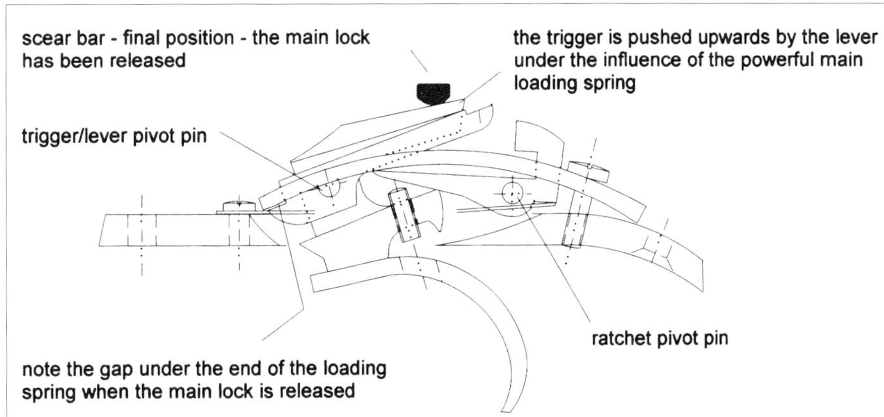

Fig. 73 Le Page set trigger – released.

Page. However, the way the 'set' pressure is changed is quite different and more difficult to control. Here you have to get a balance between the Nock equivalent of the light set trigger spring and the main loading spring, which may have to be slackened off a little to reduce the trigger release pressure.

The few pistols with double set triggers use a separate trigger to 'set' the lock, rather than pushing the single trigger forward as in the Le Page.

Appendix II

The Open and Closed Shoots

	MLA Pistolfest – Wedgnock (April)	Army Meeting – Bisley (April)	Phoenix Meeting – Bisley (End May)	MLAGB National Pistol Champ' – Bisley (End June) (Closed)	Black Powder 200x – Wedgnock (Early July)	Imperial Meeting – Bisley (Mid July)	Euro or World Champs – (August) (Closed)	English Champs (Int' Team Select') (Sept)	Trafalgar Meeting – Bisley (End Oct)
REVOLVER COMPETITIONS	:	:	:	:	:	:	:	:	:
10/10 or 10/13 Repro	X	X	X	X	X	X	X	X	X
10/10 or 10/13 Original	X	X	X	X	X	X	X	X	X
10/10, 10/13 or 15/15 Free	:	:	:	:	X	X	:	X	X
Bow Street Runner	:	:	X	:	:	:	:	:	:
Cavalry Officer's Match	:	X	X	:	:	:	:	:	:
America Match	:	:	X	:	:	:	:	:	:
25Y/M Slow and Timed Fire	:	:	X	:	:	:	:	:	:
Advancing Target	:	:	X	:	:	X	:	:	X
Bobber	:	:	:	:	:	X	:	:	X
Ambidextrous	:	:	:	:	:	X	:	:	X
Surrenden	:	:	:	:	:	X	:	:	X
Pocket Revolver	:	:	:	:	:	X	:	:	X
100/200 Yards	:	:	X	:	:	X	:	:	:
2*10/13 Original + Repro	:	:	:	X	:	:	:	:	:
English Trigger Cocking	X	:	:	X	:	X	:	:	X

☐ Either but not both

	MLA Pistolfest – Wedgnock (April)	Army Meeting – Bisley (April)	Phoenix Meeting – Bisley (End May)	MLAGB National Pistol Champ' – Bisley (End June) (Closed)	Black Powder 200x – Wedgnock (Early July)	Imperial Meeting – Bisley (Mid July)	Euro or World Champs – (August) (Closed)	English Champs (Int' Team Select') (Sept)	Trafalgar Meeting – Bisley (End Oct)
	:	:	:	:	:	:	:	:	:
SINGLE SHOT COMPETITIONS	:	:	:	:	:	:	:	:	:
10/10 or 10/13 Repro Percus'	X	X	X	X	X	X	X	X	X
10/10 or 10/13 Orig' percus'	X	X	X	X	X	X	X	X	X
Free Percussion	X	:	:	X	X	X	:	X	X
10/10 or 10/13 Repro Flint	X	:	X	X	:	X	X	X	X
10/10 or 10/13 Original Flint	X	:	X	X	:	X	X	X	X
Free Flint or Free S/B Flint	X	:	:	X	:	X	:	X	X
Duelling Percussion	X	:	:	:	:	X	:	:	X
Duelling Flint	X	:	:	:	:	X	:	:	X
Shoulder Stocked	:	:	:	:	:	X	:	:	:
Pocket Pistol	:	:	:	:	:	X	:	:	:
OTHERS									
50M Deliberate Pistol/Revolver	X	:	X	:	:	X	:	:	X
Others	:	:	:	:	:	:	:	:	:

The above represents the typical competition schedules at the two main muzzle-loading UK venues about the year 2000. These schedules will almost certainly change year on year – watch out for content and rule changes!

Appendix III

The 'Wish I Had Remembered It' List

How many of us have got to the range, only to find out that we have brought the wrong balls, powder etc?

To do this in a major competition is a bit disastrous. So make a list – the following is the one I use!

VARIABLES	Le Page 44 Percussion (R)	Free 36 Percussion (R)	Kirner 44 Percussion (O)	Le Page 45 Smoothbore Flint (R)	Le Page 44 Free Flint (R)	Nock 42 bore Flint (O)	Pieta 457 Remington New Army (R)	451 Remington New Army (O)	Adams 120 bore (O)	Remington M1863 31 (R)	Bass 28 bore Flint (O)
Balls	440	360	440	457	440	476	457	451	0.342	315	535
Powder	#2	#2	#2	#1	#1	#1	#2	#2	#2	#2	#1
RWS Caps	1075	1075	1075	.	.	.	1075	.	1075	1075	
CCI Caps	.	.	.	.	.	.	.	#10	.	.	
Patches	013×1	010×.75	013×1	013×1	013×1	013×1	.	.	.	013×1,2	
Priming	.	.	.	Y	Y	Y	.	.	.	.	Y
Flask nozzle	15g	12g	15g	25g	15g	25g	18g	18g	12g	11g	27g
Nipple key	No.1	No.1	No.1	.	.	.	No.2	No.2	No.3	No.4	
Flints	.	.	.	5/8	5/8	5/8	.	.	.	.	5/8

THE COMMON BITS

Starter	Semolina filler	55 cleaning rod	Pricker
Ramrod	Filler dispenser(s)	44 cleaning rod	Patch puller
Loading funnel	4×2 cleaning patches	36 cleaning rod	Ball puller
Flask filling funnel	3×1.5 cleaning patches	22 cleaning rod	Spare Flints
Flask of #2	Knife	BP solvent	Spare flint clamps
Flask of #1	Chamber reamer – 4.5mm	WD40 spray can	Screwdrivers
Phial box with phials	Chamber reamer – 6mm	Sight black	Small Pliers
Glove	Muffs	Scope and stand	Stapler
Whistle	Stop watch	Copper drift	Spare staples
Small hammer	Ballpoint pen	Felt marker	Corkscrew/bottle opener
Firearms certificate	Black powder licence	Euro firearms pass	RCAT Document

It helps if you write this out in one long list, and check each item off as you pack it. It's also a good check on the state of the spares in the cupboard. It's very easy to look there on the morning of the shoot and find no 440 balls, no priming powder in its dispenser, or that you had forgotten to repair the flask that was dropped on the range the week before. Of course, when you have a dedicated box for all these bits, it becomes a lot easier.

Appendix IV
Calibres and Bore Sizes

A. BORE SIZES AGAINST CALIBRES

Bore	*Diameter (in)*	*Diameter (mm)*	*Bore*	*Diameter (in)*	*Diameter (mm)*	*Bore*	*Diameter (in)*	*Diameter (mm)*
230	.273	6.93	75	.397	10.07	31	.532	13.52
225	.275	6.98	70	.406	10.31	30	.538	13.67
220	.277	7.04	65	.416	10.57	29	.544	13.83
215	.279	7.09	60	.427	10.85	28	.551	13.99
210	.281	7.15	59	.430	10.91	27	.558	14.16
205	.284	7.20	58	.432	10.97	26	.565	14.34
200	.286	7.26	57	.435	11.04	25	.572	14.53
195	.288	7.33	56	.437	11.10	24	.580	14.73
190	.291	7.39	55	.440	11.17	23	.588	14.94
185	.294	7.46	54	.443	11.24	22	.597	15.16
180	.296	7.52	53	.445	11.31	21	.606	15.40
175	.299	7.60	52	.448	11.38	20	.616	15.65
170	.302	7.67	51	.451	11.46	19	.627	15.92
165	.305	7.75	50	.454	11.53	18	.638	16.21
160	.308	7.83	49	.457	11.61	17	.650	16.52
155	.311	7.91	48	.460	11.69	16	.664	16.86
150	.315	8.00	47	.463	11.77	15	.678	17.23
145	.318	8.09	46	.467	11.86	14	.694	17.63
140	.322	8.18	45	.470	11.94	13	.711	18.07
135	.326	8.28	44	.474	12.03	12	.731	18.56
130	.330	8.39	43	.477	12.13	11	.752	19.10
125	.335	8.50	42	.481	12.22	10	.776	19.72
120	.339	8.61	41	.485	12.32	9	.804	20.42
115	.344	8.74	40	.489	12.42	8	.836	21.24
110	.349	8.87	39	.493	12.53	7	.874	22.21
105	.355	9.00	38	.497	12.64	6	.920	23.38
100	.360	9.15	37	.502	12.75	5	.978	24.84
95	.367	9.31	36	.507	12.87	4	1.054	26.76
90	.373	9.48	35	.511	12.99	3	1.160	29.46
85	.380	9.66	34	.516	13.11	2	1.328	33.72
80	.388	9.86	33	.521	13.24	1	1.673	42.48

B. CALIBRES AGAINST BORE SIZES

Diameter (in)	*Diameter (mm)*	*Bore (nearest)*	*Diameter (in)*	*Diameter (mm)*	*Bore (nearest)*	*Diameter (in)*	*Diameter (mm)*	*Bore (nearest)*
0.200	5.08	585	0.430	10.92	59	0.660	16.76	16
0.205	5.21	543	0.435	11.05	57	0.665	16.89	16
0.210	5.33	505	0.440	11.18	55	0.670	17.02	16
0.215	5.46	471	0.445	11.30	53	0.675	17.15	15
0.220	5.59	439	0.450	11.43	51	0.680	17.27	15
0.225	5.72	411	0.455	11.56	50	0.685	17.40	15
0.230	5.84	385	0.460	11.68	48	0.690	17.53	14
0.235	5.97	361	0.465	11.81	47	0.695	17.65	14
0.240	6.10	338	0.470	11.94	45	0.700	17.78	14
0.245	6.22	318	0.475	12.07	44	0.705	17.91	13
0.250	6.35	299	0.480	12.19	42	0.710	18.03	13
0.255	6.48	282	0.485	12.32	41	0.715	18.16	13
0.260	6.60	266	0.490	12.45	40	0.720	18.29	13
0.265	6.73	251	0.495	12.57	39	0.725	18.42	12
0.270	6.86	238	0.500	12.70	37	0.730	18.54	12
0.275	6.99	225	0.505	12.83	36	0.735	18.67	12
0.280	7.11	213	0.510	12.95	35	0.740	18.80	12
0.285	7.24	202	0.515	13.08	34	0.745	18.92	11
0.290	7.37	192	0.520	13.21	33	0.750	19.05	11
0.295	7.49	182	0.525	13.34	32	0.755	19.18	11
0.300	7.62	173	0.530	13.46	31	0.760	19.30	11
0.305	7.75	165	0.535	13.59	31	0.765	19.43	10
0.310	7.87	157	0.540	13.72	30	0.770	19.56	10
0.315	8.00	150	0.545	13.84	29	0.775	19.69	10
0.320	8.13	143	0.550	13.97	28	0.780	19.81	10
0.325	8.26	136	0.555	14.10	27	0.785	19.94	10
0.330	8.38	130	0.560	14.22	27	0.790	20.07	9
0.335	8.51	124	0.565	14.35	26	0.795	20.19	9
0.340	8.64	119	0.570	14.48	25	0.800	20.32	9
0.345	8.76	114	0.575	14.61	25	0.805	20.45	9
0.350	8.89	109	0.580	14.73	24	0.810	20.57	9
0.355	9.02	105	0.585	14.86	23	0.815	20.70	9
0.360	9.14	100	0.590	14.99	23	0.820	20.83	8
0.365	9.27	96	0.595	15.11	22	0.825	20.96	8
0.370	9.40	92	0.600	15.24	22	0.830	21.08	8
0.375	9.53	89	0.605	15.37	21	0.835	21.21	8
0.380	9.65	85	0.610	15.49	21	0.840	21.34	8
0.385	9.78	82	0.615	15.62	20	0.845	21.46	8
0.390	9.91	79	0.620	15.75	20	0.850	21.59	8
0.395	10.03	76	0.625	15.88	19	0.855	21.72	7
0.400	10.16	73	0.630	16.00	19	0.860	21.84	7
0.405	10.29	70	0.635	16.13	18	0.865	21.97	7
0.410	10.41	68	0.640	16.26	18	0.870	22.10	7
0.415	10.54	65	0.645	16.38	17	0.875	22.23	7
0.420	10.67	63	0.650	16.51	17	0.880	22.35	7
0.425	10.80	61	0.655	16.64	17	0.885	22.48	7

Appendix V
Blueing and Browning

Anyone who takes the odd 'antique' pistol under his wing will be faced, at some time or another, with the decision on whether to refinish it. My golden rule is that, if a pistol has been acquired for display or investment, clean it but do not refinish it. If you intend to put more than a few dozen balls through it then refinish it by all means. Some of the 'antiques' available on the market, including those from the major arms fairs, are covered in a fine layer of hard rust and it is a kindness to give them a decent make-over. Refinishing by the average amateur may not return the pistol to its original glory, but he can fairly easily produce a pistol with a pleasant appearance as well as an excellent protection against black powder residues.

Now 'professional' blueing is now almost certainly blacking and not blueing, and is often produced by boiling the cleaned metallic parts in molten caustic soda. This is no field in which the amateur gunsmith should become involved since it needs special equipment and, in any case, results in the wrong colour for either antiques or repros. Another thing to avoid is attempts to replicate the translucent blues on the Boutet and the Le Page original presentation pistols, unless you are prepared to do a good deal of experimentation first. These finishes were originally achieved by heating the highly polished barrel in a reducing atmosphere and, while the finish looks superb it is very thin and a little soft, and is not really up to being handled in transit or on the range.

Small parts such as screws can be coloured a blue/black by the selenium-based, cold 'instant creams', but I have had little success with them on parts which are constantly handled, such as barrels, cocks and trigger guards, since the finish slowly but surely wears off. If you do use them, degrease the parts thoroughly before applying the blueing cream. The easy alternative for small parts is to heat them until a spot of oil dropped on to their surface disappears in smoke, and then to drop the hot part into a small container of clean engine oil. You end with a hard-wearing, blue/black finish. However, you have to watch out for parts that have been hardened, such as the scear on the end of the Remington trigger, since these may be softened by overheating. Keep the hard part cool by gripping it in a pair of heavy pliers while you direct the heat only on the surfaces to be oil blued.

This really leaves the amateur with the traditional cold blueing and browning methods used extensively in the gun trade for centuries until the modern finishes took over. These traditional finishes are often called 'controlled rusting', which is an excellent description because that is exactly what is involved. The colouring itself is a layer of complex iron oxides, the oxides being formed on the prepared surface of the metal as a part of the 'rusting' process. It is the mixtures used to accelerate the rusting process that define whether the final result will be blue or brown. It is not possible to match the existing blues or browns on a new part which you want to fit to an old pistol. You will have to re-finish the complete pistol from scratch if you want overall colour compatibility. Any rust refinishing process follows the same pattern: strip, smooth, clean, degrease, 'rust-up', clean, repeat the rust-up and cleaning processes a number of times, and, finally, seal.

STRIPPING AND SMOOTHING

The stripping and smoothing part of the process is dictated largely by the state of the pistol to be refinished. Some pistol finishes, such as the original Pedersoli Le Page 'London Bright' on the author's 'free' pistol or the typical Belgian pin-fire pistols often found in antiques fairs, are nickel-based, electroplated surfaces. The best way to strip them is to 'reverse plate' them by using some battery acid, the car battery and a sheet of lead. An alternative is to abrade the unwanted or worn finish from the surface using wet and dry emery paper. Take care not to take off the sharp corners on the frames and especially the corners of hexagon barrels since this spoils the end product and reduces the value of antiques, refinished or not.

Once you have the exterior parts of the pistol down to their original metal surfaces you start the meticulous process of getting the dents and scratches out. This normally means removing the surrounding metal around the dent or scratch until the bottom of it is lost in the new surface. There is obviously a limit to what can be done here, especially on items such as trigger guards, lock plates and standing breeches that are covered by foliate engraving or hot rolled patterns. For flat surfaces such as octagonal barrels, start with 120 grade wet and dry emery paper wrapped around a hard flat surface and work round the barrel flat by flat. Protect any engraving on the barrel by covering it with masking tape. Once the dents are out, start the process again using the next finer grade of emery. On barrels always work along their length, never across them since this is where you lose the sharp edges. By the time you have got down to 320 grade, you will have the sort of surface that is ideal for refinishing by the rusting process. Note that there is no need to go down to the really fine grades of emery, and a brightly polished surface is a positive hindrance for this type of refinishing. You are looking for a smooth and consistent surface over the whole of the area to be refinished. Look at the light reflected from it at several angles to find the odd parts that you have missed.

CLEANING AND DEGREASING

In refinishing, cleanliness is next to godliness. If the surface to be refinished is not clean the final finish is guaranteed to be patchy. You will be doing a great deal of cleaning, so plan it properly before you start. You need quantities of absolutely clean cotton cloth, and a roll of paper towelling should be on hand. You need quantities of cotton swabs – cotton wool balls used as make-up removers are good – and a pair of plastic tongs or some similar non-metallic clamps to hold them. You will need pints and pints of clean water; a good source could be someone with a dehumidifier. The next best alternative is distilled or battery water, if you can afford it, but a cheaper source is rainwater collected in a new plastic bucket and filtered through a paper coffee filter before use. Tap water may be acceptable to drink but has too many dissolved minerals in it for our purposes. You also need containers in which to put the parts for boiling, which is all part of the process. A problem could be finding something long enough to boil a pistol barrel in – long vessels also tend to be wide and it can take a lot of water to cover them. This matters since you have to throw the water away after you have used it once. In the end I persuaded a sheet-metal worker to make me a 12in-long, shallow tray in mild steel, which I quickly had to replace with one in stainless, which was more practicable. Add to all this a degreasing method. The original method was to boil the metal parts in a strong solution of caustic soda (sodium hydroxide). You then spend a further half-hour boiling it in ever cleaner water to remove the remains of the caustic soda. These days, it is easier to buy a cold degreaser from a tool shop; use it twice, remembering to handle the parts with a clean strip of paper towel once they have been degreased.

Before starting the rusting process, you need to build a 'damp box' in which to hang the parts to be rusted. The easiest way is to use a cardboard box resting on one end. Poke some stiff wire through the top and turn the ends over inside the box from which you can suspend the parts. Finally put a damp sponge in the bottom of the box to raise the humidity.

THE RUSTING PROCESS

Using these guidelines, first degrease the parts, followed by boiling in water for 10 minutes. Take them out and vigorously wipe them with a clean cotton cloth. Then, taking the rusting solution, apply it liberally to the surfaces to be finished with a new cotton swab and hang the parts in the damp box for 4 to 6 hours. At the end of this period they should be covered with a bright, reddish-brown rust. The first time you see this you may wonder whether you have done the right thing. But this is just what you want, since underneath, adhering firmly to the metal surface, is the initial layer of the brown or blue finish you are looking for. Having done this, the next stage is to take all the lose rust off.

Use a carding brush to remove the rust if you can find one.[1] These brushes have short, densely packed, thin, steel wires, which remove the loose surface rust quite easily. They have a surprisingly little effect on the fine blue or brown finish which has started to form under the loose rust. You may scrub away quite hard without removing the finish. For awkward shapes such as trigger guards, the little rotary wire brushes fitted to a Dremel (one of those little, variable-speed, lightweight drills) are excellent. Other alternatives to the carding brush are wire wool and sets of nylon pads, both of which come in various grades. Surprisingly, even the fine grades of nylon pad take off more rust than the carding brush, and may even take off some of the blue/brown finish. Wire wool in its finer grades is a good alternative, but there is always a fine bloom of oil on wire wool, so you should degrease the parts again after you have used it.

Having removed the loose rust, boil again in water for from 10 to 15 minutes. This serves both to stabilize the oxide surfaces and to float off any remaining rust particles. Cool and wipe with a clean piece of cotton cloth. You will probably find that a little of the newly formed surface finish marks the cloth. This is quite normal, you are simply removing loose particles from the surface. Then start the rusting process again. If you want a really durable finish you will probably have to do this for a minimum of six times on fairly soft steels such as barrels, and even more on forged or cast parts, such as the receivers of revolver frames or standing breeches on single shots. When browning Damascus or stub twist barrels you can probably manage with a smaller number of re-rusting cycles. Here you need to reach a compromise between a finish which enhances the pattern in the steel and its protective properties, which are definitely improved as the film on the surface gets thicker.

Once you are satisfied with the finish, spray with WD-40 or some other dewatering fluid and rub the oil well into the surface. If you have refinished the pistol for display purposes only, use a good wax polish instead of the WD-40.

THE RUSTING SOLUTIONS

Rusting solutions for both blueing and browning used to be widely available from gun shops. I was recently told that EU regulations or the HSE now prevent their sale,

1. If you can't get a carding brush from your local tool supplier, try a good ladies' haberdashers, where they are sold for bringing up the pile on certain knitted fabrics.

presumably on the bureaucratic principle that their users are incapable of handling them safely. However, they were freely available at the last arms fair I went to, so do look around. The alternative is to make your own, which – I can assure you – is a great deal more fraught than buying it made up in a bottle. One problem in making your own is a ready source of the small quantities of acids and the other chemicals required. Another problem is that, even if it is made up in a modest quantity, you finish with enough solution to refinish a fair-sized armoury. Now you can find the essential ingredients for blueing and browning rusting mixtures in any of the specialist books on metal finishing, as well as in most gun books such as R.F. Dunlap's *Gunsmithing* (Stackpole Books, 1963). To see how effective they were I tried the simplest of Dunlap's blueing mixtures, reputed to have been used by professional gunsmiths since the eighteenth century. While the formulation is exactly that of Dunlap, the hard-won experience in its concoction is that of the author, which is completely ignored in all the books on the subject.

Take 4oz of concentrated nitric acid and 3oz of concentrated hydrochloric acid in separate bottles down to the bottom of the garden. Make sure that there is a fair wind blowing away from your own and your neighbours' houses. Pour one of the acids into a large, open-topped, glass container with a pouring lip. Add the second acid. This mixture forms aqua regia (Kings liquid). It fumes and you must not get these fumes in your mouth or up you nose. It will dissolve almost anything, including gold (hence its name), your clothes and you. Wear goggles and rubber gloves. Into this mixture lower up to half a pound of clean 3 or 4in nails. Leave this to stand, and walk well away. After a short time the mixture starts to dissolve the nails. As it continues the mixture gets hot, and the hotter it gets the faster the reaction. Do not use small nails since the reaction becomes too violent. The problem is that it produces prodigious quantities of dense, brown, choking fumes, which are much to be avoided; hence the location away from the house and the requirement for the wind to disperse the fumes. When all reaction appears to have ceased, slowly add two and a half pints of distilled water. Leave for a couple of hours to settle, and then pour off the upper part of the brown coloured liquor into a large glass or thick polypropylene storage jar. Dispose of the remaining brown sludge safely, remembering that it is highly acidic, corrosive and poisonous.

Leave the storage jar for a couple of days to allow more solids to fall to the bottom of the container. Then decant a few ounces into a wide-necked glass or plastic bottle with a plastic top, and use this when you need it for the blueing process. Plan whom you can sell or give the remaining liquid to since the contents of the small bottle will last you for a lifetime. In the meantime, label both the storage jar and the working bottle and keep them in a secure location.

Despite its manufacturing problems, the mixture really works, and produced a dark blue, dense, glossy coating on the barrel of my Lefaucheur gallery pistol. It also gave a pleasing dark blue effect to both the receiver and the trigger guard, enabling the 'engraving' to be clearly seen, even though I had not completely removed the pits from the original rusty surfaces. With this success behind me, I went to work to blue the original barrel on my Le Page 44 percussion repro and some other guns beside, with equal success.

In summary, my view is that to make your own blueing or browning mixture is expensive, time-consuming, anti-social and not a little dangerous. Most of the mixtures described in the books are more complicated variants of the mixture described above, but, I suspect, with many of the same pitfalls. My recommendation is to spend the time searching for a commercial source for these blueing and browning liquids.

Appendix VI
Balls, Powders and Velocities

THE BACKGROUND

Many people ask how fast the balls are going when they come out of the muzzle-loading pistol barrel. I never did know until I borrowed a chronograph and, with the help of several club members, investigated the matter. Now, as anyone who has used a chronograph knows, the more measurements you take of a single ball/load/patch/barrel combination, the more accurate your results will be. We worked on the principal that, if three consecutive readings were within a ±5 per cent spread of their average, those readings were as good as we were going to get. When the spread was greater than this, five readings were taken and we used the average of the middle three. In general, when corrected for barrel length, reasonably consistent graphs could be drawn from the results. This appeared to be the best approach since most shooters just want an idea of the approximate velocities and what difference a change in load might make. We saw no point in trying to relate these data to accuracy – there are far too many variables to take into account, none of which would be under our control.

THE METHOD

The pistols used were a smooth-bore Lefaucheur (335 ball), a rifled Pedersoli Le Page (360) a rifled Greathead underhammer (395), another rifled Le Page (440), my smooth-bore Nock flintlock (476) and a Green original rifled percussion (527). The only rifled and smooth-bore barrels taking the same ball we had available were the Greathead and my newly arrived matchlock pistol. The initial results showed no significant difference between velocities with the rifled or the smooth-bore barrels when using the same load and powder. Barrel length does make a difference, since black powder burns all the way up the barrel and out of the muzzle. The experiments on the effect of barrel length were carried out using the Le Page 440, with 8, 12 and 16 grains of Swiss No.2 and ever-increasing quantities of filler to get the ball closer and closer to the muzzle. Considering the comparatively small number of tests we carried out, a reasonably straight line was achieved between 3½in and 8in barrels. The different velocities were used to factor the data taken by the chronograph to get the effect of a common barrel length, irrespective of the pistol used.

For the normal velocity testing, the loads used started at 8 grains for the smaller calibres and went up in 4-grain steps, with the maximum load being 40 grains. I know some flintlock shooters stoke up their pistols much higher than this, but we had our shooting hands and the effect of a misplaced ball on the chronograph to think of. Once velocities started to creep over 1,000ft/sec in any one series we stopped that ball/load combination and moved on. Besides, we soon found that the muzzle blast from the higher loads affected the chronograph: too close and we had dubious readings. Another problem with having the chronograph too close was that the patch followed the ball through the screens and gave false readings. In the end the chronograph had to be placed nearly 3m down the range, with pieces of writing paper clipped over the front screen to stop the odd patch. We used the powders already mentioned in the body of the book, including a little comparative work at a single calibre with Pyrodex. It was necessary to use a small measure of semolina over the load before loading the ball when using the lighter loads in order to ensure that the ball did not bottom on the lip of the patent breech. This also obviated the problem of the patch lubrication affecting the burning of the powder, and was finally used in all loadings. It is of interest that the spread of velocities dropped quite markedly after we adopted this technique. We even made up a small quantity of serpentine powder, that is, the way powder was made up to the middle of the sixteenth century – just a well blended mixture of 75 per cent potassium nitrate, 15 per cent sulphur and 10 per cent charcoal by weight, and no attempt at corning.

A further observation was that the spread of velocities dropped when the cock was left closed over the nipple when loading the finer grades of powder, preventing the powder from being expelled through the nipple. We had to ensure that the nipple was cleared with a nipple pricker before each cap was put in place.

RESULTS

Tables are presented giving the velocities of balls of different sizes, the actual figures from the chronograph being reduced or increased to a common barrel length of 8in, the conversion factors being taken from Table 1. The barrel length in all cases was the free barrel length after the ball had been seated on the semolina filler. The powders used were Swiss No.1 and No.2, and Nobel's TS2 for the detailed testing. Comparisons were also made with a single ball size using these powders against Pyrodex and the serpentine powder.

The final tests to satisfy our curiosity were of the effect of an ever increasing amount of ramming of the ball on to the powder. The only discernable result of these was that the greater the degree of ramming, the wider the velocity variation between shots. It made little difference to the average velocity, however.

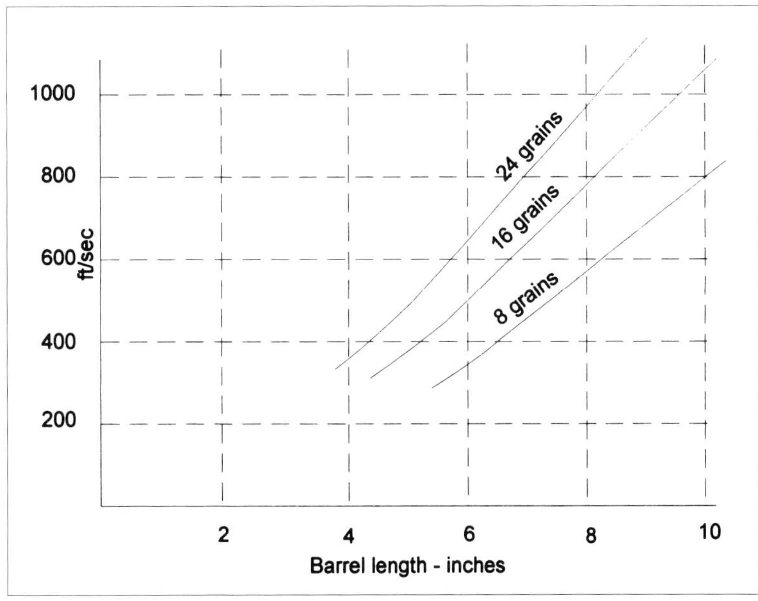

Table 1: Variation of velocity with barrel length.

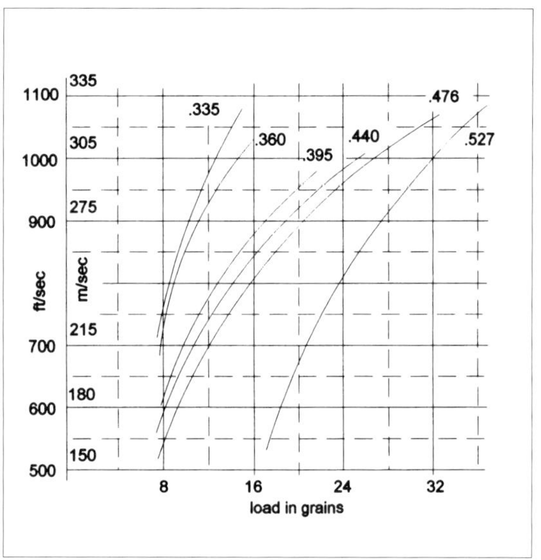

Table 2 Variation of velocity with load – Swiss No.1.

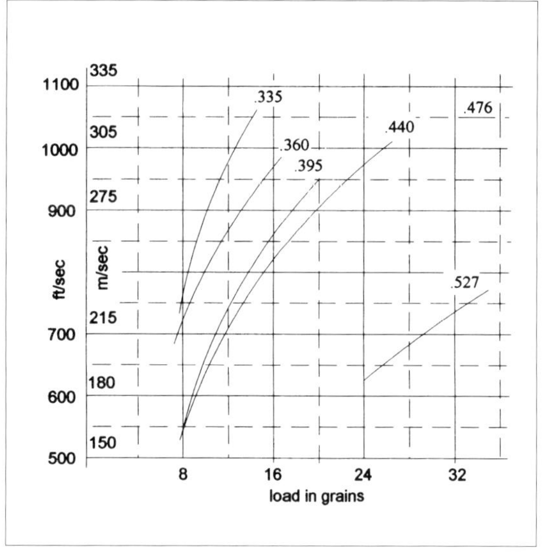

Table 3 Variation of velocity with load – Swiss No.2.

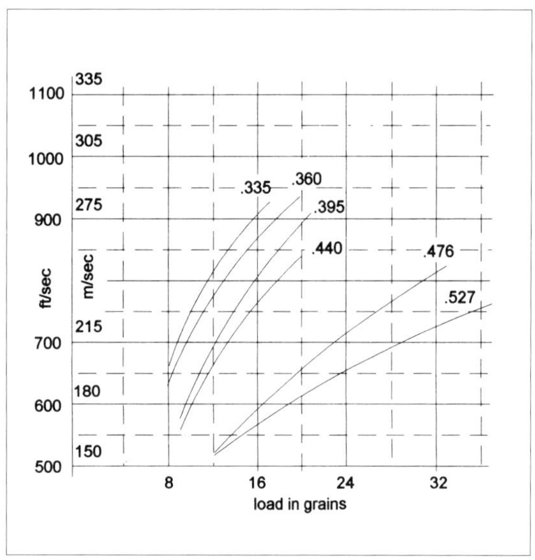

Table 4 Variation of velocity with load – Nobel TS2.

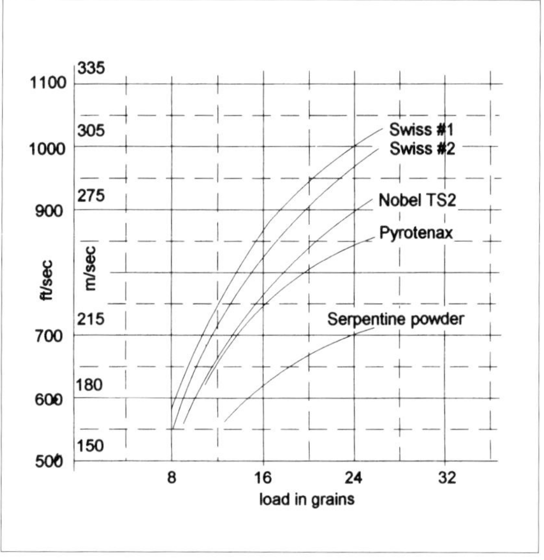

Table 5 Variation of velocity between powders.

Index

Index